MW01285571

Praise for And Life Continues

"Trafficking is one of the most brutal and misunderstood crimes here in the United States. Wendy's story and voice spotlights the horror of what is happening close to home. *And Life Continues* is an honest, thought-provoking look into the depravity of exploitive 'love' and the cycle of abuse that can be overcome with the triumphant soul."
—Michael Cory Davis, American actor, activist to end modern-day slavery, and director of *Svetlana's Journey* and *Cargo: Innocence Lost*

"Some will read this book to try to understand what went wrong. How could we have intervened to stop the mind games that created her alternate world? But the real story here is Wendy's resilience. We are told that the primary factor in resilience is having positive relationships. You will be surprised as you meet the people who pulled Wendy out of her distorted world and into theirs, where they treated her with dignity, respect, hope, and love. You may also be dismayed as you recognize lost opportunities you could have had to pull someone like Wendy into your world with kind words, concern, and expectations of something more. Reading this book will challenge you to see the person more than their circumstances."
—Sandra L. Morgan, RN, PhD
Director of the Global Center for Women and Justice
Vanguard University

"Wendy takes readers on a journey in the life of a girl who is abused in childhood and then becomes a young mother; the father of Wendy's child ultimately becomes her trafficker, using the baby to coerce Wendy into prostitution. Wendy helps us to understand the mindset of a young woman who is so broken that she is unable not only to stand up for herself but unable to stand up for others who are victimized by the same man. If you are working within the movement against human trafficking, and especially if you are working with survivors of sex trafficking, then I highly recommend reading Wendy's book. It's a powerful account of survival, and it offers an important personal perspective that we aren't hearing often enough—the perspective of a girl who is victimized in childhood, victimized in adulthood, and then sentenced as a criminal offender. Wendy is an expert on the needs of young women victimized via sex trafficking, and I can't wait to hear more from her!"

—Holly Austin Smith, Author of *Walking Prey*

And Life Continues

Sex Trafficking and My Journey to Freedom

Wendy Barnes

Published by CreateSpace Independent Publishing Platform

ISBN-13: 978-1502304179

ISBN-10: 1502304171

Disclaimer: The events are portrayed to the best of Wendy Barnes' memory. While all the stories in this book are true, some names and identifying details have been changed to protect the privacy of the people involved. This book contains graphic language and explicit scenes. It is not recommended for a young reader.

Cover photograph Copyright © 2015 Latasha J. Arnold, Photographic Dreams

Cover design by Paul Kinni

Print book interior design and eBook formatting by Lis Sowerbutts http://BookFormatter.com

Edited by Susan Foster de Quintana

Article from *The Oregonian*, Portland pimp gets life sentence after third conviction, by Aimee Green. Copyright © 2013 Oregon Live LLC. All rights reserved. Used with permission.

Wendy Barnes was introduced to sex trafficking by her first love, the father of her children. *And Life Continues* is her story: how she became a victim of human trafficking, why she was unable to leave the man who enslaved her for fifteen years, and the obstacles she overcame to heal and rebuild her life after she was rescued.

Printed in the United States

Dedication

To my daughter, Beautiful Princess Latasha. You are my best friend and my source of strength. You have triumphed over all the adversity in your life to become an amazing, loving, forgiving, happy human being. You are my life's biggest blessing—you are my miracle.

To my older son, Gregory. No child deserves to go through what you have experienced, and I know those experiences continue to weigh heavily on your spirit. I am grateful for your forgiveness and love, and I treasure the connection I have with you. I am proud of the steps you have taken to grow into an honorable man; your actions demonstrate that while you can never change your past, you can direct your future.

To my younger son, Michael. You so lovingly share hugs and smiles, even though we do not have a typical mother–son relationship. I am thankful for your forgiveness and love, and I treasure the relationship that we have. You are the apple of my eye.

To my mother, Susan Corning. Your sometimes complicated but unswerving love gave us purple pumpkin memories that will last forever. May you rest in peace and know that I love you dearly and appreciate everything you did for me.

To my older brother, Steve. Your encouragement today erases the childhood pain in little Wendy's heart, and your accomplishments and high ethical standards have given me direction for my own life. In part because of the choices I made as a teenager, you had to make many hard decisions as a young man, and those decisions have made you what you are today: a wonderful person and a *great* big brother. The day you told me you were proud of me was the day I knew for certain I was headed in the right direction.

To my father, Floyd Barnes. In spite of a rocky start between us, you faithfully and persistently made an effort to build and nurture a solid father-daughter relationship. Your yearly visits have made me feel like I am my father's favorite daughter.

To my little sister, Darla Corning. Your teenage wisdom redeemed the missteps in my own life. When you were thirteen years old, I asked you, "How did you become so smart, mature, and level headed?" "I give you all the credit, Wendy," you replied. "I learned what *not* to do from you."

To my stepfather, Tom Corning. You have provided me with a beautiful home where I can safely progress on my healing journey. Every day when I wake up in this home, I know I am blessed. I am grateful for your loving generosity.

To my little brother, Daniel. Thank you for the countless deliveries of rocky road ice cream. I don't care what the neighbors say; your "drug deliveries" have soothed my soul and given me time to keep writing.

A bridge of silver wings
stretches from the dead ashes of an
unforgiving nightmare
to the jeweled vision of a life started anew.

Aberjhani, *Journey through the Power of the*
Rainbow:
Quotations from a Life Made Out of Poetry

Table of Contents

Foreword

As I read *And Life Continues*, I was struck by the quality of the writing, the ability to share a very brutal and profoundly personal story with such a clear voice...a voice filled with compassion for all the girls victimized by traffickers, buyers, and society, as well as for herself, the broken child in a woman's body that was Wendy. This book provides a very real account of the "Romeo" pimp's ability to destroy and control others and the complexity of the relationships in a pimp/trafficker's "game." It is hard to understand for someone outside that world, and Wendy is able to help the reader follow the thinking pattern that kept the girls locked down under Greg Hightower's control.

And Life Continues is, at times, a difficult read. There are moments of frustration as you begin to hope Wendy will actually leave the life and start over, just to find the lies and the beaten down self-esteem overtake her again. But there is hope. Members of law enforcement that saw and treated her as a person with dignity, family that never gave up, school counselors, probation officers, co-workers who heard the full story, and instead of jumping to judgment, showed compassion, and saw it all for what it was— enslavement. And in Wendy, they saw not a criminal, not a scarlet letter, but a survivor! Throughout the reading of the book, you witness the metamorphosis, slow and steady. With each new struggle, a little more confidence and a little more strength gained, until there's finally enough to break the cycle and emerge victorious.

Reading this book made me ponder just how many of the adolescents and young adults walking the street, turning tricks, beaten and coerced, are actually gifted artists, business people, writers, athletes, mathematicians, teachers, and lawyers who are being denied the chance to develop—who have been deemed throwaways of our society and have begun to internalize and believe that message themselves. My hope for each one of them, and, in turn, for all of us as a society, is that we would not accept a class of people as disposable. And my prayer is that each one of them would be met with compassion, respect, and kindness, so that those seeds planted by people they encounter, who see them as the people they are truly meant to be versus what they are being forced to do, would grow and blossom, and we will all be the better for it.

Kylla Leeburg
Deputy Director
Truckers Against Trafficking

Preface

Write hard and clear about what hurts. ⁻
Ernest Hemingway

I TOUCH THE KEYS ON THE PIANO and the heavenly melody of dream songs moves from my soul to the instrument. I had discovered music as a child, and then lost it in a fifteen-year chaos of torture and abuse. When I rediscovered the music, it fed my soul once more—and the healing journey began. It was in the music that my spirit soared and hope embraced me. Dreams do come true, even for me.

Through a childhood of poverty, neglect, and abuse, I formed the beliefs that would write the script for my life. At fifteen, I left home to escape the chaos and traded in a childhood of violence for a fifteen-year "adult" relationship of violence. I did not dare to dream of better days. Daily, in order to save my life and protect others, I followed the dangerous, often illegal, and destructive demands of a brutal and controlling husband. The demands ultimately cost me a twenty-three month prison sentence and the greatest price of all: I lost the ability to parent my three children. This is a consequence I paid for each day as I rebuilt my life and my relationship with my children.

While completing a year-long drug and alcohol treatment program, I was able to discern between the harmful beliefs I had always held about myself and the actual truth. The truth, I discovered, is that I am an intelligent, compassionate, and creative woman, capable of loving and caring for myself. I also realized I could only go as far as I dared to dream. I found hope and began to set goals.

And Life Continues is the story of a survivor of human trafficking in the United States. It is my story: how the events of my childhood contributed to my becoming a victim of sex trafficking, the challenges and thought processes that kept me trapped, and my journey into healing after I was rescued. I am often asked how I was able to rebuild my life and who I was at a core level. *And Life Continues* answers those questions in the hope that my experiences will increase awareness about human trafficking and its victims. I hope my book will be useful to professionals and volunteers who work with or around trafficking survivors in understanding the kinds of circumstances that enslave children and young adults.

My greatest hope is that the survivors who read my story are able to see that there is hope for a better world, that they are not alone in facing the emotional, financial, physical challenges. If my story offers even a glimmer of hope to a victim who feels trapped, or who is struggling with her own healing journey, I will be eternally grateful.

Acknowledgments

They say it takes a village to raise a child, and I've learned that it also takes a village to write a memoir. There are so many people who have had a deep impact on my life and on the telling of my story. I want to express my appreciation to all the villagers who have made it possible for me to write this book.

Susan Foster de Quintana was willing to edit this book on only a promise; without her, it is possible the project never would have come to completion. Her ability to let my own voice shine through her editing has been amazing and something no other person has ever been able to accomplish. I am truly blessed to have found her.

I don't even know the names of many of the people who have made a difference in my life. What I've learned from the kindness of strangers is this: Never underestimate the power of caring about someone, of making eye contact, sharing a smile, a gentle touch. Those seemingly simple gestures could be the difference between someone attempting suicide and choosing to live. To all the nameless people who smiled at me when I didn't think I existed, who gave me a hug when I needed one the most, and who gave me a helping hand along the way: I thank you from the bottom of my heart.

In order to protect their identities, I cannot tell you the real names of Greg's victims, but I must acknowledge the vital part they played in my life. They kept me alive when I chose to give up. They loved my children as if they were their own. We will forever be connected by the pain we endured together and the love that we showed each other. I am forever thankful to each girl and woman who was brave enough to speak out for truth. Because of their courage, Greg's reign of terror is over. Because of them, I have been given the chance to live free.

People in many walks of life have shown me love and caring throughout the years: family, friends, police officers and other law enforcement officials, teachers, counselors. These people did not judge me; rather, through their kindness, they gave me strength and hope—not only for myself but for mankind. In some cases, it was the simple act of including me in their circle; others devoted countless hours to supporting me on my journey. They emboldened me to explore possibilities, encouraged me to enjoy life, and taught me how to responsibly have fun. Each and every one of these people did or said something so profound that it made it possible for me to be the person I am today—a gift that to me is priceless...because today, I love who I am.

My family has supported me and loved me through thick and thin: Latasha Arnold, Floyd Barnes, Gladys Barnes, Joshua Barnes, Lory Barnes, Steve Barnes, Daniel Corning, Susan Corning, Tom Corning, Gregory Hightower II, Michael Hightower, Margie Martin, Mike Martin, Darla Molina, Julie Etscheid, Wendy Rollins Holt, Janice Putnam Sherman, Dolly Sundstrom.

A score of parole officers, police officers, correctional counselors, and other state officials supported me when I was first released from prison and gave me the guidance I needed to succeed: In order to protect their identifies, I am not listing them by name. I hope my expression of appreciation to them in person has given them a sense of my gratitude for their positive contributions to my life.

Friendships have taken many forms as I have traveled my long road to recovery. Many people have helped me, cared about me, and become my friends. Some appeared in my life when the road was still a mirage—childhood friends who tried to stay in contact with me even when Greg forbade it as well as people who may not even realize that their kind actions or words helped move me to a better place. There have also been men friends who have shown me that not all men are pimps, tricks, or gay—and that the only good man is a gay man. I am grateful for all these friendships: Daryl Bargy, Troy "Toby" Bodine, Karen Brabham, Janet Callahan, Janine Carver, Maureen Clark, Deb Clark-Griffith, Damen Crane, Michael Cory Davis, Mark Dormaier, Crissy Eco, Mark Edward, Lily Eichert, Kelsea Olivia Gaynor, James Austin Gaynor, Millie Gess, Laurie Ishii, Chong Kim, Jennifer Lucier, Claudia Massarelli, Heather McIntosh, Sandi Morgan, Yvette Ollada, Tammy Joy Pritchett, Ellen Pyle, Kristin Ross Lauterbach, Brian Rowe, Dawn Smith, Lanita Stark, Tina Szigetvari, Meg Vallee Munoz, Nina Vatani, Kim Vu, Carol Wheeler, Linda Winters.

The telling of my story is much stronger because of those who graciously read early drafts and offered comments and suggestions. I would especially like to thank Kylla Leeburg for her insightful and generous foreword, as well as Michael Cory Davis, Sandra Morgan, and Holly Austin Smith for their encouraging reviews.

I'd like to give a special shout out to my Hacky Sack team: Chris Brightwell, Antoinette Bucknam, Staci Harrison, Mike Keller Jr., Peter Lecki, Boyd Machtolff, Erica McHenry, and Gemma Pucci Watkins. You taught me to laugh at myself and at life, to embrace the joy in accepting myself and others, to understand what it means to be a team. Most important, you taught me that it is okay to be me and it is okay to trust people.

My heart is willing and grateful but my mind can be weak. I know I may have failed to acknowledge people who have made a vital difference in my life, and I apologize now for that. I may have forgotten a name or two or three, but my spirit remembers and glows with gratitude for their loving light.

Chapter 1
The Rain: Fall 1986

Let the rain kiss you. Let the rain beat
upon your head with silver liquid drops.
Let the rain sing you a lullaby. —
Langston Hughes

I LOVED THE RAIN, and by the time I was seventeen, it had become my best friend. Raindrops drumming on the window soothed my spirits; on working nights, the rain gave me hope that I could stay home.

I stood in our small studio apartment holding my baby girl and gazed out the window. I looked down at Latasha in my arms. Only six months old, she had completely captured my soul. As she stared up at me with dark brown eyes, I spoke to her in a gentle voice.

"You're the most beautiful baby in the world. I love you, my Princess Baby." I longed to stay home with Latasha for the evening.

It didn't seem like so much to ask for, but it was just one of many wishes that were not likely to come true any time soon. If wishing could make it so, Latasha's daddy and I would have jobs, and a nicer place to live, and we would spend every evening with our beautiful baby—but her daddy, Greg, had different ideas, and he was calling all the shots.

The heavy rain had turned to drizzle. I didn't need for Greg to get home to hear his verdict; I knew I would have to go out. It was almost seven thirty;

darkness was setting in and the dim street lights began to shimmer. I sat down on the bed to put on my tennis shoes, but instead I lay down with Latasha next to me. I gazed at her, now in sweet sleep, and placed my index finger in the palm of her hand. She squeezed my finger; surely she, too, wanted me to stay nearby? Her touch comforted me; she was the one blessing in my life. Latasha was the reason I wanted to live.

When I heard the faint sound of Greg walking to our apartment, I lifted myself up to finish tying my shoes. Sadness crept into my spirit, but I quickly blocked it out. His large dark frame appeared in the doorway, and I could see he was alone. Denise was already out working; I needed to hurry.

His strong, deep voice pierced the gentle darkness. "Are you ready to go?"

My voice was soft, with a tint of frustration. "Yeah, I'm going."

I walked the seven blocks from the rundown apartment I called home to my station, one of the many ghetto areas that dotted Seattle. A warm sweater, jeans, and a light coat protected my body from the drizzling rain, but I leaned my head back to catch the raindrops on my face as I walked. As the rain streamed down my face, I allowed the tears that I had been fighting for days to fall. This was the reason I loved the rain so much; even though people could see me, the rain masked my real feelings, the despair I didn't dare let anyone see.

I arrived at my destination—Yesler Way, a rundown street lined with low-income housing. As sad as it was, I yearned to live there instead of my tiny studio apartment. The homes were two-story townhouses, with eight apartments to each building that stretched for four blocks on the north side of Yesler. The bus stop shelter was decorated with overflowing garbage cans and graffiti, as was the building that housed the washing machine and dryers for the low-income housing residents. The laundry facility was a microcosm of everything that was wrong with Yesler Way: The floors were dirty, the washing machines were dirty, the coin machine had been smashed into pieces and no longer worked. A few small businesses dotted the south side of Yesler but were always closed up at night. There was also one small apartment complex that wasn't low-income: Regular people lived there, and we all knew to keep our distance for fear the manager would call the police if we went near it.

I scanned the darkening sidewalk and glanced into the passenger seats of passing cars, keeping an eye out for Denise. As I approached 16th and Yesler, the empty street gave me pause. The police must have recently driven through, or the streets would have been filled with girls desperate to make a few dollars. I feared that the police may have nabbed Denise. I was, of course, concerned for her; but my real fear was for me. Working the street was hard enough; working alone was a nightmare.

A light blue Toyota slowed to a crawl, the driver silently waving to get my attention. My gut cramped, but I knew what I had to do; and in order to do it, I would need to ignore my emotions and turn off any feeling I had inside. Taking a deep breath in and pushing my chest out, I turned to face the car so that he could get a better view of me. I knew the reason men stopped for me and I used that to my advantage. I was just a regular-looking girl with lots of freckles, curly strawberry-blonde hair that fell down around my face, and a few extra pounds that some men appreciated more than others since most of it was on my chest. This is the reason most men picked me up: They all wanted to see and touch my big breasts.

The Toyota circled around the block and came to a stop about five feet in front of me. I started to walk toward the car. For a brief moment, traversing the few feet between me and the car, my confused emotions screamed for my attention, not quite believing what I was about to do. *You're not a prostitute!* Yet I was walking the steps of a prostitute that night.

Damn it! Where is Denise? The fear of being alone forced my full attention to the job at hand. *NJD-NJD-NJD.* I concentrated on mentally repeating the last three letters of the license plate of the car. It was Denise who should have been there to memorize the license plate so she could report it to the police if I disappeared. I always did the same for her. I knew it was futile for me to do it for myself, but somehow it still made me feel safer. *NJD-NJD-NJD. Please God, I don't want to be alone.* As I reached out to open the passenger door of the car, I glanced one last time across the street. My desperate little prayer had been answered. Denise's eyes met mine; she gave me the nod, letting me know she had the license plate number and would remember it until I returned.

It was bittersweet that I was so dependent on Denise. Greg had only recently met her, and she had spent a few hours a day with us since they met. She was fourteen years old, a homeless girl who, Greg had led me to believe, wasn't wanted by her mother. I later learned that she had been living in Greg's car. I didn't like her being around Greg so much, but I also felt sorry for her because she had no place to live.

I opened the car door and settled into the passenger seat. Neither of us spoke as the man started driving slowly down the street. Most of the men who roamed these streets were Chinese, as Chinatown was only a few blocks from my post on Yesler and 16th. I didn't look at the man as he began to talk; my job was easier if I could keep the men faceless in my mind's eye.

"Twenty dolla' for sex."

The tricks from Chinatown were very cheap, but they were safe and very fast. Greg had always warned me: Don't get into a car with a white man, and never with a black man. Even though the white men will pay more, he had cautioned, they take longer, and some will rape you. Greg had convinced us that *every* black man would rape us, but I suspected he had other concerns; there was an air of jealously to his warnings about black men.

I quickly countered, "It's forty dollars for sex and twenty dollars for a blowjob. Which one do you want?" I couldn't believe I was hearing myself speak these words. I wasn't that kind of girl.

The faceless man responded in his broken English, "Twenty dolla', no condom, you suckie."

Although I knew the men finished much faster when I didn't make them wear a condom, I really hated the taste, and the thought of it always made me gag. I wasn't too worried about disease; it was 1986 and the only reference to AIDS that I had ever heard was that it was the gay man's cancer. In my naïveté, I thought any sexually transmitted disease a girl got could easily be taken care of during an afternoon visit to the King County Public Health STD clinic. All I really wanted was to be with my baby. The faster I made the money, the faster I would be able to go home.

"Thirty dollars if you don't want to wear a condom."

The man started to drive down the dark side streets, trying to find a place to park.

"Just pull over here, we won't be long," I directed.

"Too dangerous."

"It's not dangerous. I can't go far, I have to hurry back."

The man pulled over on the dark side street between two houses. A light shone in one of the houses, and I decided that would be the house I would run to if the man tried to hurt me. I was always careful to observe my surroundings and to pick the direction I would run if anything bad happened. The faceless man unzipped his pants and pulled them down around his thighs. I knew what would help him go faster: I pulled down my sweater, reached into my bra, and pulled out my left breast. I bent over the seat; the repulsive smell made my stomach lurch, and I forced myself to hold back the vomit surging in my gut. Quickly composing myself, I bent even further down so the man could cup my breast in his hand.

I hated where I was. My body did what it needed to do to make the money to go home, but my mind withdrew. I emotionally retreated to the safe place I had discovered many years ago: a dreamlike state where I could be an observer, an onlooker who could turn away and not witness my body's degradation. Nothing bad could happen in my safe place.

Two minutes later, it was over. My mind rejoined my body, and I sat back in my seat while the faceless man ejaculated into a napkin. I patiently waited and stared out the window, wondering how I ended up in this place. *I'm out here because I love my daughter. I'm out here because I love Greg and I need to show him that I am worthy of his love in return. I'm out here because I am a piece of shit not worth being loved by anyone and my only status in the world, the only purpose for my...*

The hum of the car engine shifted my thoughts to more practical matters. I knew I didn't want to go home with less than ninety dollars. Greg wouldn't be too hard on me as long as I made ninety dollars. *If I can just do two more blowjobs for thirty dollars a piece, I won't have to have sex with anyone tonight.* I hated that the most, having intercourse with the faceless men. I detested it and I tried my hardest to make the money without having "real" sex.

The car pulled to the side of the road at my corner and I exited as quickly as I could. Denise was walking toward me, and I could see she was visibly upset. *We're not so different*, I thought. She was wearing jeans and a big sweatshirt—neither of us wore miniskirts or heels. She had shoulder-length dark, wavy hair and was about my size but without the added bra cup size. Neither Denise nor I had the attitudes or the looks of the prostitutes we had seen in the movies, much less on the streets. Neither of us felt like prostitutes, either. We each believed that we were only going to do this for a short time, each for her own reasons.

"What's wrong?" I asked.

Denise's voice trembled, "A weird guy picked me up and he wouldn't let me out of his car. I had to jump out at a stop light and run back here to get away from him."

Somehow when others were in trouble, I was able to center myself, remain calm, and assess the situation. "Did you get the license plate?"

Denise looked down, ashamed. "No, I forgot to get it."

"What color was the car? What did the guy look like?"

"He was a white guy in a big old blue truck."

"Didn't Greg tell you to never go with a white guy?"

"But he said he would pay me a hundred dollars."

I didn't know what to say to Denise. If I had been offered a hundred dollars I might have done the same thing.

"Wendy, why don't we go on the dates together? That way if something bad happens there'll be two of us to fight 'em off."

Silently, I rejected the idea. *No! That will just slow me down! I'll never get home to Tasha.* But then my voice spoke.

"That sounds like a really good idea Denise. Let's go."

Although it would take us longer to make enough money to go home, staying together on the dates was worth it for the feeling of safety. It wasn't uncomfortable for us at all. While one of us would perform whatever kind of sex the guy wanted in the front seat, the other would sit in the back and stare out the window. There was comfort in knowing the other girl was there, giving us a sense of power in a helpless situation.

Denise and I got out of the silver Honda Civic after turning our last date for the evening. It hadn't been a great night for either of us, but I had a good outlook and shared it with a smile. "If you're still alive at the end of the night, it's a good evening," I gushed.

It was nearing eleven o'clock, and the drunken men and addicts were starting to rule the streets. Other girls in their high heels and miniskirts—the real ladies of the night—strolled along the street. If Greg could have his way, we would work the street all night long—but even he knew that the later it got, the less likely we were to make any more money. The drug addicts would rob us and the drunks would rape us or waste our time. Denise and I needed to get home. After all, we were only kids.

Chapter 2
My Childhood

Grown-ups are complicated creatures, full
of quirks and secrets.
‾Roald Dahl

WHO IS THIS BEAUTIFUL LITTLE GIRL? I see pictures of myself as a child, and I wonder, Who is this child? She looks sweet, almost happy. How can these possibly be pictures of me?

Only small segments of my childhood come in and out of my memory—and the little bit that I do remember rarely brings a smile to my lips. One vivid scene is a typical memory remnant: Little Wendy is crying and frightened, locked in the bathroom to stave off her tormentors—her big brother and his friend, who are threatening to beat her up. All she wants is for Mommy to come home and rescue her.

Otherwise, the few memories I have before I was eight or nine years old have been recreated from other people's stories and pictures. I watch videos of my dad playing with my brother and me; I struggle without success to recall first-hand the sense of fun that we were clearly having the day that film was made. I am my dad's only biological child, and I know that he loved me dearly when I was a child; but I can't bring forth an image of little Wendy feeling loved.

I do know that I was born and raised in Kent, Washington, a small suburb south of Seattle. The year I was born was stormy; normally relatively safe from natural disaster, the Seattle area even experienced a tornado that year. An omen, perhaps, of the tempestuous journey that Baby Wendy was about to begin.

Until I was eight, there were four of us in the house: my mother, my father, my older brother Steve, and me. My parents struggled financially. Seattle's "Soaring '60s" had soured in the 1970s; when the U.S. Senate canceled projects that had fueled the Puget Sound economy, my father's jobs at Boeing and Lockheed disappeared in the waves of layoffs. So, perhaps it is no surprise that it was my mother who was vocal about our not having enough money and how we had to save every penny. There was never enough money even for the things we needed; if there was something special I wanted, I learned early not to ask. All that I gained was a feeling of selfishness for even asking.

My earliest "real" childhood memory is my mother teaching me notes on an old piano that sat in our living room. For some children, that would be a happy time, but I was miserable. She would make me practice touching the keys on the piano that coincided with the notes on the pages in front of me. When I made a mistake, she would get very upset, and insist that I do it over and over and over again. For at least thirty minutes a day from what seemed like the time I was born, I would be forced to press the keys on the piano and memorize the names of the notes on the pages. If I played well I could stop after half an hour; if I made a lot of mistakes, my mother insisted that I play longer. The notes didn't make any sense to me. It was a ritual, a memorization game that I hated; but it was important to my mother, and I would do it to keep her happy. How I wanted my mother to be happy! Like most children, I loved my mother, even though she was frustrated and angry so much of the time, and I felt responsible in the way children so often do. Making her happy was the most important thing to me, even though I rarely succeeded.

My mom and dad were divorced on Valentine's Day when I was eight. We drove as a family to a strange building. They didn't tell us much about what was going on, but I overheard part of their conversation. "When we walk out of that building," I remember their voices saying, as if singing an unhappy song, "we will no longer be married." As my dad began to park the car, my mother turned to me and Steve in the backseat and said, "You two wait here."

I didn't want to wait in the car with my brother. He was always very mean to me; and since he was two years older, and much bigger than me, it was never a fair fight. "I thought Valentine's Day was for love," I sheepishly said to my brother.

"Shut up," was his only response. He repetitiously kicked the back of the front seat, knowing that it irritated me.

After the divorce, my father moved two hours' drive north to Bellingham, where he was born and raised and where most of his relatives still lived. The divorce did nothing to help our financial situation; it left my mother the house in Kent, its house payments, and us two kids. My mother's income was low. She would only buy food when it was on sale, and then she would stockpile. At times we would have barely any food at all; and at other times we would have enough tuna fish, boxed macaroni and cheese, and TV dinners to last what felt like a lifetime. Once my mother went to the welfare office to ask for assistance;

but they said that she made two dollars over the limit, so she was denied any financial help.

We were left alone quite a bit as children, not because our mother was unfit but because she had to take on extra jobs whenever she could. Sometimes she worked two full-time jobs. With her leaving for work just as we got up and not getting home until after six o'clock in the evening, on most days we had to fend for ourselves. I knew that working and taking care of the house was hard on my mother, and I tried to help out as much as I could. I would wash the dishes and clean the house—although that was mostly futile. My brother, not having anything better to do than to make me cry, would come through like a cyclone, destroying everything I had worked so hard to accomplish.

My mother knew my brother was unkind to me. I often felt alone with the pain that she did not stop him from hurting me, but I was wise enough even at eight to understand that she was probably too tired to deal with it. Years later, when I discovered her journal, I realized that she did appreciate how hard things were for me.

About Wendy

She was personally neat, and although not too clean with her own room, she did more than her share of keeping the rest of the house clean. She often did the giving when it came to conflicts between her and Steve. Wendy always got me the expensive Mother's Day and birthday cards, and wrote a very complimentary song dedicated to me for all I had done for her. She knew I had to work more than one job for just our necessities, and she always wanted to make life easier for me however she could.

It would be easy to say that every day was as painful as the next, but that would not be entirely true. For a few magical days each year, our home was filled with wonder. Christmas time was like a dream come true. The season transformed my Mom into a different person. She would save up vacation days and use them in December, so she could stay home and be a "real" mother. Together, we would spend several weekends getting ready for Christmas: While Christmas music floated from the record player, I would help Mom decorate the house. She would bake cookies—the worst cookies, always burnt on the bottom because she couldn't really bake. Still, her doing normal mommy things made all of us feel so good.

Even when it was awful, Christmas was wonderful. One year, the tree was brimming with presents. After Mom went to work, neither Steve nor I could contain our curiosity. We carefully took the tape off of each present, just enough to get a glimpse of what we would be able to play with on Christmas Eve. We weren't careful enough, apparently; the following day, we could hear Mom yelling, "*You two peeked at your presents!*"

She started ripping all the colorful paper off the presents, lamenting all the while, "I try and do something nice for you kids and you have to go off and ruin it." She demanded that we get dressed and get in the car as she gathered up all the now-unwrapped gifts.

"You are going to return all of these presents and tell the clerks at the store why we are bringing them back."

In the car I burst into tears. I felt like I had stolen something very precious; and, in a way, I guess I had. I had stolen my mother's joy to be able to give us a nice Christmas. We pulled up to the store and she got out and grabbed a few of the gifts. I followed behind her, still whimpering but now more scared than sad. She walked right up to the store manager, handed me one of the presents, and sternly said, "What do you have to say for yourself, Wendy?"

I had no idea.

"Wendy, why do you have to take your present back?"

Softly I uttered, "Because I peeked at my presents...?"

"And what do you have to say to the manager?"

Confused and scared, I thought that maybe I could go to jail for peeking at a present. I looked in vain for support from my brother, but he had run off to hide. I had no idea what to say to the manager, so I softly said what I always said when my mom was upset.

"I'm sorry."

I guess it was the right thing to say, but I didn't say it loudly enough for my mom. In a voice that boomed across the store filled with shoppers, she declared, "*What did you say?!*"

I looked at the ground next to the manager's feet, now more confident about what to do. "We have to return the presents because I peeked at them. I'm sorry."

The next few days were bleak. We were sent to our rooms, and the only music was "I'm Getting Nuttin' for Christmas." But Christmas was still working its magic on my mom. We awoke on Christmas morning to a tree filled with even more presents than we had seen before. It was a great Christmas.

My mother made sure that none of us wasted anything. Even heat was a luxury that she could not afford. With a very stern voice, she told us, "I can't afford for the heater to be turned on. If you need heat, you need to build a fire."

The house was very cold most months. We had a wood stove with a blower, and we would build fires for heating the house. The blower would circulate the precious warmth through our small, three-bedroom home. Sometimes it would take a long time to get the fire roaring hot enough to warm even a few feet around the wood stove. The cold was painful to my body, and I yearned for warmth. One day I discovered that if I turned the knob on the heater that was attached to the living room wall, the heat would blow with great force, soothing the pain. I could hear my mother's admonishment not to turn up the thermostat, but it made no sense to me. *How could turning a knob cost money?* So, every morning I would wait for her to leave and then run to the heater, turn the knob as far as it would go, and feel the healing warm air blowing in my face. With a blanket wrapped tightly around me I would maneuver myself to put my feet on the grates until I felt the sweet sensation of being burned. It was really wonderful not having to get up in the morning and fight to get a fire burning in the wood stove, waiting anxiously for the cold air to stop biting at my skin.

Then came the day my mom got the electric bill. I had not cleaned the house that day when I got home from school. Instead, I had made two tuna fish sandwiches and decided to watch television. When my mom walked in the house, it was easy to see she was in a bad mood, and the messy house did nothing to help soften her disposition. She barely nodded hello before she walked into the kitchen, tearing open the pieces of mail. Suddenly, in a thunderous roar that shook me to the bone, she bellowed.

"Who's been turning on the heater?!"

I swear my heart stopped beating.

"Which one of you kids has been so selfish? Don't you know we're going to be out on the street with nothing to eat and nowhere to go because of you?!"

My eyes swelled with tears; I didn't know that turning on the heater would put us out on the street. I was scared to tell the truth, scared to let anyone know how selfish I was, scared that we would have no place to live and it would be entirely my fault. The sadness overwhelmed me and the truth cried out.

"I'm sorry, Mommy. I'm sorry. I didn't mean to."

My mother's face glowed with rage and pain. I'm not even sure what she said, but the message was clear: Wendy is not worth the money it costs for heat, and she is a selfish person who doesn't care about others. My inner voice repeated the message until it was solidly integrated into my whole being. *I am so worthless, I don't even deserve to be warm. I don't care about anyone.*

The first part I could not change, but the second part I could. I made the decision right then and there always to put others first. *Maybe if I care about others more, I will no longer be selfish, and then someday— maybe—I will be worth the money it costs to get warm.*

Nothing outside my home did anything to console little Wendy. The neighborhood kids were malicious, viciously teasing me as "freckle-face" and "carrot-top." Occasionally, they would be nice to me, but they were just trying to deceive me. They wanted me to put down my guard so they could get closer and make me the target of their cruel games. Once, they called me by my real name, indicating that they wanted to give me a small bunch of leaves with flowers in them. I remembered my vow to put others first; surely I had misunderstood their teasing, and they just wanted to be friends. I gladly accepted their gift, taking the sad bouquet into my hands. Suddenly, my fingers started to sting, and one of the kids pushed my hands together. The hateful neighborhood kids had gifted me with a caustic spray of thistles and thorns.

Being shunned by kids who, they had convinced me, were better than me, I chose to stay at home as much as possible. Like the fateful day we got the huge electric bill, I didn't always clean when I got home from school. Sometimes I would sit in front of the television and make friends with the characters. I knew that they really couldn't hear me or see me; but it was nice pretending that I had friends, and I would talk to them through the television screen. I enjoyed my time with the television characters and would sit there for hours on end, watching reruns and waiting for my mom to come home. My best friends, the ones I liked the best, were Michael, Peter, Micky and Davy—you may remember them as The Monkees.

When I was nine years old, I moved to Bellingham with my dad and new stepmother for my fourth-grade school year. My stepmother had three sons of her own, ranging in age from thirteen to sixteen. Family life in Bellingham was nothing like a typical day in my mother's home. We would sit down at the table for dinner as a family and talk. We didn't own a television, but we would spend many enjoyable hours listening to records. Church was a huge part of their lives, and I attended every Wednesday and Sunday with them. The church had a lot of fun activities for kids, and we enjoyed clapping our hands and singing songs. The whole experience opened a door to a different type of life, one with more togetherness, where a mother stayed home every day instead of going to work. How I wished my mother could do that for me!

When the school year was over, I returned to Kent. As pleasant as it had been with my father's family, I was happy to be home—in no small part because it made my mom happy that I was again living with her and my brother. Around the same time, my mother started dating. On occasion, she would bring the men home to meet Steve and me, but we never really paid much attention to any of them.

I was about ten years old at this point and—perhaps partly in reaction to the new men, none of whom I liked—I started to voice my hatred for reading the notes on the pages and pressing the keys on the piano. I was no longer willing to suffer this indignity in silence. When my mother would make me play, I started to resist, and she would give in and let me stop. In a way, though, that only made it worse; soon, she used sitting at the old, ugly piano and pressing the keys as a tool of punishment. Still, I witnessed my brother routinely disobey my mother without consequence. Selfish or not, I could not bear the injustice.

One day, as I was punitively pressing the keys, I stood up and screamed, "I'm never playing the piano again and you can't make me!" I have no idea what might have gone through my mother's head, but I do know one thing. She never again made me touch the piano. As relieved as I was, I am saddened now to realize that little Wendy did not at that moment also learn the power of screaming "*No!*"

Chapter 3
The Snakes

Childhood should be carefree, playing in the sun;
not living a nightmare in the darkness of the soul.
—*Rob Pelzer,* A Child Called "It"

WHEN I WAS ELEVEN my mother met Ray. I think she liked him so much because he worked two jobs. Steve and I liked him because his house had heat and a fridge packed with a variety of food and, best of all, cable television. I was eager for the weekends to come; we would all go over to Ray's where we would eat and watch television and be warm. Ray would even take us all to the drive-in movies on occasion. That was a real treat for all of us—something we otherwise could never afford to do. More and more we started staying with Ray. Soon it expanded from a weekend adventure into an everyday routine.

My mom found a job working as a clerk at a local police department, and between the raise in pay and Ray's hospitality, my mom was able to quit her second job. She was happy that she could be home with us kids more; she also appreciated that, between their two work schedules, there was always an adult in the house when one or both of us kids were there. Sometime during my sixth grade we basically moved into Ray's house. Without ever making it official, we just never went back to the cold house with no food.

One day not long after I had become comfortable with this newly discovered, cozy family life, I got home from school around four o'clock; and, as usual since we had moved in with Ray, I started watching television. With my mom working swing shift and my brother hanging out with his friends, Ray and I were alone in the house until she came home, typically after ten o'clock. Usually, Ray was asleep when I got home—he was working two jobs—so I was startled when he sat down on the couch beside me. He had never sat so close to me before; I was uncomfortable but I just ignored it and tried to focus on *Mork and Mindy*.

Mork was sent from planet Ork to Earth to study human behavior, and the show was a comedy. It was one of my favorite shows because it was funny and made me happy. But on that cruel day, Mork wasn't the only alien in the room, and I wasn't laughing. Ray the responsible adult had completely disappeared, replaced by Ray the perpetrator. What happened next launched little Wendy into a lonely, twenty-year struggle to protect herself.

Ray lifted his arm around my back, then slid it down to my waist and pulled me even closer to him. He stank with cigarette smoke. I had no idea what he was doing; but he was an adult, and it was his house. I didn't feel I had the right to tell him to stop. He reached his hand into my bra and started massaging my nipples. I knew he shouldn't have been touching me in that way, but I didn't know what to say to make him stop. I sat in shock with his hand down my shirt, his fingers moving between each breast as if he expected to find something different on each one.

My body was average size for an eleven-year-old girl, with a few extra pounds, but I was already bulging out of a C-cup bra. Men would look at me in ways that made me uncomfortable, but I had never had anyone try to touch me the way Ray did. As the fondling continued for many months, I tried to figure out a way to make him stop. I tried pretending to be asleep hoping he would leave me alone, but he would lie down beside me on the couch. His arm felt like a snake, slithering under my shirt and into my bra, slinking on my skin. It would last for half an hour or more. It seemed like an eternity.

Even out in public I was not safe. Sometimes Ray would invite me to go with him on errands in his truck. Even after the abuse started, I wanted to go because he would always buy me fast-food or ice cream. The treats were an attractive lure. *He won't do it this time. I can stay far away from him in the truck so he can't reach me.* I was wrong. He would reach for me and pull me next to him, where he would gently position me to lay my head on his lap. He drove with one hand on the steering wheel and the other down my shirt. I would freeze, plotting in my mind how to pull away but too frightened to try. I was afraid, I wanted it to stop—but I didn't know how to tell him to stop, and I was too embarrassed to tell my mom.

I never knew when Ray would strike. One day, as I was walking into the room, he grabbed my arms and forced me close to him. He put his mouth right next to mine, opened his lips and forced his tongue into my mouth. I tried desperately to close my lips to keep his tongue out; but the harder I tried to stop him, the deeper he forced his tongue down my throat. Sometimes, he would take me to the drive-in movie alone, where he would molest me through the entire film. All I could do was hide deeper and deeper within myself, trying to escape the evil snakes that touched my body in ways I knew it wasn't supposed to be touched. Just as often, he would leave me alone, acting like the Ray who first took us into his home.

During the months that Ray molested me, I learned two things that would change my life forever: The first was that I was a victim of my own body, that the reason most men had any interest in me was because they wanted to see and touch my big breasts. The second lesson was that the only way I could escape my tormenters was to withdraw emotionally into a world where no one could touch me. Ray's abuse taught me that although a man could exploit my body, I could find respite by hiding my soul deep within the pit of my stomach, avoiding the feeling of his evil hands.

The next summer my mom and dad decided I should again live with my dad and stepmother, with monthly weekend trips to visit my mom. My parents felt that Steve was becoming a very bad influence, so they had decided that Steve would stay at Mom's and I would go to Dad's, swapping places the following year. However, the plans changed as soon as I arrived in Bellingham. My stepmother no longer welcomed me in their house.

"Floyd," she explained to my father, "we can't let her stay here. Look how she has blossomed. It would be too much of a temptation on my boys. I will not have it; she cannot live in the same house as my boys."

I was devastated, and frightened that I would be sent back to Ray's house of horrors. My terror turned to joy when my father told me I would be living at my grandparents' house.

My grandparents owned a big piece of land. They lived in the front house, on the street side of the property; toward the back of the lot, across a wide grassy area, was a mobile home where my dad and stepmother lived. There was also a huge shed that housed my grandpa's landscaping business equipment. An intercom system between the two homes allowed all of us to talk to each other. I didn't understand why I couldn't live with my dad, but I was more than happy to live with my grandma. She was so nice to me that I would have visited her every day anyway.

Miraculous things happened while I lived with my grandma. She took me to church and taught me about her friend Jesus, who was nothing like the judgmental, angry God who was going to send me to hell if I was bad. Jesus was very loving and kind, and he became my friend, too. He was a cool dude, and I could talk to him about anything.

My grandma arranged for me to go to a new school where I made other friends, too. My school chums in Bellingham weren't anything like the mean kids from my neighborhood. It was fun to be included and nice to be considered a friend to others. Going to church was nice, too, even though I only really paid attention when everyone was singing out of the hymnals. Thanks to my mom's piano punishments, I knew all the notes to sing. As much as I had hated playing the piano, I loved to sing.

Grandma also had an old ugly piano, but she never made me play it. One lazy Saturday, I was relieving my boredom by snooping around the house. I discovered a piece of paper labeled with the name of a song we had sung at church: "What a Friend We Have in Jesus." I liked singing that song! I looked at the notes on the paper and wondered what would happen if I pressed the keys on the piano. Would I be playing the song I liked? I sat down at the piano; oddly, it felt very comfortable. I started pressing the keys on the piano that correlated with the notes on the page. After a few bars, I could slightly hear the tune of my favorite church song. I played the notes again and again until I hit all the right keys at the right beats. Magically, to my complete surprise....I was playing a song. I was playing *the* song!

Dumbfounded and happy beyond words, I asked my father to buy me some songs on paper that I could play on the piano. I expected him to say he couldn't afford it, so I was thrilled when he agreed. I spent many hours learning how to put together the notes my mother had taught me so they would make a song. When my mother had made me play notes, I had no idea the notes could turn into music. I couldn't wait to show her my discovery! It felt good to be good at something, and I loved the way I felt when I was creating the music.

As miraculous as it was to live with my grandma, it apparently wasn't enough to keep the horrors at bay. I was so happy living with my grandma—and perhaps I had become so good at burying the pain Ray had caused—that I wasn't even aware of the nightmares. I did know that I woke up every morning with the covers torn off the bed and thrown around the room, but it didn't occur to me to wonder why. But my grandma knew. One day she said to my dad, "You need to take this girl to a counselor. She's having horrible nightmares every night."

I began my counseling sessions with a nice lady who would ask me questions about my life. I enjoyed the sessions; I felt special that someone cared about my thoughts and feelings. We would talk about my days at school and my activities with my friends. I felt so comfortable with her I even told her about a cute guy in one of my classes whom I admired from afar. I didn't understand why I was going there and I didn't really care. It was enough just to feel special.

One counseling session started a little different than the previous ones.

"Wendy, you know whatever you say to me will never get repeated. You can tell me whatever you want and I will never tell anyone. Do you understand that?"

I didn't really understand what she was saying because what would I possibly tell her that she wouldn't or couldn't tell others? My reply was simple and straight.

"Yeah."

"Has your stepdad ever touched you in ways that made you feel uncomfortable?"

Feelings and thoughts started racing through me faster than I could control them. *How did she know? Did somebody tell her? Why would she ask such a bizarre question? Do others know? I don't want to answer the question, I don't want to think about it, I want to pretend that it never happened and if I just pretend hard enough it will be real.*

"Wendy, you know it's not okay for someone to touch you when you don't want them to. If he did touch you, it's not your fault and there is nothing for you to be embarrassed about."

But I was embarrassed, and I didn't want anyone to know and I didn't want to talk about it. Egging me on, she continued to talk, which upset me more.

"Wendy, there's nothing for you to be afraid of, you can tell me the truth and then we'll talk about it and it will be over."

The entire time she talked I wouldn't take my eyes off my fingers as I continually played with them. As I rubbed my fingers I softly questioned her.

"What if he has touched me? What's going to happen?" By this time, Ray had stopped touching me when I visited his home to see my mother, and I wanted to forget it had ever happened.

"Has he ever touched you inappropriately?" Her voice was stern. I thought I was in trouble and knew I'd better tell the truth so I spit out.

"Yes."

"What did he do?" I gave her all the yucky details of his snake-like arm reaching into my bra and playing with my breasts. I was embarrassed and starting to get angry because it was no longer happening and I didn't want to talk about it.

The next week I again went to the counseling session thankful that The Talk was over. I wanted to get back to discussing the important things, such as my friends at school and the crush I had on the older boy in eighth grade. I was excited because right after the appointment I would be taking the bus to Seattle for the weekend to see my mom. I was ready to leave— my bags were packed and in the car—but when I walked into the counselor's office, I didn't like the feel of the room or the look on her face.

"Wendy," she said, "I have something I need to talk to you about."

"Okay," I replied as I sat down. *What could she possibly need to talk to me about?*

"When a child is in a situation like yours, it takes a grown-up to make the right decisions about what to do. I have contacted the authorities and have told them what Ray has been doing to you."

At first I was quiet, not understanding; after all, she had promised not to tell anyone. *Who are the authorities and what's going to happen now?*

The thoughts were so loud in my head that I couldn't even hear what she was telling me. I interrupted her to ask, "Will my mom find out? Who all is going to know? Who knows?"

"I don't know if your mom knows yet, but your dad and stepmom know."

That news only increased my embarrassment; I did not want to face them. *Thank God I am going to see my mom right after this. Thank God I can get away from here. I just want to go back to Seattle and live with my mother again.*

The counselor startled me out of my thoughts. "You're not going to be able to go visit your mom this weekend, Wendy. Ray could be there and you wouldn't be safe."

The thoughts kept reeling around in my head. My heart felt like it was going to pound out of my chest. I started to cry because I wanted to see my mom and I didn't want anyone to know what Ray had done to me. How could this evil woman promise me that she would never tell, and then go tell and ruin my life? I felt my life would be forever ruined because I had told.

Quickly, I had a great idea. I could say that I lied. I could say that I made it all up and it would all go away with only a little humiliation on my part.

"What if I lied to you?" I asked.

"Did you lie to me, Wendy?"

The answer I wanted to give wouldn't come out.

"Wendy, did you lie about Ray touching you?"

Softly I cried out the word that I didn't want to say.

"No."

I learned later that Dad had called Mom on Friday, before my counseling session, to tell her I wouldn't be able to visit. He had told her he could not discuss the reason but that she would find out soon enough. Free for the weekend, she and Ray on a whim decided to elope to Las Vegas. On Monday morning when my mom arrived at work as a happy newlywed, she received the phone call.

"Your boyfriend..."

"You mean my husband..."

"Your husband has been molesting your daughter."

Chapter 4
Unloved

*The most terrible poverty is loneliness and
the feeling of being unloved. —Mother
Teresa*

I HAD DESTROYED MY MOTHER'S LIFE. Everything she
had ever wanted was ruined because I had told the
counselor what Ray had done. The court would not
allow her to see me if she and Ray were living
together. I wouldn't have blamed her if she had
decided never to see me again, but she was very kind.
She didn't divorce Ray for financial reasons, but she
believed me and told me that I was not at fault. I was
relieved and grateful when she moved out of Ray's
house so I could live with her again. When the school
year ended in Bellingham, my mother, brother, and I
moved back into the cold house without any food or
cable.

Even though my mother told me I was not to
blame, I woke up every day to the reality that I was the
cause of my family's misery. There was never enough
money, and she once again had to work a second job.
I watched her grow more tired and angry with each
passing day—and it was all because of me. I knew she
wouldn't have to work so hard and that she wouldn't
be yelling so much if I hadn't told the counselor what
happened with Ray.

My brother had no trouble validating my guilt. He was bored and miserable. At Ray's house, Steve had discovered how to sneak alcohol so he and his friends could get drunk and have fun. Now he was back in a house with no alcohol and no cable television. He let me know every day that he hated me for causing this misery in his life.

Ray wasn't allowed to come over to the cold house. The court had given him a reduced sentence. He was required to do some sort of counseling for three months; when the counseling was finished, so was his sentence and he was allowed to live his life however he chose. He never admitted what he had done.

Steve was nearing his teens and had taken to hanging out with the wrong crowd. Their getting drunk was only the tip of the iceberg. More often than not, their activities got them into a lot of trouble; and a lot of my mother's time and emotional energy was spent dealing with the fallout of Steve's stealing from stores or other petty crimes that I did not even understand. By the time he was fourteen, Steve had checked himself into an emergency shelter, entered a child treatment facility, and moved to a boys' group home, where he lived for a year.

One day while I was home alone, I snooped through my mother's filing cabinets. The first file I came to was a thick file labeled "Steve." I grabbed the folder; it was so big that I had to use both hands to extract it from the drawer. I flipped through the folder, which was bursting with all sorts of documents regarding Steve and his life in the group home—letters to and from the counselors over the years, and oodles and oodles of pages in my mother's handwriting. The file made it clear to me: Steve was very important. I could see how much time my mother spent thinking about him and writing about him. *How important am I to my mother?* I wondered. I quickly searched for my own file folder. Sadness consumed me when I discovered my file—a skinny folder containing only my birth certificate and a few report cards.

Of my two children, one was my "good" child, and the other was my "problem" one. My son, Steve, was the one I was afraid would never finish high school or keep a job, and perhaps live on the street, if not end up in jail. When Steve was fourteen, he was sent to a group therapy home for over a year, at which time I made a written record of his life from birth to present. I ended up with a thick accordion file telling of positive and negative events of his life, and the conflicts between his father (my ex-husband) and I.

I also had a skinny folder for my daughter, Wendy, who was my "good" child. She was two years younger than Steve, and she was mature, level-headed, reliable, responsible, and goal orientated, and consequently I never worried about her.

One day Wendy found the two files, and after going through Steve's thick file, then finding only a skinny file on herself, she asked me why I didn't have more on her. I told her I didn't need more, that she was no problem to me.

I can't remember my mother's telling me I was not a problem to her. By that time, my self-image was solidly "the selfish child," and my inner voice probably blocked anything my mother said to the contrary. I wanted to be important and special like my brother. I wanted to be loved as much as my brother was loved. I wanted a thick file like my brother.

During my eighth-grade year, my mother bought a house with Ray. It was no secret that this was my mother's dream house, and that she would never be able to live in it because of me. It had been difficult to return to my old school, and I continued to struggle. I had a difficult time making friends, and I became increasingly secluded. I felt different than the other kids because of the things I had gone through with Ray and the fact that I was destroying my mother's life and there was nothing I could do about it.

To keep my mind off my life, I developed a game, which was to see how long I could go without allowing anyone to touch me...ever. Each day, I discovered new ways to make it from class to class without having to walk down the busy, crowded hallways. Whenever I was in a room full of people, I would ditch and dodge to avoid any contact. I went eight months without feeling anyone's touch. No hugs or kisses from my mother, no side brushes from passing students in the hallways. It was my way of dealing with my guilt. If I had played this game when we lived with Ray—if I had not allowed him to touch me—my mother would not have to pay the consequences.

The saving grace in the eighth grade was music. After the happy hours playing the piano at my grandma's house, I was more than willing to start playing my mother's piano again. When the music teacher discovered my ability to read notes, she asked if I would be the accompanist for the concert choir. Although I was shy and didn't think I was all that good, I accepted her offer and discovered a place where I belonged.

In the ninth grade, I was no longer without friends. I became popular at school because I was the one who played the piano. Life started going well for me, but I was still haunted by the life my mom and brother were forced to live. My mom and I continued to live in the cold house. Technically, Steve lived there, too, after he left the group home, but he would sometimes visit Ray in the dream house.

One day when I got home from school, I discovered that Steve had taken Ray's expensive camera to a friend's house. My mom had borrowed the camera from Ray, and I knew she would be worried about it. When I told my mom, she called Steve at his friend's house and screamed at him that he must return the camera immediately.

Steve did return home immediately, and he was furious. He was so upset with me for telling on him that he started hitting me. As I ran out of the house to try to get away from him, his angry taunt rang in my ears.

"You've ruined our lives. Because of you we're back in this pathetic house without heat. Why did you have to come back?"

I knew what he said was the truth but I didn't know how I could fix it. If I did know a way, I would certainly do whatever I could to change things back the way they were. But all I knew was that I wished I had never told.

I ran down the street going nowhere except away from the house and Steve's violence. In what seemed like less than a minute, I heard a motorcycle approaching rapidly behind me. I looked back to see my brother on his dirt bike headed straight towards me. I could see the anger in his eyes—the anger he had every right to have—and I started to run even faster. I could feel the motorcycle close behind me; when I realized Steve was about to run me over, I jumped into the ditch on the side of the road. He zoomed past, screaming, "I wish you were dead, I'm going to kill you."

There was my answer, the answer that would solve everybody's problems. If I were dead, my mom and brother could move into the house with Ray and they would be happy. I stood up in the dirty ditch and screamed as loudly as I could the great news I had for Steve.

"Don't worry; you don't have to kill me. I'll do it for you."

I headed home feeling hopeful for the first time in a long time. I now had the answer. I hated my life and I wasn't all that special. No one would miss me because no one loved me. If I were dead, my mom and brother would have the opportunity for happiness. My giving them that opportunity would make me a good person in their eyes, and then I would be loved. I walked into the house and headed straight for the bathroom, where my mother kept all the pills. Since I didn't know one pill from another, I took them all.

I waited in the bathroom for a few minutes and then became impatient. I wanted to do this *now*. I went into my bedroom, sat in front of the door with my back against it so no one would come in, and placed a plastic grocery bag over my head. Soon I would become the good person who everyone would now love because I was giving them the opportunity to be happy. A few minutes passed and breathing became harder and harder. I waited to pass out, but the difficulty breathing became unbearable. I removed the bag and decided to wait for the pills to kick in.

Finally the pills started to take effect. I felt woozy, and weird thoughts swam through my mind. *I want to be pretty at my funeral. I don't want to be a bother to anyone, so I will put on my makeup before I die.* I struggled to my feet, gathered the empty pill bottles, and went into the bathroom. I found a little makeup and applied it to my face; then I decided I also needed to make my hair look beautiful. I grabbed the curling iron, went into the living room, and started curling my hair.

"Wendy, I'll be back in a little bit," my mother said as she walked out of the house.

"Okay, Mom. I'll see you later."

I hadn't even known she was there, and I wondered when she had gotten home. I started feeling dopey and thought about how much I would miss playing the piano. I sat down at the piano, which reminded me of my grandma and the Jesus she had taught me about—the nice Jesus whom I could trust and talk to and he would love me no matter what. Although I had heard the rumors that if you kill yourself you will go directly to hell, I believed more in this wonderful Jesus who would truly understand why I was doing this and would surely allow me into heaven with him.

I softly pressed the keys of the piano and sang.

"We've only just begun...to live....White lace and promises...A kiss for luck and we're on our way....And yes, we've just begun."

This was a happy event for me—Jesus and I were beginning our life together! Not only was I giving my mom and brother happiness, I was also going to live with Jesus forever. I continued to sing....

I woke up the following day to disappointment. I could tell by the white walls, hospital equipment, and the nurses in crisp uniforms that I wasn't in heaven. Breaths of air went in and out of my lungs—I was still alive. I hadn't succeeded in giving my mother and brother the life they so desperately wanted. I was a failure even at this. Was my selfishness greater than my desire to make life better for others?

Soon I remembered I was scheduled to play the piano at a concert that night. I had already let my mother and brother down; I didn't want to disappoint my school friends as well. I told the doctor I was alright and I needed to go. I told him about the concert that I needed to be at that evening. They

released me from the hospital to continue to be a
burden on my mother and a thorn in my brother's
side.

Winter came and the house was even colder. One
especially cold Saturday morning, after my mom had
left for work, I lay on the couch underneath a
thousand blankets watching morning cartoons. I
didn't want to leave the warm blankets, but hunger
drew me to the refrigerator. When I opened the
refrigerator door, the warmth from inside embraced
me. I stood at the open refrigerator door, taking in the
warmth for a few moments, until I realized that
keeping the door open could cause the electricity bill
to go up. Forgetting my hunger, I closed the door and
retreated to my blankets on the couch and the
morning cartoons.

In early December, Mom said to me, "Wendy, Ray
is going to be gone from his house for two weeks over
the Christmas holidays. We can stay in the house
while he's gone."

I wanted to go. It was a nice house, and I knew it
would be warm, and I knew my mother would love
being there. I readily agreed.

We packed some belongings and went to the
warm house as soon as Ray was gone. Steve and I were
each assigned a room—the rooms we would have had
if we lived there. My mother's room had a private
bathroom. For two weeks, we all enjoyed ourselves; I
was especially happy about "my" room. I dreamed of
how I would fix it up if it were really mine.

A few days before Ray returned, my mother
approached me with a proposal.

"You know, Wendy, Ray lives downstairs…. He
very rarely comes upstairs. If we were to live here, we
would hardly ever see him. It would be like two

different families renting different parts of the house."

I knew both my mom and my brother wanted to stay at the warm house. I knew that it was the right thing to do, the right thing for me to not be selfish, the right thing to help my mother. In a soft, sheepish voice I stepped up to the plate.

"We can move in here, Mom."

"Are you sure Wendy? Are you sure you would be okay with that?" The expression on her face as she spoke revealed the excitement and happiness she felt.

No! It's not okay!! I wanted to shout, but I remembered what happened the last time I was honest and so I didn't say a word. I was sure I wanted my mother to be happy, and that meant I needed to move into the house of her dreams.

We soon moved all of our belongings into the warm house. My mother was right: It wasn't that bad. Sometimes Ray did come upstairs, but I would go into my room until he left. When I wasn't in school, I would spend most of my time playing the piano. I loved practicing the piano. On the sounds of the notes, I would float away to a peaceful place where I was safe. Playing the piano brought me the escape that I needed, and it felt so good.

I don't remember ever seeing Ray when I was in that safe place, carried away by the music. Years later my mom told me I would sit at the piano playing beautiful music for hours, but when Ray walked into the house, the music changed into some evil, pounding, horrible cacophony. Whenever that happened, she said, I went into a total trance. The minute he would walk out of the house, I would come out of the trance and my music would again transform into a lovely, soft, beautiful melody.

After the Christmas holiday, I returned to ninth grade and continued to play the piano for our school choir. The choir teacher took a liking to me and offered to give me free piano lessons. She invited me to her home, where I got to play her white baby grand piano. It sounded so good when I played it—so good that I felt like I was in the home of my dreams. A home where my mommy didn't have to go to work so she could be there whenever I came through the door, a home where I was loved and appreciated.

I didn't want to lose that feeling, and I wanted to make my dream a reality. I found an old coffee can and decorated it with pretty notes of all colors. I drew the notes with wings because that is the way I felt when I played. I placed the can on the mantel above the fireplace and put every penny, nickel, and dime I found in it. Someday I would buy my own white baby grand piano, and I would be able to float away on the notes anytime I wanted.

Chapter 5
Meeting Greg

The love that lasts the longest is the love that is never returned.
—William Somerset Maugham, A Writer's Notebook

EVERY GIRL AT THE PARTY NOTICED GREG, and almost all them were hanging around, gawking at him. Abigail brought him over to meet me, introducing him as her ex-boyfriend. I thought he was cute, but I could tell right away that a guy like him would never be interested in someone like me.

Greg. Cute, adorable Greg. I thought about him the rest of the summer in the way fifteen-year-old girls do—not unlike the way I had thought about Michael, Peter, Micky, and Davy when I was eight. I hoped to see him again; but I was still surprised when, on my first day as a high school sophomore, I noticed Greg walking into the school—still surrounded by girls who were falling over themselves just to be near him. Greg was sixteen and a junior. His outfit was a replica of Michael Jackson's, and his hair shouted *Thriller* album. Each school day, I would watch him whenever he walked by me, and my heart would pound just from being close to him.

Greg didn't know that I existed, but that didn't stop me from dreaming of him at night. Looking back,

I don't really know why I was so attracted to him. Maybe that's just a rite of passage when you're fifteen, to secretly fall in love with the popular guy at school, knowing he would never like you in return.

I let on to Abigail that I thought Greg was really cute and that I would love to get to know him—even though, I admitted, he probably would never pay any attention to me. Abigail was more optimistic on my behalf. She set up a date for the three of us to go to the Spectrum, a local teen dance club in Federal Way, a small suburb a few miles southwest of my home in Kent. Since none of us had a driver license or car, Abigail arranged for an older friend—who, she told me without embarrassment, gave her money and favors in exchange for looking at her breasts—to give us a ride. I thought that was weird but was grateful that this tiny Asian man was going to drive us to the dance club. He also bought us a six-pack of beer—Olde English 800, which the four of us finished off before we went into the club.

On the drive to Federal Way, Greg sat in the backseat with me, where the smell of his cologne made my heart beat faster. I felt like I was in the presence of a movie star. Under the best of circumstances, I was shy and timid; with Greg sitting so close to me, I couldn't think of a thing to say—and even if I could, I was afraid my voice would shake if I spoke. Only when he asked me a direct question did I answer, and even then the answer was short and to the point.

His voice was full of strength and confidence. "How are you doing tonight?"

"I'm fine," was my small and jittery reply.

I internally berated myself for not being able to make conversation, being totally uncomfortable with the situation in which I found myself. Why couldn't I talk to Greg? When Abigail spoke to me, I could respond intelligently—or at least as intelligent as an awestruck fifteen-year old in the backseat of a car with an open can of beer could be.

Abigail's friend dropped us off to dance the night away. I had never danced with a guy before, and I was very uncomfortable. I didn't know what to do. However, I quickly decided that I was being silly for worrying about this, since there was no way Greg—or any other guy, for that matter—would ever ask me to dance with him. I tried my hardest to act nonchalant, as if I went to dance clubs all the time.

After we ordered sodas at the bar, we found a small, round table where we could sit. The club was packed with animated teenagers, all of them appearing perfectly comfortable and at ease in the setting. Greg grabbed Abigail's hand and led her onto the dance floor. I stayed glued to my seat, nursing my soda. Resigned to the fact that no one would ask me to dance, I watched Greg and Abigail having fun on the dance floor, gracefully moving their bodies to the '80s hip hop dance craze. I closed my eyes so I could enjoy the music, too.

My eyes flew open in surprise when I heard a voice behind me.

"Would you like to dance?" Greg waited for my response.

My heart dropped to the floor—I could barely speak, let alone dance! But my strong attraction to him had other ideas.

"Sure."

I stood up in my high-heeled shoes and followed him to the dance floor, fearing what he might think of my dancing. The jazzy hip hop ended just as we reached the floor, and a slow song took its place. Some of the kids were leaving the dance floor while others moved closer to each other to embrace. I stood completely still, not knowing what to do. Greg reached out, wrapped his arm around my waist, and pulled me close to him. My stomach was full of butterflies and my heart was beating so fast I thought it was going to explode. His arms softly wrapped around me, he guided my body to sway at the same tempo as his. I had never been this close to a boy before. It was the best night of my entire life.

When the dance was over we walked back to the table. My spirit danced with excitement: I had just danced with Greg Hightower! Now he would know who I was at school. No longer would I be Nobody.

The next song clued all the break dancers to get out on the dance floor to show their poppin' and lockin' moves. Abigail and I stayed at the table while Greg went onto the dance floor with all the other young men. He was so good that the other dancers formed a circle around him—their way of showing respect for the best dancer. I secretly fell even more deeply in love.

Abigail's friend picked us up around eleven o'clock. Abigail and Greg talked most of the way home, while I sat quietly in the backseat with my Prince Charming who didn't even know I was alive. The magic of our slow dance did nothing to soften the reality—I had no self-esteem, I didn't think I was at all pretty, and I didn't feel special or that I had any worth. Greg's exclamation when he got out of the car cinched my self-image.

"Bye, Abigail. I'll give you a call!"...and he was gone. I was invisible.

The next few days I spent daydreaming about him, staring at him across the crowded cafeteria, knowing he could not see me and even if he did, he probably wouldn't remember who I was. One day as I was sitting in my homeroom class working on an assignment that was due, I looked up to see him walking down the hallway. He happened to glance back and looked right at me as I was looking at him. *Oh God, how embarrassing, hide, hide!* but there was no time or place to hide as Greg walked through the door, headed straight for me. I looked down at the work on my desk, acting as if I were completely absorbed by my schoolwork, when he walked right past me and up to another girl in the back of the classroom. In a split second, my heart went from panic to devastation. He finished talking with the other girl and then retraced his steps. I kept my head down as he brushed right by me to leave the room.

I spied out of the corner of my eye, watching my Prince Charming walk out the door. Suddenly he turned around, his gaze fixed on me.

"Hey, Wendy! How are you doing?"

Oh my God he remembers my name, Oh my God, he's talking to me, what do I say, what do I say?

"Hey, Greg..."

I was rudely interrupted by the blaring tardy bell. Greg bolted to the door to get to his own classroom. As he squeezed between other kids rushing into my classroom, he turned to me, smiled, and said with a quick upward nod of his head, "I'll catch up with you later."

Needless to say, I didn't hear anything the teacher said during class. I was in love and in a land far away.

Greg and I started talking between classes and occasionally he would invite me to hang out with him and his friends during lunch break. I learned that he was part of a blended family, living with his mom, stepdad, and a mix of kids—hers, his, and theirs. It was a tight fit for the family, living in a three-bedroom, rambler-style house. There were always so many people around him, always many more girls than guys. Plainly all the girls were smitten by him, but Greg never treated any of them like his girlfriend.

A few days before the school dance, Greg asked me, "Are you going to the dance?"

I didn't really know how to answer. Even in junior high I had never gone to a school dance, and I hadn't planned to go to this one. Was he asking me to the dance as his date? I couldn't tell for sure, and I didn't want to ruin that possibility by saying I wasn't going.

"I guess I'll be going." My heart started pounding as I anticipated his invitation. *My first date...Oh my God...It's going to be my first real date and it's going to be with my Prince Charming.* The excitement built inside me until I was almost ready to blow into a billion pieces.

"Great, I'll see you there," he said as he quickly walked away.

I was flooded with confusion. *What the hell is that supposed to mean?* I ran over to my best friend, Allison, and told her what had happened.

"What does that mean? Is he my date for the dance?" Allison didn't know, either; but we immediately started planning what we would wear to the dance two days away.

Allison's dad dropped us off at seven forty-five, even though the dance didn't start till eight. Out of an old, yucky green dress, Allison had created a cute, slutty, totally '80s get-up for me to wear. With black high-heeled pumps and big hair, I looked hot and ready for anything. Allison and I stood in the corridor between the front doors of the school and the cafeteria where the dance was taking place. Allison was a junior, so she knew a lot more people than I did; other girls who came alone would stop, talk, and laugh with us while I kept my eyes on the door, waiting for Greg.

As time passed, it became clear that Greg must not have asked me to come as his date. I had suspected that anyway, so it didn't hurt much. Still I wanted to see him, and he did say he would "see me there." Allison and I went on into the cafeteria to join the party. Near nine o'clock, Greg finally walked through the door—surrounded, as usual, by a crowd of mostly girls. After lingering with them for a bit, he noticed me and strode up to me. Greg looked so handsome, and he was dressed in a nice suit that made him look very sexy.

My hormones flew into overdrive and I'm sure my face was flushed when he approached and looked me up and down.

"Girl, you look *hot*."

I smiled and shyly looked down, not knowing what to say to such a wonderful compliment, especially coming from him. After a short pause he continued with a smile.

"I gotta find my friends in there. I'll be back."

I was so happy and thrilled that he liked what I was wearing and how I looked. Allison and I continued to hang out together, occasionally talking to other people and sometimes just talking to each other, trying hard to look like we fit in and belonged there.

Around a quarter past ten, Greg returned.

"Would you like to dance, beautiful?"

He held out his hand for mine, I laid my hand in his, and we walked to the dance floor. George Michael's "Careless Whispers" began to play. Just like he did at the Spectrum, Greg pulled me close and guided my body to sway with his. For a few precious moments there was silence between us and I soaked up the feeling of being held by a man...of being loved. I built up my courage to lay my head on his chest and it was as beautiful as it was in the movies. The precious moment became even better when he said, "This will now be *our* song." I couldn't contain the joy; as the smile grew on my face, it grew in my heart. This was the best night of my life. My Prince Charming and I had a song—*our* song.

We started seeing each other often. As boyfriends and girlfriends do, I confided in him about personal things, like what I went through with Ray. Greg talked about the day he could save me from the torment of living in that house. One weekend my mom went out of town. Ray was still working two jobs so was rarely at the house, and Steve was almost never around. With the house essentially to ourselves, Allison and I invited Greg and another guy to hang out. I had a feeling this was going to be the night I would give myself to Greg, and we would at long last officially be boyfriend and girlfriend.

Just the idea of being in a relationship with a man and his loving me was exhilarating—more than I could ever hope for in life. I had always felt so alone. In elementary school, a popular girl named Cheryl made fun of me and made sure that nobody else liked me either. My dad loved his wife more than anyone in the world; he had even written me a letter saying his love for his new wife came before me. My mom was too busy working to love me, and my brother hated me. I felt like no one liked me. I had friends who were good people, but I didn't feel truly connected to any of them—well, except for Allison. Allison and me were like peas and carrots, as Forrest Gump might say. All that loneliness was going to change now. I was about to be special to someone. I would never be Nobody again. Greg was going to love me for who I was forever and ever.

That night, in my mother's waterbed, we made love for the first time, and I was now his girlfriend—or so I thought. I was crazy in love with him. And even though we didn't see each other for a few days after that magical night, it did not stop me from daydreaming about how we would spend our lives together. Even though he didn't treat me at school the way boyfriends treat their girlfriends in the movies, I didn't mind much because I knew I was just lucky to be his girlfriend.

A few weeks later we were standing in the lunch line at school when a girl came up to him and started talking to him. In the middle of the conversation she turned to me and asked, "Are you his girlfriend?" I smiled because the answer I was about to give was the answer to all my dreams, but then he answered for me.

"No, we're just friends."

What the fuck? Friends? We had sex! That means we are girlfriend and boyfriend. I wouldn't have sex with a friend. Does he really believe that?

His response jerked the smile off my face and I didn't know what to say, what to do, or how to act. I was totally confused. *Maybe we're not boyfriend and girlfriend until we have sex multiple times?* I became very shy and withdrawn around him, not really understanding where I stood with him. Still, I was so enamored, I was grateful just to be near him—even if he just wanted to be friends, I was okay with that, but I really wanted more.

Chapter 6
So This Is Love

*When the first time I saw you, when you
have been totally a stranger, suddenly,
somehow everything completely
disappeared and I realized that I found
it... true love... From that moment nothing
else matters...* ⎯*Rati Tsiteladze*

*When Steve and Wendy turned sixteen
and eighteen, they did an about-face
turn. I don't worry any more than normal
about Steve who is twenty years old at the
start of this writing, but for Wendy, there
is enough to write a book, if I don't first
have a nervous breakdown! —Mom's
journal*

I WAS DESPERATE TO BE LOVED, to be special to
someone. I wanted to feel the warmth that I didn't
deserve as a child, and I felt Greg could bring me that.
I continued to go to school and play the piano for the
choirs. I developed a few friendships and would do
the things that teenagers would do: skipping school,
going to dances on Friday nights. Greg was always
warm and friendly to me at school, but he was warm

and friendly to all the girls. I wanted more. I wanted to be his girlfriend. I wanted to be important to him.

Like a lost puppy dog, I would follow him around the school trying hard not to be noticed. I wanted to be near him all the time, even if I was hiding around the corner. Always there were lots of girls around him. After a time, I started to think that my dream was hopeless. I wouldn't ever get his love because I wasn't worthy of it.

Out of the blue, he started calling me on the phone. We would talk for hours into the night but he wouldn't be at school. He told me his mom had kicked him out of the house and he was living in a shelter for runaways in downtown Seattle. I felt so bad for him and hated that he was so far away.

One day, he surprised me, arriving at my house in a car. When he took me for a ride, I felt so special— like a Princess being driven in a chariot by her Prince. He told me he had a job at Kentucky Fried Chicken and he had bought the car with his paycheck. He also told me he was living in his car.

How cold it must be in the car! Without a second thought, I said "I can sneak you in my house tonight through my window. You can sleep in my closet. My mom will never know."

He gratefully accepted my offer and said he would come back around ten after my mom went to sleep.

I was so excited to have the opportunity to help him and give him a warm place to sleep. With my mom going to work every day, we could hang out at the house together during the day without anyone knowing. I took a shower and put on my makeup to look pretty for him. At nine-thirty, I started watching out my window for him to pull up; we had agreed he would park his car down the street a few houses. I waited excitedly—the anticipation of his spending the night at my house was more than a dream come true.

Ten o'clock came and went. I continued to wait at my window. My heart would miss a beat every time I saw car lights coming close and would fill with sadness every time I realized the car wasn't his. Eleven o'clock, midnight. I could feel my makeup wearing away and my eyelids grow heavy.

I woke up to a tapping sound. Greg stood on the garage roof, just outside my window. I jumped up to open the window and invite him in. I noticed the time was two in the morning, but at that point I didn't care. I was thrilled that he was finally there.

"Sorry I'm late," he whispered.

"It's okay." I smiled. "Come on in, but be quiet. We mustn't wake my mom."

I showed him to my closet where I had made a pallet of blankets and pillows on the floor. It felt wonderful to have him in my room. We didn't talk much from fear that we would wake up my mom.

"Good night, Greg," I whispered.

"Good night, Wendy."

My mom left for work early in the morning, just as she did every day Monday through Friday. The minute Greg accepted my invitation to stay in my room, I knew I would be skipping school to hang out with him for the day. I got up right after my mom left for work, went to the kitchen, and made French toast and eggs. I brought the hot breakfast to Greg, who was sound asleep in the closet.

In a soft, lilting voice I said, "Good morning, Greg."

He could smell the French toast and eggs. With eyes barely open, he gently responded, "You made me breakfast? That's so sweet of you."

His words melted my heart. I sat down on the floor next to him and watched him eat my offering—

hoping and praying that he would love the food and love me.

Sneaking Greg into the house became a nightly ritual. I started skipping school more and more to hang out with him during the day. It was easy to do; since grammar school, my mom had given me permission to write and sign my own excuse notes. I had been signing my mom's name for so long that the school had my signature on file as hers. Greg and I spent our days making love. I hoped he shared my fantasy that he was my husband and I was his wife. Although he never put a ring on my finger or ever asked me to be his girlfriend, I assumed that we were a couple and hoped that someday we would marry.

Every day late in the afternoon, before my mother would get home from work, Greg would take a shower, put on his nicest clothes, and leave. I understood that he had to leave before my mom got home from work and would return after she went to bed, but I didn't understand why he would have to take a shower and put so much energy into looking perfect. Most nights he wouldn't come in until well after midnight; even though that would upset me, I didn't dare say anything to him for fear I would lose him.

One day he jumped in the shower right after my mom left for work and started getting fixed up.

"Where are you going?"

"I have some things to do," he said nonchalantly.

What could he possibly need to do? He doesn't have a job anymore.

"What do you have to do?"

He patiently sat down on my bed with me and told me about some homeless kids whom he had met. They had been sleeping in his car for the last few nights.

"There are teenagers sleeping in your car?" I said in shock.

In a soft, compassionate voice, he responded, "There are two girls who ran away from home because their dad beats them. They were living outside on the streets and I felt so bad for them that I told them they could stay in my car."

I, too, felt bad for these girls who were being beaten by their father and who had no safe place to go. Greg continued, "I have to find them some food somehow. They must be hungry and I can't just let them starve."

I couldn't believe my good fortune that the man I loved cared so much about other people.

"Greg, please bring them inside. I will make them breakfast."

Greg agreed and left the house while I started making French toast and eggs for four people. A few moments later, Greg returned with two young girls who looked scared and unsure about what was going to happen. I welcomed them and told them breakfast would be done in a few minutes. I showed them where bath towels were and told them they were welcome to take a shower and use the bathroom. They went into the bathroom together, and soon I could hear the shower running. They were very young and vulnerable, like lost puppies with no home to go to. I wanted to help them however I could.

The two girls didn't say much as we all ate breakfast, but it felt so good that Greg and I were helping these young girls. The good feelings shattered when we finished breakfast.

"We better go now."

Before I could say anything, the two girls were standing and heading for the front door with Greg.

"Greg, where do you have to go?"

"They need to get some of their clothes and figure out where they are staying tonight."

I felt like I was losing Greg. I wanted him there with me, not out there with them. Without thinking I blurted out, "They can stay here. I will tell my mom that they are friends from school and I'll ask if they can spend the night."

My intention was not especially altruistic. I had skipped another day of school to be with Greg, not to be left alone for the day. I didn't especially want to share our time with the girls, but it was a better option than not being with him. It was all so confusing; where were they supposed to get their clothes if they couldn't go home because of the father who beat them? The girls looked hesitant, but Greg said it was a good plan. Still, he picked up his car keys and left with the girls to "go get their clothes."

I called my mom to ask her if my two friends from school could stay for the weekend because their parents were going out of town, and she said that was fine. I waited all day for them to return. Into the evening, my mom asked where my friends were, and I told her they would be coming later in the evening. She went to bed early and I continued to wait. Around midnight, I heard the familiar tap on my window. I opened the window; Greg climbed through first, and the two girls followed him in. Since I didn't have to hide the two girls, they slept on my floor while Greg stayed in the closet.

The girls stayed a couple of nights over a three-week period; after that, I never saw them again. Greg told me that they had decided to go back home. I hoped their father would stop beating them. At first I was relieved, thinking that Greg would start spending more time with me again. Instead, Greg did not come back for days at a time.

I started going back to school regularly, but each night I waited for him by the window. When he would show up, we'd sleep until nine or ten in the morning and I would skip school. We would make love, and I always wondered silently how many times we had to have sex before I became his official girlfriend.

Summer was quickly approaching. To this day I'm shocked that I passed the tenth grade with all the days that I skipped, but I did indeed pass. I looked forward to spending all my days and nights with Greg. Sometimes he would leave for days at a time and I wouldn't know where he was. Other times I would hang out with him for days at a time, even spending the night with him in his car.

I got a job at a Dairy Queen to earn money. I wanted to make enough money for us to get our own apartment. I still wanted to get out of the house where the Troll lived downstairs. I quickly learned how easy it was to steal money from the cash registers and I did. With the money, Greg and I would put gas in his car and go out to eat or go to the lake and hang out for the day. The stolen money never lasted very long and neither would my tiny paychecks.

Life was good. All the girls at school knew that Greg and I were together and everyone was jealous of me. Classmates would ask me about Greg and it felt good to have information that the other girls wanted. Somehow, someway, this made me important. I existed to other people because I could answer questions about Greg. Many girls tried to reach him by calling my home phone or hanging out at the lake where we spent a lot of time. Although he still had never asked me to be his girlfriend—and I still wished he would—I was content.

Sitting at home alone one evening —of course waiting for Greg who was God only knows where—I looked at the calendar and wondered when my period should be starting. I counted the days since my last period and thought it was strange that it had been more than twenty-eight days. I wasn't especially concerned until a few days later, when I started throwing up. I felt so sick that I went to the hospital. It didn't take long for the doctors to figure out what was going on; they took a few tests, and within a couple of hours told me I was pregnant.

Because I was only sixteen, the hospital staff had called my mom. When she arrived at the hospital, she was very supportive. As if I had found a doll at the park, I asked her, "Can I keep it?"

"Do you want to?"

"Yes," I said softly, my voice as small as a child. I was a little bit scared, but I was also excited. My baby would surely love me, and Greg would have to love me and stay with me forever.

"Well, then, I'm going to be a grandma," she said with what I think may have been a slight smile.

"You're not mad?"

"No, of course not," said my mom, her humor breaking through. "You know, this is probably all my fault, anyway. If I hadn't just bought that brand-new cream-colored couch and chair, thinking that you and Steve are now old enough not to get them dirty, you probably wouldn't have gotten pregnant."

When we got home from the hospital, I called everyone who might have known where Greg was. I hadn't seen him in a couple of days. One of Greg's relatives lived a mile away; I walked to the house and waited outside, hoping and praying Greg would show up. About an hour later, he pulled up with a car full of people who all got out and scattered. Greg slowly walked up to me looking as sexy as could be. He had a little boy smile and his eyes sparkled.

"Hey, baby, what are you doing here?"

He started petting my hair, stroking away all the reasons that I was mad at him for being gone for days.

"I need to talk to you, Greg."

Softly he responded, "What do you need to talk to me about?"

I had planned to discuss things calmly with him, but instead blurted out my news, my voice choked with tears.

"I'm pregnant."

Silence... Nothing but silence.

Not knowing what else to say, I asked, "Are you mad at me?"

He, too, blurted out responses.

"No, baby, no. I'm just in shock. Are you okay?"

He gave me a big hug and I told him I was fine. We sat down on the curb and talked for a really long time. I loved being the center of his attention for that moment. I was carrying his baby. I now knew for sure I was going to be with him forever. I knew he would now love me more than any of those other girls. We started talking about whether it would be a girl or boy and what we would name our baby. We laughed together and connected on a deeper level than we ever had before. He was happy, and I was overjoyed that I could make him happy.

During Wendy's pregnancy, she often told me Greg would go out with girls who were so in love with him that they'd give him money to make car repairs and other spending. To my knowledge, he never took money from Wendy. At times Wendy's understanding of Greg's relationships with other girls was to just get money, but still other times she was very upset because she'd find out the relationship was something more serious.

All during her pregnancy she said she never wanted Greg to have any legal rights to the baby because she always felt he or one of the many girls who were in love with him would kidnap her baby. The rumors I heard were that all his girlfriends were jealous of Wendy because she was pregnant with his baby and they all wanted his baby. They had many fights where she never wanted to see him again, but in a short time they were lovey-dovey again.

I liked Greg, and he was the first man who ever asked me if there was anything he could do for me around the house. After seeing how much he seemed to like keeping busy, and considering he was almost living at our house, I never hesitated to ask him to do little things for me, which he not only seemed happy to do, but happy that I asked. Of all the negative things I witnessed or heard, I always gave Greg the benefit of the doubt and passed a lot of things onto his youthfulness or immaturity, figuring with time he would grow up and become a hard-working productive member of society, as he seemed to have a lot to offer.

Chapter 7
Loving Hearts, Rough Starts

[L]earn forbearance or, I'll tell you what,
You will be taught it, whether you will or
not.
—Geoffrey Chaucer, The Canterbury
Tales, *"The Franklin's Tale"*

PHYSICALLY, MY PREGNANCY WAS ROUGH, and I was on edge most of the time. I had never grown comfortable with living in the same house with Ray, and my fragile self-esteem desperately needed Greg's presence and reassurance. My pregnancy did nothing to change his constancy; he was rarely there when I most needed him. He even went to the high school prom with another girl because I was so sick I had to drop out.

I was about six months pregnant when things took another turn—and it wasn't for the better. As I had done so many nights before, I was waiting for Greg to come home. I was upset, in part because I needed him with me and in part because I never knew where he was. Like so many other nights, he walked in the door about midnight. Normally, I would relax at the sight of him and welcome him home; but that night I was too sad and scared and no longer had the psychic resources to swallow my hurt. I started to yell.

"Greg, where the fuck have you been? Are you messing around on me? Am I just too fat and pathetic for you anymore?"

Calmly, with a smile, he walked over to the bed and sat down next to me. With assurance he took four twenties out of his pocket and handed them to me.

"Hey baby, look at this."

I grabbed the money and started to count it.

"Where did you get this?"

"You are not going to believe this." He smirked with pride.

I was excited and full of curiosity.

"What? What? How did you get the money?"

Greg then started his story.

"There are girls out on the street who have sex with men for money and then they give it to me for standing out there and protecting them."

In total disbelief, I challenged him.

"What? Protecting them from what?"

"All I have to do is stand out on the street in Chinatown. Girls ask me if I will watch out for them and then they pay me a little bit of money every time they get in a car and make money."

I was confused. How did he learn about this "opportunity"? At first the whole idea scared me: What if someone attacked him? Still, I admired that he was willing to protect girls who chose to be prostitutes, and the kindness in his voice made his concern for the women seem genuine. I was happy he was going to make some money so he could be a good daddy and support our family.

"Can I go out again next week and make more money?"

I wanted him home with me but I had the feeling it wouldn't really matter what I said. I didn't want to take any chances.

"Of course you can go back out there."

For the next couple of months, Greg would disappear on Friday afternoons, and I sometimes wouldn't see him again until Monday or Tuesday. When he would come back, he always had a small amount of money in his pocket and something new: clothes for himself, stereo equipment for his car. A couple of times he had baby clothes—it wasn't much, but enough to encourage my dream of making a family with him. I was nearing the end of my pregnancy and feeling extremely fat and uncomfortable. When he was around, he would pamper me and treat me like a princess, always squashing any concerns I had about him and the girls who gave him money.

"Greg, don't these girls like you in a way that they want you to be their boyfriend?"

He reassured me with a gentle voice.

"Baby, those girls have their own lives. They only want me out there so that pimps won't mess with them. I pretend to be their pimp, they pay me to stand out there, they make their money and go home. I wouldn't be interested in them girls anyways; I'm only doing this so we can have things so we can have a nice life."

Girls would continually call the house and sometimes Greg would leave immediately after talking to them, acting like I wasn't even there. There were times that I thought I was making a huge mistake by staying with him; but I also believed that once our baby was born, Greg would grow up and straighten up. My significance in the world was being with Greg. Before I met Greg, I had never felt like anyone cared about me. Even though he was often gone and there were rumors or even evidence that he was cheating on me, he had the ability to make me feel loved, feel special and unique. He could make me feel like I existed in this world and I was somebody to him.

I yearned for that validation so desperately that Greg's professions of love were powerful enough to counteract a darker aspect of his personality: his willingness to use words to make me feel worthless. He was a master of timing. He would build me up, and then remind me that I was a nobody, and then sweet-talk me into his arms. I'm sure I was in the same place as many other sixteen-year-old girls with low self-esteem who did not know where to find their rightful place in the world. Maybe I just was in the wrong place at the wrong time and chased the wrong boy in school.

Greg didn't want me to be in contact with Allison and would get angry any time she and I got together. One day, after Greg had been gone for a couple of days, Allison came to my house to spend some time with me. We came up with the bright idea to go spy on Greg to see what he was really doing. We weren't even sure where he was but decided a good guess would be Seattle.

Even though I was eight months pregnant, it felt good just to hang out with Allison, driving around in my mom's spare car and listening to the music on the radio. We drove to the most popular section of Seattle, Dick's Drive-In on Broadway, and started watching for Greg or his car. When we spotted his car parked at Dick's, I was excited to have found him and happy that I would be able to see him.

As we looked for a parking space, I saw Greg standing with a crowd of people outside and hollered at him as I drove by. I found a parking spot nearby. I had barely stepped out of the car and was waiting for

Allison to walk around to join me when I heard Greg's voice.

"What the fuck are you doing out here?"

I was startled by the tone of his voice. "We came out here to find you and hang out."

Without warning, he grabbed my head and slammed it into the side of the car. I was in complete shock, I didn't know what was going on, and I didn't understand what I had done that was so wrong. He started yelling at me but I couldn't hear what he was saying over the ringing in my ears. As the ringing stopped, his tone started to change.

"Wendy, you can't be coming out here at night. It's dangerous. You are putting our baby in danger by coming out here."

I'd never heard that it was dangerous on Broadway, only that it was the fun place for teenagers to hang out. He started to apologize for hitting me. He was only thinking of me, he explained, and loved me so much that he couldn't stand the thought of anything bad happening to me.

By this time, I noticed a few girls walking towards us, staring at us. I had never seen them before, but I could tell they were with Greg. Greg gave me a hug, put me back in the car and told me to go straight home. On the way home, Allison wouldn't shut up about how bad Greg was and how I should leave him—but all I had heard was how much he loved me and wanted to protect me. I felt bad that I had made him so mad that he had to hit me to make me realize it.

In January, Greg turned eighteen and in February I turned seventeen. In March, I gave birth to our daughter, Latasha. From the moment I saw her, she became the most precious thing in the world to me. Because she was born with some health conditions, the doctors kept her in the hospital for a week. After two days, I was released from the hospital—but every day, I would ride into work with my mom so she could drop me off at the hospital, where I stayed all day with my beautiful child.

Latasha Is Born
A beautiful baby girl was born one month premature. Her name is Latasha. Tasha came home one week later and Wendy seemed to be totally submitted to Greg, putting all her doubts behind and trusting Greg completely. Other than Greg wanting to give Tasha a jawbreaker on her first day home, they were both very attentive, loving, and responsive towards Tasha. Wendy was barely seventeen now, and I felt with her maturity and unselfish nature, she would be an excellent mother. I could see no reason why Tasha wouldn't have at least an average life. Although not discussed with me, I got the impression they planned to marry and make a go of it.

Our plans were for Greg and I to get married and get jobs and have more kids and grow old together. They were the perfect plans in my forever dream, but the dream was very short lived. Within days of Latasha's homecoming, Greg was gone, running the streets. Even the sporadic times that he would come by to see us, girls whom I didn't know would call the house looking for him. He would play with Latasha while he talked on the phone with the girls. I could see that he loved Latasha, but I didn't feel he loved me at all.

By this time my brother, Steve, had moved back home. While he was in the group home as a teenager, he had learned sign language, which gave him an important tool for turning his own life around. After he got out of the group home and was again living at home, he began to volunteer as an interpreter at churches, and he was gainfully employed as an interpreter for the hearing-impaired at local schools. He was no longer the mean big brother I had grown up with; in fact, he had become a protective big brother to me.

When Greg would come to the house, Steve saw first-hand the way Greg treated me. At first Steve tried to handle it by confronting Greg, which Greg chose to escalate into a fist fight. Steve pleaded with me to leave Greg, but was unable to convince me. When he witnessed Greg hit me and take two-month-old Latasha from me, Steve decided to kill Greg. Fortunately, while out shopping for a gun, Steve's maturity kicked in. He realized that killing Greg would not solve the problem; as long as I continued to make bad decisions, I would probably just end up with another "Greg." Steve worried that there would be no one to protect me if he killed Greg and went to prison.

Steve could not stand watching me go through the vicious cycle with Greg. Steve also knew that he could not trust himself to stand by while he watched me destroy my life. He felt helpless to make a difference in my life and knew that he could not help me. He told me that he loved me but he couldn't handle watching me destroy myself and Latasha. He told me that he could not be a part of my life as long as I was involved with Greg. The emotions he was experiencing were so high, he decided to remove himself from the situation and start a whole new life. Within two weeks he made the twelve hundred-mile journey to start a new life in Southern California.

My mother was my sole supporter. Greg would occasionally bring Latasha a toy, but he never bought diapers or formula. I was miserable, always wondering where Greg was and wondering what he was doing with the other girls. I wanted him to love me. I needed him to be with me and Latasha.

My mother loved having Latasha around. Thank God for my mother and all she did for us. She took Latasha to get her first photos and bought her every cute outfit she saw at the store. She always made sure Tasha had enough diapers, formula, baby powder—everything she needed and wanted. My mom would sneak into my room on Saturday mornings and get Latasha from her crib and take her into the living room. Mom would play with Latasha for hours to allow me to get extra sleep.

When Greg came around, we would start fighting. I would fight with him because he was always gone, and he would say it was all my fault. One day he stayed for a couple of days and told me that the reason we were having so many problems was that my mother was in our lives too much. He told me that if we could get our own place, he would stay at home with me and Tasha.

Greg pleaded, "Wendy, if you love me and Latasha, you'll move out of your mom's house. You can't expect me to act like a father and husband if I don't have the opportunity to be a father and husband. Your mom does everything for you and Latasha and she's always getting into our lives and that's why I'm never around."

A little bit confused about how we were going to move into our own place, I asked, "How am I supposed to get my own place when I'm not even eighteen? Nobody will rent me an apartment until I'm eighteen."

His answer came quickly, as if he had planned it out. "You have to get emancipated. If you go to a shelter and get on welfare, they will consider you to be an adult and you'll be able to get an apartment."

I wanted so much for us to be a family. I believed in Greg and the dream that I had for our family. He had a solution, he gave me a bit of hope that I could have a man who would love me and care for me and Latasha. Without much hesitation, I planned my escape from my mom.

I knew my mom would never let me go and I would need to leave without her knowing. I told Greg to pick me up the following day to take me to the shelter that he had told me about. I packed our things and wrote my mom a note explaining that I was leaving to start my life. It felt more like I was running away... And I was.

I moved into the Union Gospel Mission, an old, rundown, roach-filled hotel that had been transformed into the shelter in a scary part of Downtown Seattle. Latasha and I were assigned to a room of our own on a floor designated for women and children only. My intention was to get on welfare so Greg and I could get an apartment of our own. I was frightened and felt very alone. Greg was staying at his grandmother's apartment about five miles away from the shelter. The residents were allowed to make free five-minute calls, so every chance I had, I would call him.

Every morning, Latasha and I had to leave the shelter at seven-thirty and could not return until three o'clock in the afternoon. I was given directions to the soup kitchen a few blocks down the street, but the first few days I was too afraid to go so I didn't eat. I went to the welfare office and discovered that it would take up to forty-five days to receive my first welfare check of three hundred seventy-five dollars. I spent my time looking around for apartments that I could move into the minute I received my first check. Declarations of being together aside, Greg was rarely around. Within a week, the diapers and formula that I had taken when I moved out of my mom's house were gone, and I had no money to buy more. I called Greg.

"Greg, Tasha doesn't have any more diapers or formula."

I breathlessly waited for a response from him, waited for him to release me from this dire situation. I needed a savior, a rescuer.

Chapter 8
My First Trick

Whoever digs a pit will fall into it....
—Proverbs 26:27

AFTER A SHORT PAUSE HE STARTED TO SPEAK. "I know of a way we can make some money." I was thrilled to hear this; I wanted to know what kind of job he had discovered for us. I imagined us washing windows together or cleaning somebody's house. I was not remotely prepared for his proposal.

"What are you willing to do for Latasha? How much do you love her?"

It was such an unexpected question, it was hard to imagine what he was going to suggest. *This job must be pretty bad, maybe even picking up garbage on the sides of the streets*, I thought—but I was more than willing to do even that. All I wanted was for Latasha to be loved and to have the good life she deserved. Although we were still teenagers, I really believed that once Greg and I got jobs and a nicer place to live, everything would be alright. My only concern was who would watch Latasha while we worked.

Greg wasn't giving me any answers—just questions that weren't making sense to me.

"I know how we can get diapers and formula. You just have to believe in me and trust me. Do you believe in me, Wendy? Do you trust me?"

I started to feel uneasy, but his confidence was calming. As it so often did when Greg was gentle with me, his voice inspired feelings of trust in my Prince Charming. I wanted to believe in him, I wanted to trust him—I did trust him, for the sake of our family....for isn't that what family is about? Isn't that what love is about? And I believed in love.

"Of course I believe in you, Greg. Of course I trust you."

"Meet me up on 16th and Yesler in the laundry house in an hour." He didn't even wait for me to answer before he hung up.

I knew the laundry house where he wanted me to meet him because we had hung out there a few days earlier when I had to leave the shelter during the day. It was a Laundromat in a low-income apartment complex that was open to the public. It was so dirty and rundown I wouldn't even want to wash my clothes there, but it had provided refuge from the wind and rain when we had no other place to go.

Latasha's diaper was wet as I wrapped her up tight in a blanket, heading off to the Laundromat. I was excited that I would get to see Greg, and I did have faith that he would find a way to get diapers and formula for our baby.

Greg was waiting for me when we arrived at the wash house. He took Latasha in his arms and cooed, "Hey, Princess, how's Daddy's girl doing?" He was so great to Latasha, he loved her so much. I could see the kind of father—and Prince Charming for both of us— he could be if we were in the right situation.

Greg seemed bewildered when he realized Latasha was wearing a wet diaper.

"Wendy, her diaper is wet. Why didn't you change her?"

"I told you, I don't have any more diapers or formula for her."

He didn't hesitate. "All you have to do is walk up Yesler Way and a Chinese man will stop and pick you up. He will offer you twenty-five or thirty dollars to have sex with you. All you have to do is have sex with him in the car and we'll have the money for Tasha's diapers and formula."

I couldn't speak. I didn't understand what he was asking me to do.

He added, "The Chinese men are real quick; you'll have the money within a few minutes and it will be over forever and you'll never have to do it again. You love Latasha, don't you?"

"Of course I love Latasha."

"Would you do anything for her?"

"Of course I would, but I don't know about this. I'm scared, I don't know about this."

My mind was clouded with confusion. Surely I was misunderstanding. The idea seemed so wrong, but Greg's tone was so kind. He effusively reassured me of his love for me and Tasha. He seemed to sincerely believe that I would be doing the right thing if I followed his instructions.

"I'll stay here with Latasha. All you have to do is start walking up the street. When a Chinese man pulls over in his car, you go get in. He will offer you twenty-five or thirty dollars to have sex with him. You do it right there in the car, it will be over before you know it. Then have him drop you off right back here where I'll be waiting for you."

I was amazed that he would know that a Chinese man would stop and pick me up. I didn't understand how he knew this, but I didn't question him. He reached around me with his one free arm and gave me a big hug and a kiss on the forehead.

"You can do this, sweetie, I believe in you. I know you are scared, but it will be quick and over with before you know it. It's easy money and girls do it all the time." Still seeing the fear in my eyes, he very sweetly added the verbal blow that he knew would control me.

"You love Latasha don't you? Her diaper is wet and we need to get her some dry ones."

I walked out of the wash house and onto Yesler Way. I did exactly what Greg had told me to do. I walked down the street wondering who would possibly pick me up, who would possibly mistake me for a prostitute. I was wearing jeans and a sweatshirt. I wasn't wearing any makeup because I hadn't taken any with me when I left my mom's house to go to the shelter. I had walked only a few feet when a car pulled to the side of the road in front of me. I looked behind me to see if he was pulling over for someone else; when I saw the sidewalk was empty, I knew he was waiting for me to get in.

I was scared and visibly shaking. I approached the car, held out my hand to open the car door and saw my hand was trembling from fear. I didn't want to get in. Wasn't there some other way we could get diapers for Latasha? For a moment, I considered returning to the wash house without doing what Greg had told me, and all I could envision were Latasha in her wet diaper and Greg's disappointed face. Feeling like I had no other option, I opened the car door and got in.

The car was warm but it had a funny smell to it. I glanced at the man driving the car. He was, as Greg had predicted, Chinese—and although he was petite, I was frightened even more when I saw his face. I quickly looked away and stayed quiet, unsure of what I was supposed to do or say. The man drove very slowly down the street and then he spoke.

"Twenty-five dollars for sex?"

I didn't have a clue how I was supposed to respond, so I didn't say a word. I didn't want to be there and I started to pray silently for a way out of the situation.

Oh, dear God, Please help me. I don't know what to do. God, if you're real, please don't make me do this. I don't want to do this. Please, God, if you can make this not happen I promise I'll go to church every week and I'll never be bad again.

My heaven-bound plea was interrupted by the scary man who would soon be between my legs.

"We do it in the bushes."

I remained quiet, still hoping God would rescue me. The man drove the car onto a gravel road with tall trees and bushes along both sides. Pulling over to the side, he turned the car off and got out. My body sat frozen in the seat while tears pooled in the corner of my eyes. A senseless jumble of thoughts raced through my head. I became dizzy, still waiting on God. I was too young to understand that God rarely makes bargains.

My door opened and the small man stood waiting for me to exit his car.

"Come now, we go over there." He motioned to a small clearing between two bushes. My throat felt like it was swelling shut, and I became even more fearful when I realized I couldn't scream even if I had chosen to.

It was dark and getting cold. I followed the man to the clearing between the bushes. I reached my hand out for the twenty-five dollars he was handing me—the twenty-five dollars that would rescue my daughter from her wet diaper and hunger pains. The twenty-five dollars that would prove to Greg I was a good mother and worthy of his love.

As soon as I had the money in my hand, the Chinese man started to unbuckle his belt. I went emotionally numb and pretended to know what I was doing as I started unzipping my jeans and pulling my shoe off. He motioned for me to lie down on the ground just as I was pulling my leg out of my pants and underwear. I pushed my pant leg and underwear to the side as I lay down on the ground on the twigs that poked my skin. I didn't bother taking off my other shoe or exposing my other leg. I thought as long as what he was purchasing was revealed and accessible to him that was all that mattered.

He dropped down on top of me, spreading my legs with his body. I looked up at the tree limbs that hovered over me and realized there was no God. Two minutes later he was finished. I felt like I had been raped—but I had accepted his money, made a tacit agreement not to scream or run away. Maybe it wasn't rape after all.

The five-minute car ride back to Greg and Latasha seemed an eternity. The car was full of silence and my soul was completely empty. When the car stopped, I walked as quickly as I could to the wash house where Greg and Tasha waited for me. When I saw Greg holding Latasha in his arms, I nearly swooned with the clashing emotions. His eyes were full of compassion and warmth; surely he could see that mine were full of pain and misery? I opened my arms to get Latasha from him but was suddenly overwhelmed by the urge to throw up.

I succumbed to the convulsions of my body trying to rid itself of the horror it had just experienced. What little I had in my stomach spewed onto the floor next to one of the washing machines— but my body was not relieved. My body continued to heave even harder, determined to eject the offensive event itself. A few drops of water dripped out of my eyes and a force within me bellowed through my body, violently expelling something unseen. I stood silent, totally overwhelmed by what had happened, and then went numb. I felt nothing. It was as if I weren't really there, as if I hadn't just disgorged my soul. Greg just stood in silence, waiting for me to finish, almost as if he expected it to happen, as if he had seen the same thing happen before.

We walked to the grocery store and bought diapers and formula. I changed Latasha's diaper in the store bathroom and prepared her a fresh bottle of formula. Of the twenty-five dollars that had cost me my soul, we had about seven dollars left; with that, we went to McDonald's and ate. I thought about how much I wanted to be with Greg, how I treasured the attention and love that he was showing me at that moment. But I also knew there was now something missing within me, something irretrievable. I felt lost and alone. The experience of having sex for money with a complete stranger immediately took its toll. I felt gross, revolting, and, above all, worthless and forever unlovable.

It took only a few days for Greg to violate his promise that I would never have to turn another trick. When he came to the shelter that night, I wrapped Tasha in a blanket and went outside with her to see what he wanted. He took Latasha from me and began trying to convince me to go out on the street. I was still numb, lost, confused; but his holding Latasha cheered me. It was the one piece of happiness that I had, the illusion that we were a family and that he loved Latasha.

"We need the money," he said matter-of-factly. "The more money you make, the faster you can get out of this shelter." At first he tried to be persuasive, but he could sense my resistance. His efforts to convince me quickly shifted to accusations.

"Latasha does not deserve to be in a shelter. Why would you want to keep her here? What kind of mother are you?"

I was still emotionally black from the first trick and I couldn't handle doing another one—but I was already so psychically small that it was easy for him to pound me down to nothing. I stood there before him as the worthless piece of shit I believed I was. My soul was empty, my spirit was black, and I agreed with him that I was a bad person for not doing everything I could to get my beautiful baby out of the shelter.

I began to question my commitment to Latasha. *Maybe I don't love her the way I should. Maybe I am a bad mother and she doesn't deserve someone like me to be her mother.* It killed me inside to realize that Greg was right. She didn't deserve to be in a shelter, and the only way I could redeem myself was to do everything I could to get her into a real home. The kind of home my mother could offer her but I couldn't. For a moment, I felt a glimmer of possibility; but I knew that if I went back to my mom's house, I would never see Greg again, and I might even lose Latasha.

Greg held Latasha lovingly in his arms. I knew she was safe with him. Since the day she was born, Greg had said she would be better off with him, and I knew that he was right. According to Greg, I was a pathetic, stupid slut for sleeping with him; he had convinced me that if it weren't for him, Latasha would end up just like me.

The raindrops started to fall as I turned to walk toward Yesler Way, still not sure if I was leaving them forever to give them the chance of a happy life or if I was going to attempt to redeem myself by turning another trick. In a deathlike daze I walked up the street. The tears ran down my face, flowing more heavily the closer I got to my destination. I was a block away from Yesler Way when a car pulled over in front of me. Although I had only done this once before, I knew what he wanted. I accepted the invitation to get in the car.

He took me to a motel room and offered me a beer. I drank it for no reason other than to drink it. I was lost in a world of pain, chaos, and confusion. My emotions were running in every direction, and I wanted them to stop. I grabbed another beer, hoping to quiet my misery. He offered me twenty dollars to have sex with him. I didn't want to do it, but I didn't say no. I felt so cheap and ugly. Was this really all I was worth? I emotionlessly removed my clothes and lay on the hotel bed, still as the corpse I knew I would soon be. When he finished I put my clothes on in silence, waited for him at the door of the hotel room, and then we left.

"Drop me off here," I said.

"Are you sure?"

"Yeah."

There was a small twenty four-hour convenience store and I knew of a park nearby. I bought a bottle of sleeping pills and a Diet Coke. I walked to the nearby park where I found some bushes where I could hide my broken body. The sound of raindrops hitting the leaves calmed my spirit for a moment, but my despair silenced even their life-giving music. With the Diet Coke I swallowed the entire bottle of sleeping pills.

I waited to die, but it took too long. Once again, I was a failure even at this—and to make things even worse, I realized my death would accomplish nothing except to prove that I didn't love Latasha. What kind of mother would abandon her baby, leaving her bundled in a blanket with her father standing in the rain? I cried myself to sleep on the wet dirt.

Chapter 9
Mrs. Butterworth

Don't they always go from bad to worse?
There's no turning back—your old self
rejects you, and shuts you out.
—Lilly Bart in Edith Wharton, The
House of Mirth

SOON AFTER MY SECOND FAILED ENCOUNTER with sleeping pills, I received my first welfare check. I found a rundown studio apartment for a hundred seventy-five dollars a month—nearly half of my welfare check—on 9th and Columbia in Seattle. The apartment was only a few blocks from Harborview Medical Center, one of the busiest high-trauma hospitals in Seattle at that time. Junkies and homeless people were the main scenery from my window. The apartment was tiny, with a pullout bed, small kitchenette, and a bathroom that we shared with the studio apartment next to ours. I had entered "18" as my age on the rental application and nervously pulled out my driver license to show the manager; but he did not notice—or did not really care—that my birth date revealed I was only seventeen.

Although the apartment wasn't much and I was scared to leave it without Greg, it was still home for me. I had high hopes that this would be our new beginning that would allow us to get real jobs and build our family life together. I was happy that I had the apartment and that I would never have to work the street again. I could put that behind me and forget it had ever happened. I could pretend that I was a good mother, a good wife, and a good human being.

After paying rent and bills, my welfare check was gone. When Greg left each day, he gave me the impression that he was looking for work. In the meantime, diapers and formula were running thin again. I found a blood blank that would pay eight dollars for my plasma, and if I gave twice in one week, they would pay me fifteen dollars for the second draw. When I told Greg about the opportunity, he said that he couldn't do that because there was something wrong with his blood, but he would take a break from looking for work twice a week to watch Latasha so I could go to the blood bank and sell my plasma.

Most other days, Greg would get fixed up and leave in his car. Some days he wouldn't come home at all. I would stay up late, worrying about him. Partly I worried because he never told me what he was doing, but I was also afraid he might get arrested. He had never bothered to get his driver license, and he had been given lots of tickets that he never took care of, so he had warrants out for his arrest. After two days of his absence, I would bundle Latasha up and we would walk to the King County Jail to see if he had been detained. A couple of times I found him there, picked up for driving without a license or speeding—but, usually, he was not at the jail, and I would walk home, still very worried that he may have gotten into a wreck.

We did not have a phone; I was disconnected from the entire world. He forbade me from having any contact with my mom, insisting that she was the reason we were having problems. I missed my mom. I missed the mornings she would play with Latasha and allow me to sleep in. It was easy to obey Greg and not call my mom anyway; I didn't even have a quarter for the pay phone down the street.

One day Greg had been gone for three or four days. Latasha was out of diapers and I had been laying her on towels, washing her and the towels every two hours. Her formula was almost gone and I had been crying nonstop. This was not what I had planned. I didn't know what to do. Looking fresh and rested, Greg walked through the door with a big smile, holding two bags of diapers and a grocery bag of food and formula.

"Hey, baby, did you miss me?" he called out in a cheery voice. He dropped everything he had in his hands and walked straight to Latasha. He swooped her up and held her over his head to make her laugh and giggle.

"How's my princess baby? Are you happy to see your daddy?"

He acted like nothing was wrong—as if he hadn't been gone for four days and left us here with no diapers, with no contact to the outside world. He didn't even know or care that I had been crying for days on end or that I had walked to the jail to see if he was there. I put my emotions aside to address the more pressing matter of putting a diaper on Latasha and scavenging through the bag of groceries to find something to eat. I had been eating scraps for days and I was starving.

Stuffing food into my mouth, I mumbled, "Where have you been?"

The good cheer in his voice turned to ice. "I've been out taking care of business, more than I can say about what you've been doing."

I was completely taken aback by his response. "What do you mean? I've been here taking care of Latasha. What else could I have been doing?"

His tone got rough. "I got diapers, food, and formula. I'm taking care of you and Latasha. I could be here sitting on my ass like you are, so shut the fuck up."

I quickly softened my attitude. I didn't want to piss him off. I had seen him angry and I didn't want to ever see that again.

"Okay, baby. Thank you for the food and diapers. Where did you get them? Did you get a job?"

"Yeah, you can say that."

"Where did you get a job? When do you have to go back to work? What do you do?" I was so excited that he got a job and was so proud of him. I wanted to please him as a reward for finding a job, so I added, "Can I make you something to eat? Are you hungry?"

"I'm not hungry, sweetie, I just want to go to sleep. I've been working hard. I'll tell you more about it later." He lay down on the bed, got comfortable, and fell asleep.

Latasha and I remained quiet so he could rest. I daydreamed of what our life would be like in a few years. I watched him sleep and fell deeper in love with him for providing for us. Greg had always told me that no one would ever love me as much as he did, and I believed him.

That night, he told me that he had to go back to work. He said that he was a street sweeper and that's the reason he worked at night. He started coming home regularly, and every day he had money to buy food for us. Even though our apartment was very small, he bought a huge stereo system that filled an entire corner.

Some days I felt hopeful and even happy, but the seeds of my future torment were beginning to germinate. When Greg was home, he would blast the record player so loudly that the neighbors would complain. Their complaints made him very angry, and he would blame me.

"Why did you move us into this apartment?!! You need to get us a better place to live!!"

Also around this time, Greg started making hurtful comments to me with increasing frequency.

"You're a piece of shit."

"You're nothing in this world."

"Nobody will ever love you but me."

"You can't do anything right."

"You'll never make it in the real world."

"Everything you touch you destroy."

I had surrendered what tiny bit of confidence I had when I turned the two tricks, so it was easy to believe Greg's taunts. Once I believed them, I slowly started to become them.

One day when I got home from selling my plasma, Greg was visibly upset.

"I have to go," he roared.

"Why? What's going on?" I wanted to know what was so wrong that he was so upset and needed to immediately leave.

"I have to go take care of some business, my car needs a new transmission and you're not going to get me one with your pathetic plasma money, are you?"

I didn't respond. I walked almost everywhere I went and didn't really care that the car was broken. To me that car was nothing more than the vehicle he used to abandon Latasha and me every weekend, leaving us at home alone with no phone.

Angrily he asked me, "Is this how you plan on supporting us for the rest of your life? I thought you were a better woman than to have your family living like this. Your fifteen dollars isn't even going to put dinner on the table tonight."

"But I'm going to the food bank tomorrow; we'll get enough food to get by." My tone of voice was defensive and pathetic.

"You're a stupid fucking bitch who should've never been born! I've wasted my life with you and you're a horrible mother. If you really loved us you wouldn't have us living like this. You have the choice for us to live better than this, but you're so fucking selfish you refuse to do it."

His insults inspired my own anger.

"Is that what you think I am? Am I nothing but a ho to you?"

I had barely finished the sentence when Greg grabbed the large glass Mrs. Butterworth's bottle. I saw it flying through the air straight at my head, so fast that I barely had time to lean my head to the side. The bottle smashed into the wall behind me. I looked back at the hole Mrs. Butterworth had left in the wall and looked down at the bottle. It was still totally intact, not even chipped. I stood frozen as he turned and walked out the door, slamming it behind him.

One day Latasha and I were at the apartment by ourselves when I heard a knock on the door. No one had ever knocked on the door before, and a part of me became very scared. Creeping up to the door, which did not have a peep hole, I gathered the nerve to ask, "Who is it?"

A soft female voice responded, "Is Greg there?"

My curiosity about who this person was overcame my fear. I opened the door to see a young girl standing before me. She looked very raggedy, as though she hadn't showered in a few days, and I could tell she was as uncomfortable as I was.

"Greg's not here. I don't know where he is."

She quickly turned and started to walk away without even saying good-bye. I had to speak loudly so she could hear me.

"Who are you? What do you want with Greg?"

She slowly walked back to the door of the apartment, her head hung low and her eyes on the ground. When she got closer to me she said, "My name is Denise. I'm looking for Greg."

I felt sorry for her and I wanted to help her any way I could. "Would you like to come in for a little while and wait for him? I don't know when he will be back, but you can wait for him here and have something to eat if you want."

I barely had any food in the house to begin with, but I could tell by the way Denise looked that even a cracker would be plentiful for her. She walked into the apartment and sat on the couch, which was right next to the bed.

"Would you like something to eat?" I asked.

"No, thank you."

I sat on the bed with Latasha, who was napping. I still had no idea why Denise was looking for Greg or how she knew him. I really wanted to know, but I didn't have the words to ask too many questions.

Greg came home soon after Denise arrived and was startled to see her in the house. He quickly took her outside and when he returned he forcefully told me, "Don't ever let her in here around my daughter again."

She seemed like a sweet girl, I thought. "Why not?"

"I don't trust anyone around my daughter. She's a homeless girl that's been following me around like a puppy dog. I found her sleeping in my car this morning. Just don't let her in here again and don't ever talk to her."

I felt sorry for the young girl and wished I could help her.

Some days Greg was very nice to me and made me feel loved and cared for, but those days were becoming fewer and fewer. He seemed to have a lot of money to put into his car, including stereo systems and huge speakers. I would watch him out the window as he left the apartment building, and I could see Denise in his car. I thought it was nice of him to allow her to sleep in the car. I wouldn't have minded if she had stayed with us except that Greg had told me she was never allowed to be around Latasha and I wasn't allowed to speak to her.

A few days later Latasha again was running out of diapers. I approached Greg.

"Baby, Latasha needs more diapers. Can you pick some up on your way home?"

He turned towards me with evil in his eyes.

"When are you going to start buying her diapers? I should replace you with Denise since she loves Latasha more than you do. Denise sacrifices every night to give me money to buy Latasha diapers and formula. What are you doing for Latasha? How are you showing her love by sitting on your ass every day except to go to the stupid plasma blood bank to earn close to nothing?"

I didn't understand what he was saying. My mind tried to process what he was saying and how Denise might be involved with Tasha's diapers at all. He saw my confusion and used it as an opportunity to berate me even more.

"You stupid fucking bitch!! How the fuck do you think Latasha's been getting her diapers? Denise has been working the streets to support you and Latasha. She's not even Latasha's mother and she is doing more for Latasha than you do!!! If you were a good mother, you would be out there making the money to buy her diapers. If *you* loved her, you wouldn't be allowing someone else to support her."

I had no idea. In my gut, I had suspicions about how Greg had been getting so much money to fix up his car and buy new clothes, but I had dismissed my misgivings, convincing myself I was just being paranoid. I was ashamed that a young girl had been prostituting to provide my daughter with diapers. I felt like an unfit mother. I felt like a failure.

I also wondered how Denise could do that night after night. *She must not be like me, because there is no way that I could continue to be purchased by men night after night. She must be a prostitute, because a normal girl could never endure the humiliation over and over again every day.*

My thoughts were stopped when Greg rushed over to me and put his face right in front of mine. With evil eyes and a deathly tone, he ordered, "You're going tonight. You're going to make the money for Latasha's diapers. It's time for you to prove you love me and Latasha. I don't think you love us enough. Maybe Denise needs to be Latasha's new mommy."

Greg slammed the door as he left. I looked out the window and could see Denise standing at his car waiting for him. He approached her, gave her a quick kiss, and the two of them got into his car and left. I was thankful to Denise for buying Latasha's diapers. I appreciated what she had done for us, now that I knew the truth.

Chapter 10
The Scary Streets

I'm going to spend the rest of my life
proving to you that I'm worthy of your
love. —Georgia Cates

I ROCKED LATASHA IN MY ARMS for the rest of the
afternoon. Even when she wanted to crawl around the
tiny apartment, I stayed as close to her as I possibly
could. Touching her, holding her—and all I could
think about was Greg's verdict that would soon send
me out on the street. I wondered what I could possibly
wear out on the street that night. The two times I had
turned a trick, it was Greg's spur of the moment idea. I
had not prepared myself; I did not even know that I
was going to do it until I did it. This time, I had time
to shower, put on my makeup, and fix my hair. I
didn't have any clothes that looked like the prostitutes
I had seen in the movies. I wondered what Denise
wore out on the streets and if she had anything I
could borrow so I would look like a prostitute.

I chose the prettiest dress from a box of clothes I
had brought with me from my mom's house. It was a
light blue dress that I had not worn since I had moved
into the apartment. I had a pair of white, lacy shoes
with a small heel. I looked more like I was on my way
to church than trying to pretend to be a prostitute for
a night.

I waited by the window to watch for Greg to come home to give me further instructions. I tried to convince myself that I was doing the right thing. *All I have to do is go out one more night. This will prove my love to Greg and Latasha. This will show him that I am a good woman. After this things will get better.* I tried hard to hide the fear that consumed me.

Around eight o'clock, I saw Greg's car pull up. Denise got out of the passenger side and immediately started walking in the direction of Yesler Way. This time, there wasn't a kiss between them. I also noticed that she was wearing jeans and a T-shirt, nothing like the prostitutes on television. I figured she must not have been on her way to work after all, and I was sad for that. I was hoping she would be out on the street also so that, maybe, I could follow her for guidance on how I was supposed to act.

Greg came upstairs. When he saw me he blurted out, "What the fuck are you wearing? You're not going to church."

I spoke softly, embarrassed. "This is the best I have. I don't have anything else to wear."

"Put on a pair of jeans, tennis shoes, and a sexy shirt," he instructed. He went into the closet to the pile of clothes, pulled out the sexiest shirt I had—which wasn't very sexy at all—and threw it at me.

"Wear this," he demanded.

I quickly changed clothes and Greg inspected me up and down.

"That'll do."

Suddenly, his tone changed and he became caring and loving. He pulled me in close to him.

"Sweetie, I love you so much that you are willing to do this. I knew you would be a good mother and wife. You need to be careful out there. Only get into cars with the Chinese men. Do not go with any white men or black men. The black guys will rob you, the white guys will rape you. Don't accept anything less than thirty dollars per date. Just do two dates and then come home. That will be enough money for diapers and formula." And then he added, in the most tenderhearted voice I could imagine, "I love you."

Those words always melted my heart. That's all I ever wanted to hear. Greg scooped up Latasha and started to play with her. He threw her over his shoulders and swung her around to make her laugh and giggle. I loved seeing this side of him. I loved seeing how happy he was with Latasha. All I had to do was make it through tonight and then everything would be alright.

I kissed Greg and Latasha good-bye. I felt sick, knowing what I was about to do. I also knew there was a chance that I would never see them again. The Green River Killer was legendary in the Seattle area. I had heard about him since my childhood, and I knew that the police had never caught him. The Green River Killer was known for killing prostitutes—and even though I wasn't a prostitute, he wouldn't know that, and I could be his next victim.

I walked to Yesler Way. When I had worked the street before, the avenue was quiet; but this time, a Friday night, the streets were very crowded. From a few blocks away, I could see a lot of people on the street corner. As I approached I could see that they were all girls, all different kinds of girls. Fat girls, skinny girls, black girls, white girls, Chinese girls. Girls in miniskirts, girls in high heels, girls in sweat pants. Girls with lots of makeup, girls with no makeup at all. And they were all working. I was very surprised to see how many girls were walking up and down the street. I noticed that when a car would pull to the side of the road, a bunch of the girls would run to the car and talk to the driver through the passenger side window. After a few moments, one of the girls would get into the car and the other girls would immediately start walking the street again.

There was a sheltered bus stop on the corner; being afraid and knowing I was not at all like these other girls, I sat on the bench and pretended to wait for the bus. I didn't know how I was going to find a "date" with so many girls running to the cars. That wasn't like me at all; I didn't have the nerve to run to a car and talk to a guy through the window. I kept my eye out for Denise, but I didn't see her anywhere. I felt alone, scared, and way too far out of my element.

About fifteen minutes later most of the girls had been picked up, and only a few girls were left scattered along the block. I looked across and down the street, and I saw Denise, standing at another bus stop just like I was. She didn't look like a prostitute. She wore jeans and a T-shirt with high heels. I couldn't fathom why Greg told me not to talk to her. She looked like a nice girl. I would never dream that she would hurt Latasha in any way, and I still felt grateful to her for buying Latasha's diapers. I was still looking at her when she looked right at me. Although it was too far away for me to really see her eyes, I sensed there was fear in them. I wondered if she was as scared as I was.

A large green car pulled up beside the bus stop. A tall Chinese man bent over to roll down the passenger side window.

"Are you working?"

I shrugged my shoulders. I wasn't sure if I was "working," but I got off the bench and went and got into his car. I stared straight ahead, too scared to even look at him, and waited for him to say something.

"You look scared."

"A little," I agreed softly.

"I don't do this very often. But I got lonely sitting at home and thought I would come out and see if there were any nice looking girls."

The compliment made me feel good.

"Can I take you back to my place?" His voice was friendly and he spoke good English, unlike the other two guys who had picked me up.

"I don't think I can go back to your place because it would take too long. Plus that's kind of scary. Can't we just do it in your car?" I asked sheepishly.

"I really hate doing it in my car. I promise, I'm a safe person and I don't live far from here at all. I'll pay you fifty dollars?"

That seemed like a bit of good news. *Greg told me that I only have to make sixty dollars before I can come home. I'm sure he wouldn't be mad if I only made fifty. This means that I can go straight home after this and I won't have to do this ever again in my life.* I started adding up in my head how many bags of diapers fifty dollars would buy. I looked a little more closely at the guy, who did seem pretty "normal."

"Okay, then. But you have to be quick."

He drove me to his house, about two miles away. He actually lived in the basement of someone else's house, which made me feel better, knowing that there were people upstairs. His living area was dark and small. I walked over to the bed and held out my hand to signal to him that I needed the money. He placed a fifty dollar bill in my hand, and I proceeded to take off my clothes. I held the fifty dollar bill tight in my hand and lay on the bed.

He was taller than most Chinese men, and he looked to be only twenty-five years old. His voice was soft, and when he touched me, he was very gentle. I was still scared, but not scared of him. He lasted a little bit longer than the other two Chinese men I had "dated." I made a few sexual noises to help him along, and it ended soon after that. I was glad when it was over and promptly got dressed.

He drove me back to the spot where he had picked me up. Still there were girls scattered along the block on both sides of the street, but they weren't gathered at the bus stop as they had been earlier in the evening. It was only about nine o'clock, and I was glad that I would be able to go home to Latasha and Greg.

As my date slowed to pull to the side of the road, I noticed that Denise was sitting at the bus stop where I had been. The car came to a stop, he said "thank you," and I said "good-bye." I got out of the car right in front of Denise. I wasn't sure what to say to her; I somehow felt intimidated by her. I glanced her way and saw her smile. I smiled back and said "hi." She said "hi" back to me, and I walked home.

I hadn't brought any house keys with me in case I was kidnapped or killed, so I knocked on the door and waited for Greg to let me in. He held out his hand for the money. I thought he would be very happy with how fast I returned home with the fifty dollar bill. I put the money in his hand, he took a look at it, and protested, "Where's the rest of it?"

"I only had to do one date for the fifty. I didn't want to do another one. Fifty dollars will buy a lot of diapers." I tried to take the money back from his hand so I could go to the store in the morning and buy them. I even knew what store had a good sale on them, and I could buy extra so they would last a long time.

He looked fierce. He snatched his hand back with the money.

"I told you sixty dollars. Now you have to go back out tomorrow night and do it again. Tomorrow you'd better bring me eighty dollars." He started walking out the door with the money in hand.

"But what about Latasha's diapers?" I whined.

"I'll get her damn diapers, don't worry about that."

I watched out the window as he got into his car. I knew that he was going to see Denise, and I wondered if she had made enough money to keep him happy.

He didn't come home that night or the following day. I felt like a failure. I wanted to make him happy. I wanted him to think I was a good mother. I was mad at myself for failing at everything I did. Rather than defeat me as it so often did, my self-contempt increased my determination to prove to Greg I was worthy of his love. Tonight, I would make a hundred and fifty dollars. I would make him be proud of me. I would make sure I had money to buy extra toys and clothes for Latasha.

That evening, I went through the same ritual as the previous night, but this time with the right clothes and a much different attitude. I knew what I had to do to get him to love me, and I was willing to die trying. I was still scared…but my fear was now masked by anger. I put on a little more makeup than I had the previous night—war paint that I smothered on my face to help me to turn off my emotions and be the strong, fearless girl I needed to be. When Greg came home around seven thirty, Denise wasn't with him. He strode into the apartment with an attitude, but it didn't matter to me, because my attitude was bigger. I threw on a light jacket and headed out the door in my high-heeled shoes.

It was a Saturday night and I thought the streets would look the same as they did the night before, but they didn't. Very few girls were out, and I quickly assessed that I was the best-looking girl out there. Of the few others girls who stood waiting for their tricks to arrive, one didn't have on any makeup and looked like she was half asleep. Another was so overweight she could barely walk, and a third sat on the bench picking at her zits in a world all her own.

With confidence I started walking down the street. In less than a minute, a car pulled over and I got in. I felt a little bit more comfortable with what was about to happen. I knew how to quickly turn off any feelings I had and play the role of a prostitute. The man offered me thirty dollars for oral sex. We parked in an empty area around the corner and I quickly completed the job. He dropped me back off and in no time another car picked me up. I made another thirty dollars, again for oral sex. The second date dropped me off and I started walking. I was getting tired already but I knew I wasn't going home with less money than it would take for me to be validated as being worthy of Greg's love. When I noticed Denise across the street, I just kept strutting, acting like I was a pro. She crossed the street, running towards me.

"Hi, Wendy," she said softly.

"Hi," I responded, almost abruptly.

"How are you doing tonight?" I figured she must be asking about how much money I made because I imagined that that was the only thing prostitutes would talk about.

"I've made sixty dollars so far. I'll be out here for a while." I continued to scan the streets for the next car that would pick me up, but there weren't many cars coming.

She confessed, "I haven't made anything yet."

I found this very shocking, that I had made more money than a real prostitute. I let my guard down just a bit.

"Why? Aren't there any johns out here?"

"No, there are johns, but it's getting really scary out here. I've been hearing lots of stories of girls getting kidnapped and killed and raped. I'm scared to get in the cars."

I stood frozen in shock. She had admitted that she was scared. I stared at her and saw Denise, the real Denise, for the first time. She wasn't a prostitute. She was just like me. There must be a reason that she had been forced out on the street, pretending to be a prostitute.

"Why don't you go home?"

"I can't. I ran away. My mom won't take me back."

"How old are you?"

"Fourteen." I couldn't believe it. I thought that maybe she was seventeen, or sixteen at the youngest.

"How long have you been out here?" I asked.

"A few weeks. Greg's been nice and lets me stay in his car at night."

I remembered seeing Greg kiss her and I wanted to ask her about it, but I didn't want to get into trouble. Greg had told me I wasn't allowed to talk to her, and I didn't want to do anything that would jeopardize his loving me. And I needed to hurry up and make my money. Besides, I felt so sorry for both of us that I couldn't think of anything else to say to her.

"I gotta get going. I'll see you later."

She stopped me by blurting out, "Can we stand together until one of us gets a trick? We can keep each other company at least." I saw the fear in her eyes—the fear that I had hidden deep beneath my makeup where no one could see.

"Yeah, sure. That sounds like a good idea."

A car rolled up beside us and she jumped to the opportunity since she still hadn't made any money. She talked to the guy for a moment through the passenger-side window and then jumped in the car. As the car drove away, I noticed the license plate and decided to try to memorize the numbers. If she did not return, I could provide the police with the plate number of the car she was last seen in. Her story about girls being raped and murdered did scare me. I knew the realities, but I was so determined to make enough money to prove my worth to Greg that I had put it out of my mind. Besides, I had never heard it on the streets from other girls—that comforted me a bit until I realized I had never talked to any of the other girls except Denise.

I soon got another date, who offered forty dollars for sex in the backseat of his car. By the time he dropped me off, Denise had also returned.

"Is everything okay?" I asked her.

"Yes."

"I memorized the license plate of the car when you got in, in case you didn't come back." She liked that idea, and we made a pact that from then on we would do that for each other.

We each did a few more dates and stayed by each other's side on the corner whenever we were free. It felt good to have someone out there with me. I didn't feel so alone.

"Where are you staying tonight? Will you be okay?" I asked her.

"I don't know...probably get a hotel if I make enough money. Yes, I'll be okay."

I had made a hundred and forty dollars. I turned away from Denise, feeling a little sad that I might not see her again. After all, I had surely made enough money to satisfy Greg, to stay off the streets forever. With lightness in my step, I started home.

Chapter 11
The Gravedigger

It is said that a frog will jump out of a pot of boiling water. Place him in a pot and turn it up a little at a time, and he will stay until he is boiled to death. Us frogs understand this. ⁻*Deb Caletti,* Stay

GREG WAS VERY PLEASED with the money I brought home to him, and he treated me like a queen. He told me that I would never have to go out on the street again because he now knew how much I loved him and he had confidence in giving me his love. I loved the way he treated me. He brought me a romantic single rose. He made love to me and told me that I was the best lover he'd ever had. He made sure that Latasha had diapers and formula, and he even bought her a couple of small toys.

I fell in love with Greg all over again. It seemed like a new beginning—but like all the others, it was short-lived. As Friday night approached, Greg's sweet-talk gave way to mean remarks, and he would take off in his car and leave for hours while I worried about him.

I knew that he didn't have a job, and the money I had earned the week before was soon gone. I was still getting my welfare check and going to the blood bank twice a week to earn my eight and fifteen dollars. That helped to keep us fed and the bills paid, but it wasn't enough. By Friday, Greg's loving attitude had completely changed: The only way that I could make him happy was to go out on the street.

I was miserable. Greg had reneged completely on his promise that I would never have to work the streets again. Instead, he made me go out every Friday and Saturday night. The only thing that gave me any comfort was knowing that Denise would be there and we would watch each other's back. After a few weeks, I told Greg that Denise and I were working together. He didn't like that we were in contact, but he didn't tell me to stop talking to her.

One Friday night, it was raining especially hard. There weren't any cars on the streets, and even though Denise and I were the only girls working, there was no money to be made. After two hours of standing in the sheltered bus stop and seeing the police slow down each time they drove by, I said, "Come on, let's go home. You can stay with us tonight." She looked hesitant but gladly accepted. We went back to the apartment and told Greg the police were watching us. To my surprise, he didn't seem to mind at all that I had invited Denise to stay.

I liked having a friend spend the night. A night turned into a day. A day turned into a week. Greg would leave as he always did, but I didn't mind it as much because Denise was there with me.

One day, Greg was gone and there was a hard knock on the door. I opened the door to two police officers, who asked me where Denise was. I pointed towards the bathroom in the cubby off the hallway. I watched as they banged on the bathroom door. She came out and they put handcuffs on her. We were both scared and confused as they took her away.

When Greg got home and I told him what happened, he yelled at me.

"Why did you let them take her? Why did you tell them where she was? You should have told them that you didn't know who she was!"

His anger shocked me. I had always been taught to tell the truth, especially to policemen. I didn't know why Greg was so upset. Maybe the police would help her find a place to live since her mom wouldn't let her go home.

About a week later Denise knocked on the door, asking for Greg, who, of course, was not home. I invited her in. She told me that the police had taken her home and her mom had beaten her, so she ran away again. I felt so bad for her. She was crying and had no place to go. Of course I told her she could stay with us. When Greg returned, he seemed happy to see Denise. A little bit too happy, but I dismissed the weird feeling.

She would go out every night to work the street. I didn't understand what she was doing with the money she earned because she never seemed to have any. I assumed that she was saving it up so she could get her own place, but I couldn't help but wonder if there was something she wasn't telling me.

One Friday night I came home a little bit early and found Denise and Greg sitting together on the bed. They were fully clothed but acted very suspicious. When Denise and I left for work the next night, I asked her, "Have you and Greg ever had sex?"

She gave me a crazy look and almost shouted, "No, no! I would never do that!"

I believed her because she was my friend and friends don't lie to each other. We spent the rest of the evening hanging out with each other, going on dates together when we could or taking down license plate numbers when the guys would not allow both of us in the car. When we walked back to the apartment,

I handed my money to Greg, just as I always did—but this time Denise did the same.

"Why is she giving you her money?"

"I'm holding onto it for her so nothing happens to it." He sounded angry. I was afraid to ask any more questions, but I knew that something was different between them.

Monday, I left the apartment to go to the YWCA to look into taking some general education development—GED—classes so I could finish the requirements for my high school diploma. The farther I got away from the apartment, the more my body started shaking. I started feeling queasy, and my mind shrieked, *Go back!*

I turned around and headed back home. The closer I got to the apartment, the more I realized why I was shaking. I had a feeling that they were having sex. *God, this can't be happening. He can't be cheating on me. Oh, God, I've been so stupid not to see what was right before my eyes. She's not my friend. She's been Greg's girlfriend behind my back.*

Tears were falling down my face at the thought of what I was about to find. I put the key in the door and quickly opened it to see the two of them naked on my bed having sex, Latasha asleep on the couch. I turned around and started running down the stairs. I found a cubbyhole to a fire escape where I hid, and I cried and cried and cried.

Greg soon found me and was entreating that he was sorry. He made up every excuse in the entire world, including blaming it on me. I continued to cry, he continued to plead and apologize. He pulled me close to him, holding me tight as he whispered over and over again, "I'm sorry, I'm sorry. I don't ever want to hurt you. I'm sorry. I love you."

I was speechless. I couldn't think, I couldn't talk, I couldn't move. Greg lifted me to my feet and carried me up the stairs like a baby. It felt good to be in his arms. It felt good to feel his warmth. He continued to whisper, "I love you—I'm sorry." He carried me into the room. Denise was no longer there. He laid me down on the bed, brought Latasha from the couch over to me, and then he lay down beside us. We lay there in silence for hours. He stroked my hair, massaged my temples. He whispered, "I love you," and somehow he made everything okay again.

I didn't see Denise again after that. I was sad to lose her friendship and hurt that she had betrayed me, but the incident had the happy result that Greg stopped sending me out to work on the street.

Two weeks later there was another hard knock on the door. Again, I opened the door to two police officers.

"Is Greg Hightower here?"

"No," was all I could say. The police turned and left.

I bundled Latasha up and ran about a block away to the nearest phone booth. I called Greg's grandmother, where he spent a lot of his time. I told her to let Greg know that the police were looking for him, then I went back home to wait for Greg. I waited for him throughout the day and night. The following day one of Greg's relatives came by the house.

"Wendy, Greg sent me to tell you that Denise is setting him up with the police. Greg had to get away from the police so he moved to Denver to stay with his mom. He wants you to take the car and drive down there with Latasha as soon as you get your next welfare check."

My head was spinning. I wanted to talk to Greg. I wanted to find out what was going on. Why would Denise try and set him up with the police? What could Denise possibly say to the police that would scare Greg so much that he would run all the way to

Colorado? Greg's relative handed me the keys to Greg's car and told me that I should be at his grandma's house the following day so I could talk to him when he called.

The next day, I drove the three miles to Greg's grandmother's house. Latasha and I visited with her until Greg called. I cried the moment I heard his voice.

"Wendy, Denise is setting me up with the police. She is telling them that I was pimping her. I had to get out of Washington before the police found me."

"Greg, can't you tell the police the truth? Can't you tell them that she was a runaway and you were only trying to help her?"

That *had* to be the truth. It was impossible that Greg was a pimp. I knew what a pimp was: a black man who struts with a cane and wears a big fur coat and a hat with a feather in it. A pimp has at least five skinny, pretty girls who wear miniskirts and high heels and make lots of money for him. If Greg were a pimp, that would make me a prostitute—a possibility that my mind could not comprehend. I wasn't a prostitute, and neither was Denise—so Greg could not possibly be a pimp.

Greg began to lose patience.

"Wendy, they aren't going to believe me. I am a black man. I need you to pack all our things and you and Latasha drive down here."

We talked for a little longer, hashing out the plans for me to drive to Denver. Near the end of the conversation I asked, "Can I go see my mom before I leave?"

"No! She can't know where we are. She could be a part of this. I think your mom is helping Denise's mom to convince Denise to put me in jail."

I didn't believe what he was saying, but I knew it was futile to try to convince him otherwise. I would get my welfare check on the first of the month, a couple of weeks after I talked with Greg. We had enough food and diapers to last us until then, and it was nice not having to go out on the street.

As soon as I got my check, I packed up the car with as much stuff as I could put into it. Greg was insistent that I take all of his stereo equipment, even if that meant leaving Latasha's toys and the crib we had recently bought for her. Latasha and I drove to Colorado and met up with Greg at his mom's house. Greg's mom, stepdad, and four half- and stepsiblings—two brothers and two sisters—all lived upstairs in the four bedrooms, so Greg, Latasha, and I stayed in the large basement.

Greg promised me that he had never pimped Denise. He told me that the only thing he ever did was allow her to stay in his car and sometimes given her rides. For a month or two, everything went well. Greg's stepdad had told him he couldn't stay unless he had a job, so he was getting up every morning to work as a housekeeper at a local hotel. The money he made wasn't enough; since his mom, Juanita, said she would babysit Latasha, I was able to get a job at a hotel across the street from Greg's workplace. On our time off, we would play outside in the yard with Latasha, who was now an active nineteen month-old toddler. Greg wasn't running the streets anymore. He was being the man I always dreamed he could be.

One evening we were going out to dinner when the police got behind us, with the siren blaring and the lights flashing. We both were panic-stricken, and Greg ordered me to lie about his name. They pulled Greg out of the car as soon as we stopped, put him in handcuffs, and ordered him to get into the back of the police car. I stayed in our car, trembling. When the policemen asked me who Greg was, I followed his instructions and told them he was Alexander Ramos.

I also gave them a fake birth date for Greg that we had made up as we were being pulled over.

The policemen weren't buying it. They continued to ask me over and over again his name, even adding, "He's Greg Hightower, isn't he? And you are lying for him." When the police told me they were taking him to jail, I asked if I could get his wallet from him since he had all our money. They were kind enough to allow me to walk back to the police car and get his wallet. As I stood on the side of the road, a picture of Greg caught my eye, hanging on the dashboard of the police car. Why would they come all the way to Colorado to find him? I couldn't understand why they would put so much energy into someone who hadn't done anything wrong.

I continued to work my job at the hotel while Greg's mom watched Latasha, and I visited Greg in the jail on his visiting days. Some days he would tell me that the charges would be dropped, other days I could see that he was scared and he feared that he would be going to jail for a long time. He didn't want to be taken back to Washington; but three weeks later when I visited him, the police informed me that he had been extradited. I drove back to the house as quickly as I could and called my mom. I didn't know whom else to call, what else to do. I was lost and alone. I didn't want to stay with Greg's relatives if he was going to be so far away.

My mom was thrilled to talk with me and told me I could come home any time I wanted. She sent me enough money for plane tickets for Latasha and me. Even though Ray was still living downstairs, it was wonderful being at the house. The warmth of my mother's protection and security outweighed any uneasiness I had about Ray.

The first chance I had, Latasha and I went to visit Greg at the county jail. He wasn't upset that I had moved back with my mom. He was actually happy that I was near him and would be able to visit him regularly.

"Wendy, I'm taking my case to trial. Denise is lying about everything. She is trying to put me in prison for a very long time."

He told me that if he was found guilty, he would go to jail for five to ten years. He went on to tell me how important my testimony would be. Of course I would tell the truth for him—I would do anything for him.

He often called collect and we would sit on the phone for hours on end talking. We talked about how wonderful Colorado was, and he promised that when he got out it would be the same way. We talked about our future, talked about our love for each other. I was the only one in his corner, he was depending on me, he loved me. I assured him I would stand by his side and love him forever.

When the case was about to be heard in court, Greg started going over the questions that I might be asked. He told me that he had never had a "boyfriend-girlfriend" relationship with Denise and he never had any feelings for her. I finally realized his defense: Denise was a jealous woman; she was angry and accusing him of pimping only because she wanted to be with him. He wanted the jury to think that Denise was insane and lying about everything. He wanted the jury to believe that she was infatuated with him and would do anything—even help sentence him to prison—so he wouldn't be with anyone else. But all I could see was Greg kissing Denise.

"Why did you kiss her?" I blurted out on the phone.

"I never kissed her. What the fuck are you talking about, bitch?" He wasn't yelling, but his tone was fierce. He continued in a stern, demanding voice:

"*Wendy!*" and then the short pause that told me I needed to read between the lines of what he was about to say. I knew that my mother had the ability to record all my phone calls, and we didn't know if the jail was listening also.

"I *never* kissed Denise, I *never* slept with Denise. If I had kissed her or had sex with her, I would surely be found guilty, and I would go to prison for a very long time." He continued in a slow, deep voice, "Do you understand what I am saying?"

I knew what he was saying. He was telling me to lie on the witness stand. I stood silent. I didn't know what to think. I was raised to tell the truth. I thought that if you tell the truth everything would be alright. He was asking me to lie and I didn't like that idea at all.

"*Wendy!!!!!*" bellowed through the phone. With a snappy, mean, sarcastic tone he started listing off questions without giving me the opportunity to answer.

"Do you *want* me to go to jail?"

"Do you *want* Latasha to not have her father in her life?"

"Do you even love me at all?"

"Did I make a huge mistake by ever believing in you or trusting in you or loving you?"

"I need you on my side. I need a good woman that will stand by me and fight this case. I need you to trust in me enough to do what I tell you to do."

I felt helpless, I felt I was being manipulated, I felt that I needed to prove my love so I would be worthy of being loved. His tone changed to a more loving tone, almost in a little boy's voice, he entreated, "I love you, Wendy. I need you now more than ever. Just do this one thing for me and I will show you the man that I can be. I will be the best husband and father to you and Latasha. I will love you forever and never leave your side."

The trial finally started. I was not allowed to be in the courtroom because I was a witness. When I was called, I swore on the Bible to tell the truth. I sat in the chair on the witness stand, and the prosecuting attorney began his questioning.

"Have you ever seen Greg and Denise in a romantic relationship?"

I remembered the time I saw Greg kiss her next to his car outside my window and I replied, "No."

The attorney looked at me like I was lying and then asked, "You never saw them have sex?"

I remembered the time that I caught them in my bed having sex and I replied, "No."

The jury deliberated for five hours and came back as a hung jury. Half of the jury thought he was guilty and the other half thought he was innocent. Before the district attorney asked for another trial, he made Greg an offer that he couldn't refuse: a thirteen-month sentence if Greg pleaded guilty to promoting prostitution. On a thirteen-month sentence, Greg would only serve nine months. He had already been in jail for four months, so in five months he would be a free man.

Together, Greg and I dug my grave that day. Still to this day, I feel that the next chapter in my life was my karma for my lying. How would my life have been different if I had told the truth? I wish I had told the truth but I wasn't strong enough, or maybe I was too brainwashed. The only thing I believed for certain that day was that no one would ever again love me, that I would cease to exist, if I sent Greg to prison.

Chapter 12
A Changed Man

*But even when I stop crying, even when
we fall asleep and I'm nestled in his arms,
this will leave another scar. No one will
see it. No one will know. But it will be
there. And eventually all of the scars will
have scars, and that's all I'll be—one big
scar of a love gone wrong.*
— Amanda Grace, But I Love Him

GREG WAS RELEASED FROM PRISON in April 1988. I had
written him almost every day during the nine months
he spent incarcerated. The letters I received from him
gave me hope of a changed man, the man I had
believed he was when I first met him: a man who
loved me for who I was, a man who would stand by my
side forever, a man with whom I could build a family
and home.

I had moved into a small, one-bedroom
apartment in March and prepared it as best I could
for Greg's homecoming. Latasha and I shared a twin-
sized mattress on the floor. It wasn't the best
apartment in the world, but it wasn't the worst either.
There weren't any roaches, and it wasn't in the ghetto.
It was in a quiet neighborhood and a short walk to a
discount store that provided for all our shopping
needs. I received three hundred ninety-seven dollars

a month from state public assistance and my rent was three hundred fifty. With a hundred fifteen dollars in food stamps, and my occasional visit to the food bank, we would only go hungry a few days a month. Greg had promised me in his letters from prison that he would get a job when he was released so we would have enough money to pay heat, phone, and other bills.

Greg had also written to me that he had a ride home from prison, which was a relief for me since I hated driving, which caused me too much anxiety. The morning he was to arrive, I put on my makeup and did my hair, a routine I had long forgone since I no longer needed to present myself for sale. Latasha wore a pretty pink dress my mother had bought her, and for hours we waited nervously at the window for him to arrive.

It was around noon when a car pulled into the apartment complex and we saw Greg get out. Latasha and I ran outside to greet him. I almost jumped on him to give him a hug while Latasha waited her turn. Greg was happy to see us, too, and returned our hugs and kisses. We then walked into the apartment for me to present to him the home I had prepared for us.

Although I was nervous and uneasy, I was also excited and hopeful for the future. The man who would someday be my husband was home; we had the opportunity for a fresh start, full of love and happiness. We had a quiet afternoon. I cooked something for him, and Latasha and I watched him while he cleaned and played with his car.

While I put Latasha to bed on the living room couch, Greg went into the bedroom. When I came into the bedroom, he was already underneath the covers, and I began to undress to join him. I wasn't especially eager to make love that night, but I thought he would expect it. It wasn't that I didn't want to have sex with him, but what I wanted most of all was to talk and listen to his voice, which I hadn't heard in many months. But he had been in jail for so long, and my first intention was to keep him happy so he wouldn't have to stray to other girls like before. All these thoughts were swirling through my head when I lifted the covers and saw that Greg was still fully clothed in the outfit he had been issued at the prison when he was released.

"Don't you want to do it?" I asked.

"I don't know....It feels weird to be here with you."

I didn't know what to think of this, so I decided to use it as an opportunity to open the lines of communication and just talk.

"What do you mean? How is it weird to you?"

I was full of understanding and ready for any response he had...except for what was coming. He grabbed me and pulled me onto the bed. At first I didn't think anything strange of it; he had been without sex for a long time. As he held me down on the bed he began to kiss me, not in the gentle way that I had imagined, but hard and hurtful. I tried to make him stop by keeping my mouth shut and making boisterous cries in my throat, but my efforts were useless. His entire mouth covered mine, smothering any sound I made and nearly smothering me. He covered my body entirely with his heavy body and fumbled to lower his zipper, I tried to move away from him, but the more I struggled, the harder he pressed on me to hold me still. He took my wrist in his hand and pinned it to the wall to prevent me from struggling. He then shoved his manhood inside of me with an angry force that created a pain not only in my body but in my soul. I struggled for only a moment more; realizing there was no escape, I mentally started making excuses for his behavior. I could not bear to lose the fantasy of having a man who truly loves me, who would stand by me forever and would never hurt me again.

It was over in moments. He rolled off me to the side of the mattress, turned his back on me, and fell into a deep sleep. I laid there wondering what had just happened, chalking it up to his being upset about being away for so long. As the teardrops welled in my eyes, I fought back the whimpering sounds coming from deep within my heart. I didn't want Greg to know I was crying. I didn't want to upset him any more than he already was.

The following morning I brought Greg breakfast in bed.

"Are you okay? Did I do something wrong to upset you?" I asked.

My heart dropped when he looked up at me. I saw the "old" Greg in his eyes, the monster Greg I had hoped I would never see again. *It* was supposed to be dead. I got defensive with protest.

"It felt like you were raping me. Is that what last night was about?"

"Rape doesn't exist between girlfriend and boyfriend. We are together, you are my girlfriend, and your pussy belongs to me."

I stood speechless as the thoughts reeled in my head. How could I have been so stupid as to think he would change? Now that he knew where I lived, I was stuck. I knew I wouldn't be able to kick him out without devastating consequences.

As if he could read my mind, Greg started to harass me with the words he knew would affect me the most.

"What? Do you want me to leave now? Are you going to kick me out with no place to go just after getting out of prison?"

I remembered from my childhood how selfish my mother made me feel, and the only way I would be worthy of love was to stop being "selfish" now.

"Of course I wouldn't kick you out, Greg, but maybe we shouldn't be together after all. Maybe we should just be roommates."

"As a roommate you can't control what I do, or who I have as a girlfriend," he sneered as he walked out the door, slamming it behind him. He knew he had won this round.

Greg's moods became more erratic. One night he came home after Latasha and I were asleep and gently woke me up.

"Wendy, wake up," he said in a sweet, soft voice.

I opened my eyes to see Greg sitting on the floor next to the mattress, fiddling with something on the nightstand.

"What's going on?"

"Wendy, I want you to try this."

"Try what?"

"Just inhale when I tell you to."

He inserted a glass pipe into my mouth and put fire to the other end. I waited for his instructions.

"Inhale slowly now."

I did what he told me to; when I had taken as much smoke into my lungs as they could hold, he added, "Hold it in as long as you can."

I wasn't feeling anything and had no idea what I was smoking—and then I could hold it no longer. I exhaled. The most amazing, wonderful, exhilarating feeling washed over me. My entire body tingled. I sat quiet for a minute mostly because I couldn't talk. I was frozen in time.

Once my brain could connect with my mouth to create words, I asked, "What is that?"

He barely glanced at me while he took a hit himself, and by this time, the wonderful feeling was starting to wear off. I desperately wanted to feel it again.

"Can I do another one?"

And of course he obliged.

This went on for a couple of hours. I didn't care what it was. It made me feel good and took away all my problems—that was all that mattered.

Much later I learned that we were smoking crack cocaine during that pleasant interlude. By the time I knew that, we were both addicted.

We settled into our life together, but our relationship was rocky. One minute he wanted his freedom to see other women, without any apologies to me. "We're not together," he would hurl at me when I protested, reminding me of my suggestion that we just be roommates. The next minute, Greg would pour out his love to me, pulling me close into his web with romantic proclamations. "You are the only woman I will ever love or trust."

With hope renewed, I would rededicate myself to my dream of a happy family—with the fog of our friend crack cocaine obscuring the truth, I could easily convince myself that Greg was a changed man.

Chapter 13
Escort Call

*As she grows older she gets stronger. She
learns to do what she is told with the
utmost compliance. She forgets everything
she has ever wanted. The pain still lurks,
but it's easier to pretend it's not there
than to acknowledge the horrors she has
buried in the deepest parts of her mind.*
—*Margaret Smith,* Ritual Abuse

AFTER HE GOT OUT OF PRISON, Greg quickly got a job at
the local Kentucky Fried Chicken where he worked
about 30 hours a week. Between my welfare check and
Greg's minimum-wage job, we made ends meet, but
scarcely. It should have come as no surprise that he
would be scheming about ways for me to make more
money.

One day Greg walked in the house after work and
asked me; "Do you know the lady Carlie next door?"

"I've met her, but we've never really talked."

With a sparkle in his eye and a plan reeling in
his head, he said, "Did you know she works for an
escort service? She gets paid a hundred and fifty to
three hundred dollars per date."

"I guess that's good for her then."

I had heard of escort services and knew that
women made a lot of money. But escort services were

for prostitutes and I wasn't a prostitute. In my head I justified my "dates" in the same way Greg had presented them to me: I was only having sex with men for money so I could survive, to give my baby girl what she needed, and to show that I was a good mother who loved my daughter. Besides, that was all in the past. Greg had promised I would never have to do that again.

Greg waited for the right moment to bring this matter up a second time. He sprung his trap when the money from the welfare check ran out, which was, as usual, the day after I got it and before the food stamps had arrived in the mail.

"Wendy, Carlie said she would hook you up with one of her dates from the escort service. You'll get paid a hundred and fifty dollars; then you'll give fifty back to Carlie for hooking you up."

Disgust for Greg filled my heart. How could he even think this if he loved me so much? I stayed quiet, revealing my hesitation about the very idea and my hatred for Greg for even thinking of it. The sparkle in Greg's eye extinguished and his voice hardened, his proposal no longer a suggestion but a demand.

"If I were a girl, I would go out and make lots of money to keep my man happy. What kind of woman are you that you would turn down the opportunity for your daughter to have some nice things? I knew I shouldn't have had a child with you. Maybe I should find another woman to replace you. I should get another mother for Latasha. Tasha would be much better off without you around."

Latasha sat on the floor in front of us as we had the conversation. Occasionally she looked up at us, but mostly she played with the toys sprawled out on the floor in front of her—toys that I could not afford to buy her. My mom had given her some of the toys; most of the rest were donations from the food bank.

Once again, I didn't feel that I had a choice. Greg countered every excuse I had not to "date," preying on my fear that I was failing not only him but our daughter. Any resistance I put up only fueled his anger. I was afraid he would soon blow up; I didn't want him throwing things and trashing the apartment like he had done before. I really wanted to keep this apartment nice for Latasha.

"Fine," I said, succumbing in frustration to his will. "What do I have to do?"

His eyes flashed with victory. "I'll talk to Carlie and let you know. Just be ready."

I sat next to Latasha and laid my head in her lap. Tasha wasn't aware that anything was wrong—only that mommy's head was disturbing her playing.

"Mommy...Get up!"

I rose to my feet and headed to the bathroom to apply the war paint. I coated my face with layer upon layer of makeup, creating a mask that obscured the person who was Wendy. With her face and emotions concealed, she became another person, a person who could be a prostitute if needed, maybe even a real prostitute. I knew I didn't really have two different personalities, but my brother's bullying and Ray's abuse had taught me that I did have the ability to trap my own naïve, innocent soul in a safe place within me. When I did this, a brave, strong girl with lots of power and attitude came forth to do the things Wendy couldn't possibly do.

Around seven thirty, Greg ran through the front door. He had been at Carlie's for nearly three hours.

"Why have you been over there for so long?" I asked.

"Don't worry about it, I got you a date. Come over and talk to Carlie. She has some things she needs to tell you."

I had never been in Carlie's apartment before. Although the layout was the same as mine, it had a much different feel to it, perhaps because her apartment was filled with furniture, crowded with knickknacks. It was the home of someone who was living a life. Carlie was about thirty-five years old and a very kind woman.

Her first question to me was, "Are you sure you want to do this?"

Hell no! I don't want to do this! cried out Wendy's soul. But Greg was standing there, and I had already been transformed into the emotionless prostitute Greg wanted me to be.

"I don't know, I guess so."

Carlie handed me a cup of tea. She was trying to be kind but didn't know I hated tea, so her hospitality only made me more uncomfortable.

"Have you ever done a dominance call?"

I didn't need to answer; the look on my face told her the answer.

Carlie looked at Greg. "Are you sure she is ready for this?"

I thought Greg would be furious that I had let Carlie know I was inexperienced; instead, he encouragingly replied, "You just need to school her Carlie. She'll do fine."

Greg drove me to a Motel 6 in North Seattle. He gave me a hug and kiss, assuring me of his love and that I was doing the right thing for the sake of the family. Latasha sat in the backseat of the car, asleep from the drive. The black high-heeled pumps hurt my toes; I hadn't worn them in a long time. Slightly wobbling from my shaking knees, I walked up the stairs leading to Room 225. Biting hard on my upper lip—attempting to feel pain instead of the fear that consumed me—I knocked softly on the door, half hoping there would be no answer. A nice, normal-looking, older gentleman opened the door.

"Hi, I'm Wendy. Carlie sent me."

"Hi, Wendy, it's nice to meet you." He opened the door wider for me to come in.

The room looked like rooms in any other Motel 6—a bed on one side of the room and, on the other side, a long desk of drawers holding a television. Beside the television were an extra-large cucumber, a woman's store-bought douche, a belt, and many shoe laces. I hoped my camouflaged face would hide my confusion, but it was clear the man could see that I was bewildered by the array of objects. Without embarrassment he started to tell me in great detail what my job would be for the next hour.

"First we will put some towels down on the bed and you will insert the douche into my ass and clean me out. Then you will use the shoe strings to tie my feet and arms to the bed. Next you will insert the cucumber into my ass and fuck me with it, followed by beating me with the belt while you say things like 'Bad boy, you've been a very bad boy, and now you must be punished.' During that time I would also like for you to grind the heel of your shoe into my scrotum; and no matter how much I beg you to quit, you need to continue until you are satisfied. When that is complete, we will have straight sex."

I couldn't imagine that my jaw was not almost hitting the floor. I stood in total shock listening to this and wondering *Why?* The man gathered up the towels to lay on the bed where I would be sticking a douche up his bum. He undressed while I just stood quietly, still in shock. I observed the size of the cucumber sitting next to the douche. *Oh my God, how am I going to get through this?* Before I knew it the man was laying on the bed naked, making some sort of weird animal noises interrupted with pleas of "Please don't hurt me, please don't hurt me." I didn't know if he was talking directly to me and telling me not to do as he had instructed, or if this was a part of his cucumber fantasy. I wondered if the man could see the fear and confusion that filled every cell in my body, since I hadn't moved from where I stood the entire time.

"Grab the douche. I'm ready now." I realized then that he actually wanted me to hurt him.

My heart seemed to stop beating; I couldn't even remember the last time I had taken a breath. Slowly walking over to the bottled douche, I closed my eyes and inhaled deeply. I exhaled Wendy and allowed the powerful woman within me to take over. I did what the man asked, although even the powerful woman reacted with the shock a small child would experience if she accidentally walked in to find her parents having sex. Even the powerful woman was grossed out, confused, and amazed all at the same time as I fulfilled the man's cucumber fantasy.

"Okay, I'm ready to be tied up, but take your dress off while you do it. Keep your underwear and shoes on."

I took the shoe strings, and making tiny bows I tied his hands and feet to the bed's head and foot board. I grabbed the belt; I knew I was supposed to hit him, but I didn't want to hurt him. *What could he have possibly been through as a child to make him want this? Does he have a wife? Children? What does he do for a living? Has he ever seen a therapist for this problem?*

I raised the belt above my head.

As hard as I could, I spanked the man with the belt. My voice quivered, "Bad boy. You've been a very...bad...boy."

With Wendy's spirit breaking through, the beating was a disaster. It probably felt as harsh as if I had caressed his skin with fleece. After only a few minutes, the man gave up on the fantasy he was trying to experience.

"Wendy...You can untie me now."

I untied the bows from the shoe strings, hopeful that I would be free from this insanity soon. All I had left to do now was have sex with him. The man rose from the bed, went over to his pants, and reached into the pocket. He handed me a roll of money.

"You can go now, Wendy."

My heart overflowed with happiness. *I don't have to have sex with him after all!* I threw my clothes on and in moments had my hand on the doorknob ready to leave.

"Here, take this." I turned to him and watched as he reached his arm out with his closed fist. He opened his fingers; it was a bag full of white powder. He said with a slight smile, "Do me a huge favor: Don't ever accept a dominance call again. Really. You're no good at it at all."

Even though I knew this was true and I was relieved that the trick was over, the words, "You're no good" penetrated my heart. The man quickly saw how these words affected me.

"It's okay, Wendy. It's no big deal, really. Some girls are good at this. You're not because you are sweet and kind. Keep your sweetness. It has much greater value." I hesitated for a moment, and then smiled at the man who was being kind to me for no reason at all.

I opened the car door and handed the money and bag of cocaine to Greg. He gave me a huge hug and said, "Atta girl! You make me so proud."

Those were the words that I lived for. Greg's pride in me validated my existence. As we drove back to South Seattle, I told Greg all the gory details and the reason I was dismissed so quickly.

"Wendy, these freaks pay a lot of money. You should learn how to be good at dominance calls. You probably wouldn't have to have sex with them at all."

Carlie would occasionally set me up on escort dates, but they were few and far between. She was a drug addict herself and needed all the business she could get to soothe her own habit. It was fine with me not to get many escort calls. Living close to Pacific Highway in north Federal Way, it was easy for me to pick up tricks, sometimes even while walking to the grocery store to buy food. Greg would not allow me to date white men from the street (only through the escort service), but in that area there were Mexican and Asian men who would purchase me.

My mom knew where I lived and would stop by often to bring Latasha toys or new clothes. Finally divorced from Ray, she had started dating a man named Tom. He would play with Latasha and was always nice to her and treated her as his own grandchild. Soon, my mom and Tom decided to get married. I was invited to the wedding, but—even though I liked Tom and was happy for them—I was so caught up in my world of drugs, prostitution, and Greg's degradation, I forgot about it and never showed up.

I made enough money to keep Greg satisfied but never happy. He brought another girl around for a couple of days. It was bittersweet. On one hand, I hated the attention and love that he showed her while he acted like I did not exist. On the other hand, it was nice being left alone and being able to spend more time with Latasha since I didn't need to cater to his every want and need. Still, money was tight, so there were a few more fights where I was thrown around, choked, and smacked; and it wasn't long before one of them was the straw that broke the camel's back for the apartment manager.

After we received the eviction notice, I couldn't find another apartment that would rent to me with only my welfare check as income. We stayed in seedy, rundown hotels for a few weeks. It was harder for us to get drugs, especially with all my earnings going to hotel and food and gas and taking care of Latasha. Greg called his mom, who had recently moved to Rialto, California, and arranged for us to live with her for a few months.

That night, Greg told me not to come home until I made enough money for us to drive to California. It was a slow Wednesday night, with very few tricks on the street. When I came home at two in the morning with only a hundred fifty dollars, he yelled at me and sent me back out. I walked up and down the empty street, crying, until five o'clock. At that point, even Greg had to concede that we would have to wait until Friday night when I could make more money and my welfare check would arrive.

We moved to California to stay with his mom, stepdad, and three of his half/stepsiblings in their three-bedroom townhome. Just as she had done when we had lived with her in Colorado, Juanita was kind enough to let us have one of the rooms to ourselves. And, just as he had done when we were in Colorado, Greg promised me that this was our new start. He promised that I would never have to work the street again, and for a short while, he kept his promises. He actually went out and got a construction job that his stepfather had arranged for him. He worked every day for a couple of weeks while I stayed home, playing housewife and being the mother I had always wanted to be to Latasha.

It wasn't long before Greg stopped going to work. He would hang out with friends throughout the day and would sometimes leave for two or three days with no contact at all. I would worry about him and cry. When he would show up, he would act like nothing was wrong. If I questioned him, he would push me around and yell.

"What the fuck are you doing for our family? Sitting on your ass all day while I bring in all the money. You're pathetic."

He had stopped bringing in any money, of course; but if I pointed that out, he would bring up the fact that he had worked in construction for two weeks. By that time, I had transferred my welfare check to California. Greg refused to acknowledge that all of that money went to paying our share of the rent and buying gas for his car so he could "go out and look for work."

Six weeks after we moved to California, I discovered that I was pregnant. My second pregnancy was similar to the first, with morning sickness that lasted the entire day. I was too weak to even care that Greg wasn't around. Thank God Greg's mom was there to help me with Latasha.

My own parents wanted to be around, too, but over the years Greg had made that nearly impossible. Greg hated it when my mom visited our apartment with toys for Latasha. Although he was always on his best behavior when she showed up, he would berate me and start to hit me as soon as she left. It didn't take me long to see the correlation between my mom's visits and the beatings. I stopped answering the phone when she would call, or I would tell her that we would not be home when she wanted to visit Latasha and me. Although this slowed her visits down, she continued to find ways to be in my life.

Greg would also beat me when I received letters from my dad, and I soon began to throw his letters away without even bringing them into the house.

There was no point in reading them. I knew I wouldn't respond...What could I possibly say? I certainly didn't want him to know what my life had turned into.

While Greg was in prison and I was living with my mom, she and I finally had a chance to work on our relationship. Although still not perfect, it was nice. By that time, she only had to work one job to make a livable wage, so she had the time to be a good grandma to Latasha. She would buy her toys and clothes and spend hours playing with her. Mom even took Latasha to Sears to get her picture taken.

My father and I hadn't spoken in many years except for quick, occasional phone calls on Christmas or my birthday, but he also had taken advantage of Greg's prison time to reach out to me—first by writing a couple of letters and then asking if he and my stepmom could make a trip to visit Latasha and me. The visit was uncomfortable. My life was so complicated; it was like we were strangers. So when my father told me that he loved me. I stood speechless, not knowing how to feel, not knowing if he was even telling the truth—but it did mean something to me that he was trying. I could see that he saw me. For that moment, I existed to him and it felt strange.

Once Greg was out of prison, I continued to keep my dad at arm's length. He would visit once a year or two, staying at a nearby hotel. He would take the kids and me out for the afternoon, typically to a restaurant to eat and then on a nature walk. I always made excuses to keep the visits short. I knew what would happen with Greg if I spent more time with my dad.

Chapter 14
Through a Mother's Eyes

*Q: What do you regard as the lowest
depth of misery?
A: Living in fear.
—David Bowie, responding to a* Vanity
Fair *questionnaire*

1989

 *After Wendy went to California [with Greg to be near
his mother], things did not go well for her. One night she
called me and asked me if something were to happen to
her, if I would take Tasha, or would Tasha end up in a
foster home. I told her of course I'd take her. She told me
she was so stressed out from Greg that she went to the
mental health ward of a hospital, and they treated her like
dirt and like she was crazy. I received the following letter
from Wendy:*

 *How are you? I'm not too good. I want to come
home Mom. I'm going crazy, I'm losing it. Each day I
can feel my sanity slipping away from me. Greg
doesn't care about me—I'm just a slave to him. Every
night I go to sleep thinking about killing him. But I
don't want to kill him. I tell him this but he doesn't*

care. I just want to die, but I don't want to kill myself. I want to get away from him—he plays games with my head—and tortures me with things that he does. He hates me, mom—He hates me—He's trying to drive me crazy. He wants me to kill myself—I'm afraid I might lose it and kill him. I want to come home before something really awful happens. Please Mom, please help me. I need help; have no one to talk to. I'm gonna go. I'll mail this tomorrow if I don't kill myself tonight.

Love, Wendy

Fortunately, Wendy didn't continue in this bad a shape, and there wasn't anything I could do but pray.

Unexpectedly, five weeks early, I gave birth to a baby boy, Danny. My son Steve, Wendy, and Tasha made a surprise trip up [to Seattle] to see me and the baby. Things were still not going good between her and Greg, and before she left she asked me if she could stay with us for a month if she decided to move back up here. I told her "yes."

When I was about six months pregnant, Greg's mom was evicted from the apartment we shared with her in California, and she moved back to Seattle. I was still sick and weak from my pregnancy, and uncertain about my future with Greg. My mom bought plane tickets for Latasha and me to fly home to live with her in Bellevue, Washington, near Seattle. Greg promised that he would drive back to Seattle as soon as he could come up with the gas money.

I was happy to be going home to my mom. She was now settled into a happier life with her new husband, Tom, and their newborn baby. She was no longer stressed out like she had been when I was a child. She had a better paying job and had a little bit in savings, which gave her comfort, and she had grown and matured a lot over the years. Not only was she better at showing love to the kids and me, she was a wonderful grandma. I always knew that she would take care of Latasha and me and that by living with her and my stepfather, we would enjoy being part of a warm family. Maybe she didn't make the best meals, but there was always food in the house. She could never afford cable, but there were many shows on regular television that would make us laugh together. On days I felt okay, I could help my mom out with her newborn baby, which not only gave me an opportunity to get to know my little brother but also gave me a sense of value.

Wendy and Tasha ended up moving back in with me around June, and she considered herself still going with Greg who was still in California. She was in constant turmoil regarding him, and spent a lot of time and money calling him. Shortly before she had her baby, he finally did come back up, and Wendy still spent a lot of time very upset and distraught because of her suspicions he was with other girls.

When Greg returned to Seattle, he was moving from place to place, doing whatever he was doing—but I still held out hope we would create a happy life together. After our second child was born, my welfare check would be increased and I might be able to get an apartment for us to be a real family.

One morning in September 1989, I woke up feeling uneasy. My mom and stepdad had already left for work, and, suspecting I might soon be going into labor, I didn't want to be alone. I called Greg's mom; grateful to find him at her house, told him I wasn't feeling well and I really wanted him to come sit with me for the day.

When he showed up an hour later, he was accompanied by a girl I had never met before. He introduced us as if it were an everyday occurrence to bring a date to the birth of our baby. I didn't dare say anything, and even if I had, I was too tired to argue. An hour or two later, I had no doubt that I was in labor. Greg drove me to the hospital, with his new "girlfriend to make money for him" in the backseat.

Wendy gave birth to a little boy, Gregory. I wasn't too happy about her naming him that, but it wasn't my choice.

Wendy was now trying to get her GED, although Greg couldn't understand why she wanted a GED when she could get welfare.

I stayed with my mom for another two months. Greg still had total control over my mind and heart. I would drop anything to be at his beck and call. He had other girls to make money for him, so he never demanded that I go out on the street; but he always needed to know that I belonged to him and I was under his control. At the time, my heart jumped with joy to think that he "wanted" me. Looking back now, I see that his real motivation was to look good when the police were scrutinizing him. I could give him an appearance of family stability that none of his other girls could offer.

With increasing frequency, Greg would visit me at my mom's house and involve me in his life. He would tell me that he needed me to drive him and the girls because none of them had a driver license. It felt good to be needed and wanted by him. It felt good to not be a pathetic piece of shit to him.

Early one evening he called and told me he needed me to drive him and some girls to Aurora Avenue in North Seattle. I didn't know what he needed to do on Aurora Avenue, but I was more than willing to go. My mom was home from work and agreed to watch Latasha and Gregory. Since I hadn't seen Greg in over a week and there were going to be girls with him, I fixed my hair and put on makeup. I wanted to look my best so I wouldn't embarrass him.

Greg arrived alone, came in to say hello to Gregory and Latasha, and made small talk with my mom. He and I got into the car and I drove, following his instructions, to a store down the street, where four girls climbed into the backseat. Greg did not introduce us, but the girls included me in their conversations as if we were all best friends. It felt good to be included, to be a part of something.

We parked at a restaurant, and all four girls got out of the car and started walking to the street. One by one I saw each of the girls get picked up by a car. I noticed that the men picking them up were white.

"Greg, who are all these girls?"

"They are all friends of Bridget's. They work for her and I'm helping her out."

I didn't want to ask too many questions and take the chance of his getting mad; I knew he was being intentionally vague. I assumed that Bridget must be one of the four girls.

The girls got in and out of different cars without ever bringing any money to Greg or Bridget. We had only been parked for about thirty minutes when Bridget came back to the car and jumped into the backseat with a smile.

"Damn! Money is freakin' easy tonight." She started counting the money; when she had finished, she turned to me.

"Wendy, don't you want a piece of this? It's so freakin' easy and the tricks are coming quick. Easy fifty bucks."

Except for the tall Chinese man who had taken me home, fifty dollars was more than I had ever made working the streets. The Asian and Mexican men typically paid twenty or twenty-five dollars, maybe thirty-five at the most. Still, I wasn't interested.

"No, I don't do that anymore." I smiled to be able to say that, but one look at Greg and I could plainly see that was not the right answer.

"Wendy, how the fuck do you expect us to ever get our own place? We cannot live on your welfare check alone. These girls out here are making bank, and you want to get all stuck up on me." He must have seen the fear on my face, because his voice softened a bit.

"Wendy," he coaxed, "these guys are white guys, they pay a lot of money. Just try it one more time. Go out there and make me proud, baby. Bridget will help you get a date."

I was scared to death. This was a whole new territory for me—almost like I was turning my first trick all over again. It had been nearly a year since the last time I had been out on the street. Greg had always told me never to go with a white man. "They take longer," he had warned, "and some will rape you." Why was he now so eager for me to put myself in danger?

Bridget walked me to the street and a car quickly pulled over. We both stuck our heads through the passenger-side window.

"This is my friend Wendy. She's a little scared. Will you take good care of her?"

The driver was a decent-looking white man with a tie.

"I'll take very good care of her."

Bridget opened the door so I could get in. He offered me one hundred dollars to go back to his apartment and have straight sex with him. It was easy money and I knew it would make Greg happy—and when Greg was happy, I felt I had value.

Over the next few weeks, Greg would pick me up every Friday night to drive the girls to Aurora Avenue. I quickly became one of the girls, working side by side with them. I saw the other girls give Bridget their money and Bridget would give some of it to Greg in appreciation for the transportation and protection. I always gave all of my money to Greg. I never would dare ask to keep any of it for myself. If I had made enough money and told him I needed cigarettes or diapers, he would almost always be "kind" enough to give me twenty dollars to take home.

Juanita moved again to an apartment in South Seattle. It wasn't the best part of town by a long shot, but she was enthusiastic about the place because they were easy-going with their credit checks. All I had to do, she told me, was to write down a fake job and they would accept me. At the same time, Greg was becoming increasingly insistent that I get an apartment for us, threatening to get a "new wife" since I wasn't doing what a good wife was, in his mind, supposed to do. He maintained that the reason he could not get a job was because I could not provide him with a stable place to live.

"How can I work if I don't know where I will be sleeping at night or if I will have a shower to clean myself?" It was all my fault that our lives were not "the happy family" that I so badly wanted.

I decided to take a chance. During the interview with the apartment manager, she mentioned to me that there was a nursing home about five miles down the street from the apartment that offered certified nursing assistant (CNA) training and employment opportunities. I was intrigued. *If I have a real job, a job where I can make enough money to pay my rent, Greg won't make me work the street anymore.* I wanted to have a career. Even though I had no idea what a CNA did, the lady made it sound easy—and the money was more than I would earn on welfare. I took a flyer from the stack on her desk and called as soon as I got home to set up an interview for the following week.

That night Greg called. "Hey, baby, how did the appointment go? Are we getting our apartment?"

"I don't know. They didn't give me an answer yet."

"When are you going to get an answer?"

I felt frustrated. I didn't have the answer, and I knew by the tone of his voice he was getting ready to explode.

"I don't know. They said they would contact me."

And then it started. "Are you the fucking most stupidest bitch in the world? What the fuck is wrong with you? They aren't going to let you in the apartment, you are too fucking stupid and dumb to do anything right. That's why I need to get a real woman. You ain't shit. You are a pathetic piece of shit. You can't even take care of your man. I should come over there right now and beat the shit out of you. That's what you deserve, you know that, right? *Right?!* You fucking know you deserve a good ass whooping."

I started my apologetic mantra, the same one that I had repeated many times before.

"I know Greg, I know I am pathetic and I can't do anything right. *I am sorry!* I am sorry that I'm not a good woman for you and I don't deserve you."

I was doing so well acknowledging my shortcomings and the error of my ways when, without any effort on my part, the tone of my voice started to change from pathetic to sarcastic. It was as if the words themselves had gotten weary of being said so many times before.

"You are right... I'm not a good woman and you should find a good woman who will take care of you and cater to your every need, who will go out and work the street for you and make you money so you can sit on your lazy ass all day long and not do anything at all."

I had much more to say, but he cut me off.

"You fucking *bitch*!!!! Do you want me to break out all the windows of your mom's house? Are you going to make me hurt your mom and your little brother? You asked for it, bitch... You are the one making me do this... Make sure your mom knows that what is about to happen is *all your fault.*"

Around November, Wendy was having some heated conversations with Greg on the phone, and I was delighted one night when I heard her hysterically yell at him to "Go ahead and break all the windows in my mom's house, come on Greg, if you're going to kill my mom, do it! Hurry up, Greg, do it!! Come over here right now and kill my mom, break all our windows, do it Greg, do it!" I was so relieved to hear her talk like that, I thought she was cured—that he would never again be able to threaten her. She then got a restraining order on Greg.

Towards the end of November, I found this handwritten note:

> Mom,
>
> I am sorry but I have to get out of here. I feel my life is at a standstill, going nowhere but down. I need a new start in life, just my children and me. Please forgive me for running out on you like this; this is just something that I need to do. I love you and I thank you for everything you have done for me. I'll call in a couple of days and I'll try and come back to get the rest of my stuff. I just don't know how Greg is going to react, so I'll play it by how mad he is.
>
> I Love you! Love, Wendy

What I didn't know is that Greg had been making lots of threats against our house and myself, saying he was going to break all our windows, kill me, etc., etc. Wendy had to leave to protect me.

Chapter 15
Mona

We are stardust
(Billion year old carbon)
We are golden
(Caught in the devil's bargain)
And we've got to get ourselves
back to the garden
—Joni Mitchell, "Woodstock"

I CONTACTED A DOMESTIC VIOLENCE SHELTER and moved the next morning with Latasha and Gregory. The center was a huge, three-story house in North Seattle, an area of the city I did not know well. We shared a room on the third floor with two other families: a woman with two children and another woman with three children.

It was a long, hard climb up all those stairs with Tasha and Gregory. They hated it at the center and wanted to go back to their grandma's house. Even more heartbreaking, Tasha would whine that she wanted to see her daddy. I lasted only two days before I called Greg and apologized. He picked us up and took us to stay with his mom.

The next morning, I contacted the apartment complex regarding my application and they said that I was approved. They had a special going on that waived the renter's deposit, so all I needed to do was come up with the first month's rent.

I started going out every night to work the street to make the money to get into the apartment. I didn't want to stay out long, because I didn't want Juanita to suspect what I was doing. I would tell her that I was going to the store and would turn one or two quick tricks on my way to and from the store. To cover my tracks, I would buy whatever we needed that didn't need to be refrigerated. Greg enjoyed the money I was making; every night that I went out to get money for our apartment, he would take half of it for himself, using it to put gas in his car or to buy a new stereo system or whatever else his heart desired that day.

I was excited about the appointment at the nursing home, which was quickly approaching. Greg was very encouraging; he said he wanted me to get a good paying job and would watch the kids while I went to school.

A class was starting the day after my appointment, and I jumped to sign up. It was also the day that I had enough money to move into the apartment. I dropped the money off at the rental agency and gave Greg the keys; he then drove me to the class where I started to learn to be a "nurse." It felt good to be in a learning environment and to meet other people. Classes lasted four weeks, and we were in class for eight hours a day. The course included a small stipend, but it wasn't enough to survive. I still had to go out on Friday and Saturday nights.

Greg was a good stay-at-home dad. Latasha loved having him around; Gregory at five months was still too much of a baby to know any difference. Most days Greg would clean the apartment while I was in class, and he even made dinner for me a few times. I started to see a glimmer of hope that the dream family I had always wanted was finally going to come true.

One day, I came home and there was a young woman at the house. Greg introduced me to Mona, telling me that she was there to help him with the kids—a babysitter of sorts. I thought that it was very nice of her to help with the kids while I was gone during the day. Greg explained that he needed someone to stay with the kids while he looked for work.

"How are we going to pay her, Greg?"

"She's going to watch them for free. She is living in a hotel room with her mom, dad, and four siblings. She just wants a place to get away every day."

Although she looked well over eighteen years old, this last statement made me wonder.

"How old is she?"

"She's eighteen."

I felt sorry for Mona that she didn't have a real home and I was more than happy to give her a break from her surroundings. By the way she treated Latasha, I thought Latasha was going to get the best part of the deal. Mona seemed to be a real natural with both of the children. I never felt that I really knew how to be a "real" mommy. Mona knew lots of fun games that she and Latasha loved to play together.

My impression was that Greg was out looking for work during the days. Mona would clean the house, wash all the dishes, and make really good meals for me to enjoy when I got home from work. One day when I got home, Greg was still gone and I asked Mona to stay and eat dinner with me so we would have a chance to get to know each other a little better. It was nice having a girlfriend, another thing that Greg had taken away from me. He never allowed me to stay in touch with the friends that I had made in high school—including Allison, my best friend, whom I very rarely got to see.

When I graduated from the CNA program, I was so proud of myself—and even Greg was proud of me. I was still only twenty, but the store down the street never asked me for ID, so I bought some beer to celebrate my new achievement. Thinking Greg would be home to celebrate with me, I invited Mona to come over and have a beer with us. Greg never showed up, but Mona and I had a very enjoyable evening getting drunk together, laughing and giggling.

I was offered a shift at the nursing home that allowed me to work thirty-six hours on the weekend and get paid for forty. My shift was six in the morning to midnight every Saturday and Sunday, allowing me to stay home with the kids Monday through Friday while Greg worked—once he found a job—and Greg could watch the kids on Saturdays and Sundays while I worked. I thought prostituting was behind me forever. Once Greg found a job, everything would be perfect. Again... I saw a light at the end of the tunnel, or maybe I just saw what I wanted to see.

The light soon dimmed. I started getting a weird feeling about Mona and Greg. I wondered what they were doing behind my back. There were times that Greg would get upset if Mona didn't tell him where she was going or where she had been. This seemed odd, but familiar to me. *Is this the way he treats* all *women? or just his "girlfriends"?*

One day Greg and Mona went outside together and I could hear them arguing. I could occasionally hear Mona scream, "Greg! Stoooooooop it!!" I was afraid to get involved, but it was enough to confirm to me that Mona was more than just our free babysitter. But without proof, I didn't dare make any accusations. I turned the television up so Latasha couldn't hear what was going on.

Greg came into the house and shouted out his ugly demand. "Wendy!!! Put your makeup on and go with Mona!"

I knew from his tone that I'd better not object or disobey. I ran into the bathroom, threw on my makeup, and reported back to him for his inspection. Since I didn't know exactly where I was going or what I was doing, I didn't really know how much makeup or what to wear. He must have read my mind; as he nodded his approval of my look, he barked, "You're going on a date with Mona."

I was confused. I didn't understand why both of us needed to go. I went outside to find Mona standing at the front door.

"You ready to go?" she asked.

"I guess," I said almost to myself as we started walking down the hill to Rainier Avenue.

After a few yards, I spoke up. "What's going on? Can you give me any info?"

"There is a guy who likes having two girls. He'll pay us each fifty dollars to have sex with both of us."

Even though I had turned tricks while Denise sat in the backseat, I had never performed sexual acts on a man with another girl. From Mona's response, I assumed that she was experienced in this type of thing and had done it before. I was glad that Mona was easy to be with and glad that she was more experienced. I hoped she would walk me through what I was supposed to do.

A man named Richard picked us up and drove us to his house in Bellevue. I sat in the backseat and Mona sat in the front. He had a six-pack of Olde English 800 for us.

"Are you over twenty-one?" he asked. Mona indicated she was, even though I knew she was only eighteen. I was too honest and explained that I would not be twenty-one for another week. He handed me a can of beer.

"Happy birthday a week early."

He took us into his bedroom where he handed us each fifty dollars and we all undressed. He lay down in the bed and Mona and I lay on either side of him. He took turns kissing us, even though I tried to keep my lips closed. Greg always told me to never kiss a trick, but I noticed that Mona was kissing him and thought I should follow her lead. He put a condom on and started having sex with Mona while he kissed and fondled my breasts. He climbed on top of me and had sex with me while he kissed and fondled Mona's breasts. It was over pretty quickly, and he gave us each another beer for our ride home. On the way back he asked, "Can we do this again next Friday night?" Although I would have to be at work at six the following morning, I agreed, knowing Greg would be mad if I were to decline.

Soon, Mona was living with us, and she was just as much Greg's girlfriend as I was. Greg started bringing crack cocaine around again, and it didn't take much for us all to become consumed by the drugs. Soon I was working as a CNA on the weekends, staying up the entire night doing drugs, and going back to work in the morning without any sleep. Mona and I would work the streets together a couple nights during the week, and Mona worked by herself on Friday nights while I slept and on Saturday nights when I worked at the nursing home.

There were a few clues that Mona was not really eighteen years old. One time I overheard her tell Greg that her mom had reported her as a runaway. *How could there be a runaway report if she is eighteen?* One night as we were alone out on the street and there weren't many tricks driving by, I asked her.

"Mona, how old are you really? I heard you say your mom put a runaway report on you, so you can't be eighteen."

"Greg will kill me if I tell you, so don't tell him that I told you. I'm sixteen, but will be seventeen next month."

I was speechless. *Sixteen is kind of young to be living this life. Nobody deserves the life that we were living, but what can I do?*

Between the drugs, the prostituting, and lack of sleep—plus my trying to be a good wife and mommy to Greg and the kids—things went downhill fast. Once I turned twenty-one, I could buy beer whenever I wanted, and I wanted it almost always. Greg would take Mona in the bedroom and I knew what they were doing, but at that point I didn't care.

Or so I thought. One day after a few too many beers, I grabbed a knife and walked into the bathroom. I sat on the edge of the bathtub cutting my wrists, never going deep enough to hit a vein. The knife hurt my wrists, but the pain in my heart was so much worse. Greg started banging on the bathroom door; when I didn't answer, he broke the door down. Even in the pain, my fantasies rose to the occasion. As the door strained against his weight, I envisioned my knight rescuing his princess. He would see me with the knife in my hand and realize that this was too much for me. He would proclaim his determination to change, to get a job. He would never have sex with another woman again.

His reaction could not have been further from my delusion.

"You stupid fucking bitch. You want to die that bad, I'll fucking kill you for you."

He grabbed the long metal hose attachment of the vacuum cleaner and smashed the mirror. He held a piece of the broken glass at my neck and screamed,

"Do you want to die, bitch? Do you want to fucking die?"

I cried, I just cried. I couldn't answer him. I wanted to die, but I didn't want to die. I wanted the pain to end, but even I couldn't understand the pain that I was in.

Greg didn't make me go out to work for a week. That was all I needed—not to work the street for a week—to feel blessed and nurtured by him.

Occasionally I'd bring my baby, Danny, over to Wendy's apartment for her to babysit. Danny was almost a year old now, and he was very close to Tasha. Once when using her bathroom, I noticed the mirror was broken. My gut feeling told me it was Greg's temper that broke the mirror, although Wendy claimed it was an accident. Wendy had also cut herself quite badly with a kitchen knife right around this time, needing several stitches. Often when I called or went over there, there was a friend of Wendy's there named Mona, who Wendy eventually told me didn't really have a home and so she was almost living there. One night Wendy called me and told me she was so stressed out from Greg she was unable to take care of her kids, and she asked me if I would call CPS [Children's Protective Services]. She told me Mona is one of Greg's girlfriends, that he's always bringing girls over, and that he calls her apartment and her car "his." I asked her how she was managing right now, and she said Mona was taking care of them, but that Mona, too, was feeling very stressed out.

My letter to CPS:

February 8, 1990
While talking to my very distraught daughter (Wendy Barnes) last night, it was hard to keep looking the other way as her voice carried so much

distress. She has told me for months that the only reason she stays with her very verbally abusive boyfriend (Greg Hightower) is because she is afraid of him because of the constant threats he makes against her, me, or my house. She feels forced to give him part of her welfare check so he won't destroy my car, or break every window in my house, or harm me, or run off with her kids, etc. I've told her to ignore the threats, not to give him the money, and let him break our windows. She eventually moved out of my house thinking my husband and I would be protected, and she moved into her own apartment, where her boyfriend resides with her.

I've seen Wendy so stressed out she could not nurture her children. One night in January she told me the only time she smiles is when she's thinking of killing Greg. Another time she told me she is going to end up in prison. After receiving a very sharp knife as a gift, she has had two "accidents" on her hands, one requiring stitches and now further surgery is needed. I know some people don't believe in accidents, but I do. However, I'm convinced these "accidents" were deliberate self-destructive acts of her subconscious. Wendy has never been accident prone. Last night she requested I not contact her for a while and pretend like I don't have a daughter. This was not a request because she thinks I meddle, but because she is afraid of Greg carrying out threats on me if she continues to be friends with me. If only I had a recording of the conversation, the message would be so much clearer. I asked her if her kids were being abused, and she said she is abusing them by staying with Greg. She recently got a restraining order on him, and I found out he was served, but she is too scared of him to call the police. She even suggested maybe I call welfare fraud, and maybe they'd come and take the kids and cut her off welfare.

Wendy used to go to the blood bank to sell blood, then give Greg the money which he spent on other women. That stopped for a long time, and I know she is now going to the blood bank again, but I haven't asked what she does with the money. At one point in the conversation, I asked her if she was going to be all right. She knew what I was really asking, and assured me she wouldn't try anything. She then said something about the bathroom ending up a mess and the bathroom mirror breaking. The guy has brainwashed my daughter, she has no will anymore, and even though the kids are not being beaten, some authority has to step in.

She's been to shelters, and Greg knows where to find her. Her children are her life, and if she were to give up her kids temporarily she would have no desire to go on. She's been suicidal before, and I know it's her kids that keep her from doing any such thing.

Before Greg came into her life, Wendy was my mature, reliable, level-headed daughter. I saw her go down the gutter, but I also saw her mentally come back up, but never to the point of leaving Greg for good. She told me she is no longer "allowing" Greg to ruin her life—that she is only with him because of all his threats. One of which is if she calls the police, he will throw rocks through her apartment windows. Then she would get scared of the rocks and/or glass hurting the kids. He has complete control over her. She has told me how much she wished she had listened to me years ago and how right I was about everything. His threats are affecting her mind, and her mothering.

The copy of the letter I've enclosed is only one of many letters I've seen of hers; however, this one is very typical. Like most of them, it was never finished and never given or mailed to him. I do not want her to know I found this letter or made a copy of it, however.

Unfortunately, Wendy has left Greg and gone back to him many times. All he has to do is pour on the "I love you, I can't live without you, I'll change, I'll get a job" routine. She softens. However, she also told me that since she moved into her apartment and he made himself at home, that even when he gets all nice, she now continues to hate him. She's told me many times Greg knows I am her weak point. As soon as the threats are against me, she's putty. I, however, am not afraid of the creep.

She knows she needs counseling, but she never goes through with it. In last night's conversation, at the same time she asked me to pretend I don't have daughter and not to contact her for a while, I could also hear she was begging for some kind of help. Not knowing what I could do, I asked her if she wanted me to contact CPS, and she replied "yes." Wendy needs to be talked to, obviously, while Greg is not there.

I know Wendy's mind can be down or up from day to day (as with everyone), but please keep in mind if things sound okay on the day you talk to her, don't let that be the last time.

Attached to the above letter was a copy of this handwritten letter I found 12/10/89 when cleaning her room after she had moved out.

> *Greg,*
>
> *You are the biggest Fuck-head in the world. You're not a player, you're a murderer. You don't care how many people get hurt by your games. You don't care about your kids, your mother or anyone else. You don't even have a heart, you know that? Do you? You are sicker than a person that goes around molesting 3 year old children, then killing them. You go around making people crazy and you enjoy it. God didn't make you, the devil did. The devil made you to go*

around and hurt as many people as you can. You don't have any feelings, you don't even care if someone kills themselves because of you—you! You Greg Hightower just go and try to find your next victim, who will be the next girl who falls victim to your childish, cruel games. You go around telling everyone that you Love them. Love doesn't mean shit to you; you don't know what Love is. I know you so damn well, I know you're laughing at this letter right now. I know you so damn well that you don't give a Fuck about this letter; you don't care if I'm hurt. You just laughing and think it's a big joke. Well fuck you!! you keep this letter Greg, take it out in six months and read it again. Maybe after you lose everyone that truly loves you.

CPS did contact Wendy, but I don't remember any changes because of it.

Shortly after this, Wendy had left her apartment with only the clothes on her back and her two children, even leaving her purse and ID behind. She was scared to death of Greg and wanted to go far away. However, by the next day, Wendy was no longer in that frame of mind and, out of fear, she went back to Greg.

Soon after, I got a call from Juanita, Greg's mother, who lived right next door to Wendy, and who was able to see a lot of goings on. She had been told by her stepson, Spencer, who had recently returned from California, about drugs and prostitution going on in the apartment. She also told me Greg also made sure he is not there when this happens so he cannot be connected to any of it.

The nursing home was offering overtime during the week. In addition to my thirty-six hours on the weekends, I volunteered to work Tuesdays,

Wednesdays, and Thursdays from six o'clock in the morning to three in the afternoon.

The first Wednesday when I came home from work, the front door was locked, and I could hear Gregory crying through his bedroom window. I banged on the door and screamed for Greg or Mona to open the door.

"Gregory is crying, Gregory is crying! Open the door!"

I pounded on the door until, finally, I heard movement in the house. Seconds later, I could hear Greg yelling at Mona and Mona screaming in pain. Gregory was still crying and I continued to bang and scream at them to open the door. Moments later, the entire apartment building shook from something being thrown inside my apartment. I could hear the *thud* and Mona's screaming.

I could tell from her cries that she was getting closer to the front door, so I screamed to her, "Open the door! Open the door!"

"Help me, Wendy, help me!" Her screams were now muffled, and then another *thud*. I knew what was happening; each time Greg threw Mona against the wall, the building shook again.

"I'm going to call the police! I'm calling the police if you don't open the door!"

I ran next door to Greg's mom's house and called the police, and then ran back to my apartment to again bang on the door. Suddenly the door flew open. Greg with Latasha in his arms and Mona with Gregory in her arms barged over the threshold, headed towards the car.

"Wait, stop!!! What are you doing?"

"You call the police on me, bitch, I take your kids," adding as he turned, "Come on Mona."

Mona followed him with my baby. I ran after them, but Greg kept pushing me down. Ten minutes later, the police showed up. I told them what happened and they asked me, "*Is* Greg the children's father?"

"Yes."

"Possession is nine-tenths of the law. He has just as much right to have the children as you. There is nothing we can do. And if Mona is not reporting that he beat her, there is nothing we can do about that, either."

I sat down on the spot and cried and cried and cried. I cried for a couple of days waiting for them to return. I was desperate. He had taken my children, he had taken my car—a gift from my mom for earning my GED—and all the rent money, and he had robbed me of every tiny shred of hope. Distraught without my children, I was in no shape emotionally to go to work even if I had had transportation.

After a few days, Greg contacted me with his decree. He would let me have Latasha because she was too much to handle and kept asking for me. He was keeping Gregory. Latasha and I moved back in with my mom. Every day I missed Gregory and would reach out to different lawyers, who always gave me the same answer: With a past like mine and no money or a stable place to live, there was nothing they could do for me.

My stepdad, Tom, made some contacts with some police officers he knew. Greg had warrants out for his arrest for driving without a license and not showing up in court. They were all misdemeanor charges—not especially serious, but the officers told Tom they could leverage the warrants to make a deal: If Tom could find out where Greg and Gregory were, the officers would tell Greg that he could avoid jail in exchange for returning Gregory to me. Tom did not tell me about his contacts with the police or the agreements they had made because he didn't want to get my hopes up high. Without my knowledge, Tom would sit outside Greg's mom's house on most evenings, just waiting for Greg to show up.

Since Greg had taken all my money, I contacted Richard, who lived near my mom. I would see him every Friday night; he would take me out to dinner and then we would go back to his place, watch movies, have sex, and he would pay me. One of Tom's relatives gave me his old car, and Richard would change the oil and take care of all the mechanics. He was really nice, and a friendship, although strange because of the sex, actually started to develop between us. My mother knew what the relationship was, but she also thought Richard was a really nice guy. If he hadn't been a trick, he would have made a good husband to someone.

One Friday, about six weeks after Greg took Gregory, I was at Richard's when my mother called his number. When he handed me the telephone, she sounded close to panic.

"Wendy!"

"Yeah...What's up?"

"Wendy, Gregory is on his way home. Tom is bringing Gregory home right now."

"What? How?" I couldn't believe my ears.

"I'll tell you everything when you get home. Just come home now so you can be here when he gets here."

Greg had finally shown up at his mom's, and Tom was there. He called the police officers, who did exactly what they had agreed to do. They confronted Greg and told him they could either take him to jail and they would give the child to me because I was the mother, or Greg could willingly hand Gregory over and they would look the other way on the warrants this time. Greg knew he was cornered, and for once, unbeknownst to me at the time, I had won a battle in our life-long war.

On a very stormy Friday night, we either had knowledge or suspicion that Greg was at his mother's apartment with Gregory. My husband took the restraining order to the area they lived, called 911, and waited three hours for a policeman to show up to accompany him to the apartment to get Gregory. All went well, and Greg appeared very sorrowful that he had to give up Gregory. When Tom arrived home, I immediately called Wendy and told her we had Gregory. She was very excited and came home.

For the next three and a half years, Greg and I continued our perverse tarantella: breaking up, getting back together; moving from apartment to apartment; my moving to my mom's, moving back in with Greg; working the streets, not working the streets. Drugs, beatings, the fleeting declarations of love that bound me to Greg. Throughout this time, new girls would come and go. Mona and Bridget would also come and go, but they were more of a constant in our lives than most of Greg's girlfriends.

Chapter 16
The Demons

Hell is empty and all the devils are here.
—William Shakespeare, The Tempest

WHILE LIVING WITH MY MOTHER, I put my name on a waiting list for low-income housing. Gregory was about three or four, and Latasha about six. Only three months later, I got the call saying I had been approved. As I prepared to move out of my mother's house, Greg insisted that he move into the new place with us.

Greg and I had been on a roller coaster of breaking up, getting back together. He would tell me he was never going to pimp again, and then he would show up with four girls in his new Cadillac. Whenever I would attempt to break up with him and move on with my life, the threats toward my family would begin anew.

"I know where your mother lives, and I know where she works."

Or, "Do you want to be responsible for her house getting burned down?"

And, "I'll break every window in her house."

If those didn't work, he would up the ante.

"If you take my kids, I'll cut the brake lines on your mother's car."

I was scared for my children, and I was scared for my little brother and sister who were, like my son, just three and four years old at the time. I would envision a rock smashing through the window, sending the glass flying through the air and cutting the children. Greg would wear me down with the threats, and then build me up.

"You are the only woman for me and I love you so much."

But his loving attitude had an evil undercurrent.

"You can leave if you want, but you're not taking my kids with you. They are staying with me."

His malice would disappear the minute I would say, "I won't leave you, baby. I just can't handle this life anymore. It's not healthy for the kids, and it drives me insane." With that, he would soften his tone and offer me hope.

"You know how much I love you, Tasha, and Gregory. I want the best for all of you."

Those words were all I needed to hear. I believed that he loved me, even though I was not worth being loved, which put him in the position of being my savior. But even then I knew he wasn't offering hope so much as an avenue of survival, and at this point I was so worn down, mere survival was a blessing.

"You don't have a job, and you don't have enough money to care for the kids. Latasha and Gregory deserve to have a good life and I can offer that to them and to you if you just let me do what I need to do."

He manipulated my feelings about my childhood experiences to reinforce my self-image that I wasn't a good mother to my children. I could see no other options; the only way I could redeem myself was to be with him and do as he said.

"Wendy, you're just a ho without me. Your children will never have anything. Your mom and Ray damaged you so bad emotionally that you don't even know what's really important in life. All you have to do is believe in me. I will take care of you."

Giving up my power to him was not difficult—in fact, it was a relief. If I had no power to make decisions, I could not be held responsible. I couldn't be blamed for anything. All my life it seemed like everyone's misery was always my fault, and Greg plainly laid it out to me: Everything I touched, I destroyed. I believed that completely. I needed him in order to be a good mother. I needed him to love me since no other man ever would.

We moved into the two-bedroom apartment and within days he was bringing his girlfriends to "just stay for the night"—and then two nights, three, indefinitely. I had mixed feelings about the other girls. My sensitive heart felt bad for them if they had to stay in motels or in the car. And, honestly, it was nice having female companionship around. Greg would leave, and the girls and I would just hang out together, watching television or playing card games while Tasha and Gregory would play in the living room. The girls were always a big help with the kids, keeping them entertained while I would take a bath in peace and quiet with no interruptions. We even became allies. When we would discover that Greg was with another girl and not one of us, we would get jealous, and together we'd make plans of revenge. Together in our despair and anger, we created the strong, painful ties that bound us together.

Unfortunately, we had another "friend" that helped us deal with our pain. Within a couple of weeks after we moved into our apartment, Greg met Lou Ann, a financially successful girl who worked the escort services. She was heavily into drugs, and Greg started smoking crack again. Whenever I lived away from Greg, I was drug-free; but when Greg was in the picture, the drugs were never far behind. This time it was Lou Ann who reintroduced me to my old friend cocaine.

There were so many girls coming and going, I couldn't keep them all straight. I can't begin to remember all the details—it was such an insane time—but I do know that Mona and Bridget were there much of the time. Greg worked his black magic to integrate his girls into each other's lives. We would all work hard for him, competing for the spot of the girl he would claim as his own. When Bridget made more money, Greg would humiliate me in front of her.

"You're a pathetic bitch who can't do anything right. I wish you would just go kill yourself. The kids would be so much better off without you. Bridget makes enough money to support your kids...Why don't you give them to her? They love her more than you anyways."

When I made more money than Bridget, he would similarly humiliate her. As unkind as he could be to me, he found ways that would hurt her more.

"I see now why your mom didn't love you and left you. You're pathetic and stupid. Your mom did the right thing by abandoning you. You're not worth her time, and you're not worth mine."

Then the crack pipe would be presented to us as if it would take away the hurt he had caused...and for thirty seconds, it did. Greg would allow us, out of the kindness of his heart, to alleviate the pain of his cruel truth.

Bridget and I were only occasionally working the street and when we did get out, we were lucky if we each brought home a hundred to two hundred dollars—so Greg made arrangements for me to work with an escort service again. One day the lady who ran the escort service called.

"Wendy, can you handle a weird call?"

My life was weird, I was used to weird. She then added, "It pays four hundred dollars."

I wanted to know more.

"What is it?"

She wasn't even laughing when she responded. "It's a man who dresses up like a baby and wants you to pretend to be his mommy and sexually abuse him."

My life was so out of control and I was so deep in my living hell that this shit didn't even amaze me anymore. Between my war paint transformations and the knowledge that Greg would reward me with crack when I got home, I thought I could handle the situation with grace and ease.

Mona drove me to the North Seattle address, where a man wearing an adult-size diaper, baby bonnet, and bunny slippers answered the door with a baby bottle in his hand. A mental mantra helped me stay calm: *four hundred dollars, four hundred dollars.* I hoped that if I made four hundred dollars tonight off this one date, Greg might let me have a few days off. I imagined the time I would get to spend with the kids and thought of the movies we could rent and watch during the time off. All I had to do was make it through this one hour in front of me.

In a baby voice the man informed me of his desires. As he described what he wanted "Mommy" to do to him, my heart dropped to my stomach. Did his mother really abuse him sexually, or was it some made-up fantasy stemming from seemingly nowhere? Struggling to turn my emotions off and not think about what I was about to do, I inhaled deeply and tried to reconnect with my confident inner girl who could handle this.

The man then started to softly cry and whimper. In a mommy's voice I asked, "What's wrong?"

He started crying and whimpering even more and in a soft pathetic voice he cried, "I wet my diaper."

Ah, shit! This is starting now. I had thought I could stall, acting like I didn't understand, but it was futile. He was starting his fantasy and I needed to earn my money.

Once a week a man from the neighborhood church would knock on the door to invite the kids and me to attend Sunday services. Trying not to be rude I would always reply "maybe." He would appear on Sunday mornings in a big church bus, picking up all the neighborhood kids. Sometimes the other girls and I would still be up from the night before, smoking crack and recovering from the painful torture Greg had put us through. Sometimes when the church man arrived at the door, I would politely tell him we would not be able to make it, while other times we all stood quietly waiting for him to leave. This went on for months.

One Saturday night, the girls and I had gone from one escort date to another all night long. Dressed in high heels and miniskirts, we were unmistakably prostitutes. After picking up some drugs from our dealer, we headed home; and when we got out of the car, the church man was standing in the driveway. When he tried to speak to me, I quickly passed him by without even looking at him. I was so embarrassed for him to know what I really was. But he was not deterred; the next Sunday, he knocked on our door to invite us to church. This man was getting to be very irritating.

Greg was by this time collecting even more girls, more than my small two-bedroom apartment could hold. He started renting motel rooms and staying away more often. It was such a welcome relief to not have him or the drugs around as much. I still had to go out on the street occasionally, but not nearly as often as before.

One day he stopped by and I was having such a lovely time with him not being around, I told him I thought we should break up.

"Greg, you don't need me, you don't love me. I'll still let you see the kids as much as you want, I just don't want to be with you anymore."

He turned and walked out of the apartment without even slamming the door. Even though I was scared, I was hopeful that maybe he agreed with me.

The following morning the kids and I got into my car to go to the store. When I put the key into the ignition, it didn't start. I knew a little bit about cars from all the broken-down cars Greg had owned, so I opened the hood. For a moment I stood in shock: All the wires had been cut to pieces and parts of the engine were in places I knew they weren't supposed to be. For all I knew, Greg had put a bomb in the car. I grabbed the kids and took them back upstairs to wait for the next phase of my punishment.

For days he didn't call or come to the apartment. Imagining what he would do was excruciating, as psychically painful as anything he could actually do to me. When he finally called me, he acted as if nothing had happened.

"Wendy, I want to see you and the kids. I'll pick you up in an hour and take you guys out to dinner."

He picked us up and drove us first to a motel where he was staying. He had so many girls at this point he had to rent three hotel rooms to house them all. There were a total of fifteen girls between the three rooms.

Some of these girls were real prostitutes. Maybe I was wrong, but it seemed to me that some of the girls wanted to live the wild and crazy life, and Greg was the pimp who could provide that to them. Most of the girls, though, were there because they thought Greg loved them and they needed to prove their love to him. It was so unreal, seeing all these girls running from one room to another, all of them under Greg's control. Even stranger was how I felt about it: powerful, special, loved. Even though Greg could have any one of these girls—in fact, he did have all of these girls—I was the one he had picked up and was taking out to dinner. How could I doubt that he still loved me and wanted to be with me?

"Wendy, all I have to do is take these girls down to California, and I'll make enough money to support us so you won't ever have to work again. You can stay home and raise the kids, take care of the house, and I'll get a job when I get back and give up the game forever."

His promise for the future sounded like heaven to me, too good to be true. I also thought how wonderful it would be without him around while he got his act together: no drugs, no girls, no fear, no crazy-making in my life.

After dinner, Greg dropped me off at my apartment, saying and doing nothing about my still-sabotaged car. He gave me a big hug and kiss good-bye, told me how much he loved me, and then drove away, headed to California for God only knew how long. I was on cloud nine. In my mind I was a mother and a wife whose husband was out of town on business.

While Greg was gone, I flourished emotionally, and financially I made do. Richard would date me when I needed money and would even bring dinner for the kids and buy us groceries on occasion. I got a job as a CNA doing in-home elder care on a part-time basis. It was happy and serene not having Greg around, but I did miss him—not the Greg that he had become, but I missed the Greg who had so many years ago captured my heart, the Prince Charming who would love me forever and would always rescue me.

The church man would still stop by every Sunday morning to see if the kids and I would like to go to church. Even though I would always politely say, "Not this week, but thanks for stopping by," he must have planted a seed. One Saturday night as I was flipping channels on the television, I stopped on a Billy Graham special. I don't know why I didn't switch to something else, but I didn't. I sat and listened to the sermon, and as I did a powerful feeling washed over me. For the first time since I was a small child at my grandma's house, I felt God's love, and the sheer joy of it overwhelmed me. I said a prayer giving my life to God and instantly I was happy. I threw my cigarettes into the garbage and made the commitment to live a clean life. I wanted to be special to God. I wanted to love him as completely as I felt loved by him.

I'm sure Gregory and Latasha could not possibly have understood my dramatic mood change when I asked with a smile, "Do you guys want to go to church tomorrow?" Giving me a weird look, but also happy to get out of the house, they chimed an enthusiastic, "Yeah!"

The kids and I got up early in the morning and dressed for church. It felt so natural—what still amazes me to this day is that I didn't have any cravings for the cigarettes. I waited for the knock on the door, the knock that came every Sunday morning. Instead of dreading the knock, I welcomed it and wanted it. The children were excited; Tasha was in her pretty pink frilly dress and Gregory in a cute little boy's suit. It wasn't very often that they had an opportunity to wear their Sunday best. I heard the bus roll up and waited and waited. I peeked out the peep hole in the door to see if I could see him coming, and I watched through the peep hole as he walked past my apartment to the next apartment on his round.

My heart broke. I didn't know what to do. Had he forgotten me? The kids were jumping up and down; they wanted to go out the door, but I didn't want to go out there unless I was invited. I took a deep breath, fought back my fears of rejection, opened the door and walked outside where the church man could see me.

"Aren't you going to knock on my door?"

He looked over at me in shock.

"Well, I just figured you wouldn't want to go."

In a voice just loud enough for him to hear me, I said, "Well, now I want to go."

I started going to church every Sunday and studying the Bible. When Greg called I told him how I had been saved and how happy the kids and I were now that we were following Jesus. When I informed Greg that I couldn't be with him as long as he wasn't following God's Word, he took it as a joke.

"Yeah, we'll see about that."

But he also professed to be happy that I was happy.

"I'm glad you're so happy, Wendy. Keep going to church until I get back."

When Richard next visited for a date, I politely told him that I wasn't going to have sex for money anymore. In fact, I wasn't going to have sex until I got married. He was very pleasant about it and continued to bring me money and groceries, and he would come over and play cards with me and the kids on lonely afternoons. He was supportive but not nearly as pleasant when I talked to him about Greg's surprisingly positive reaction.

"Wendy, he is not going to let you go easily. Take this gun as protection and keep it in your closet just in case you need it."

I had never even held a gun before. I was frightened, but I put out my hand. The gun was a lot heavier than I ever thought a gun would be. The next few nights I couldn't stop thinking about the black handgun in my closet and what Greg would do if he knew I had a gun for protection from him.

One night, from out of the swirl of fear came not a voice but a feeling that was so strong and powerful I could not possibly mistake its message.

"You don't need the gun, Wendy... I've got your back on this."

The solution came to me in an instant. I didn't need the gun because God was going to protect me.

The next time I saw Richard, I returned the gun.

"God's got my back," I assured him with complete confidence. He looked skeptical, but he took the gun with him when he left my apartment.

Greg had been in California for three months when I got a collect phone call at three o'clock in the morning.

"Wendy, I'm coming back. Be ready for me."

"I told you, Greg, I don't want you around until you have changed your life."

He pleaded with me. "Wendy, get real with it. You ain't no Christian. God don't want you. Now get ready—I'm on my way back up there."

I had not forgotten the message God had sent me. With strength and conviction, I proclaimed my commitment.

"You cannot come here. You cannot be in my life as long as you are living in sin. I am not going to do drugs anymore, and I will not have sex with you unless we are married."

Greg was no longer plaintive.

"You fuckin' stupid ass ho. You think God can take the place of me? You think you can change, bitch? I will come up there and fucking *kill* you. You are *dead*, bitch. When I get my hands on you, I'll show you who's god."

He hung up the phone and fear started to overwhelm me. At least he wouldn't arrive for another day or two; it would take at least twenty-four hours for him to drive back from California. Maybe he would call again and I could try to calm him down. I stared at the phone, willing it to ring—but something told me I should make the next call. I picked up the phone and dialed "0."

"Operator, how can I help you?"

"Can you please tell me where the collect call I just accepted came from?"

There was a short pause that seemed like eternity.

"The call came from Federal Way, Washington."

My heart dropped. Federal Way was only twenty minutes away. I started to cry from being so scared and I wondered where God was. He said he would have my back. He said he would protect me, but God was nowhere around.

I ran into the kids' room. "Tasha! Gregory! Hurry! Get up, we gotta go."

"Where are we going, Mommy? Is everything okay, Mommy?" Tasha's voice was sweet and trusting.

"Please honey, just get your brother dressed quickly and get in the car."

I took nothing with me except my two children—they were more important to me than anything else in the world. As I drove away from the apartment, I knew I could never go back. I took one last look at the place where I had been so happy for the past three months and wondered what Greg would do to it when he got there. I knew it would be destroyed.

I drove around for a while trying to think of how I could escape. I only had twenty dollars and a quarter tank of gas. I couldn't go running back to my mother, not again. I couldn't let her know that I had once again destroyed my life by going back to Greg. I entreated God to give me an answer.

"Please, God, tell me what I'm supposed to do?"

There was no response, no wonderful feeling of protection, no reassurance at all. I knew Greg would find me because I had no place to go. I would have to go back to the apartment sooner or later, and when I did he would kill me. I started envisioning what would happen, what my death would look like. The only thing I knew for certain was that I didn't want Tasha and Gregory to see their father kill their mother.

"Mommy, where are we going?" Latasha asked as the sun began to inch its way into the sky.

"I'm taking you to Grandma Juanita's, sweetie. Do you want to go see Grandma Juanita?"

The kids were excited by that possibility. "Yeah!"

I dropped them off at Juanita's, telling her only that I needed her to watch them for the day. I gave them a big hug and kiss good-bye as I fought the tears that were welling inside of me. I got into my car and started to drive, thinking about how much pain Greg would inflict on me before he killed me. The punches, the pushes, things being thrown at me—and perhaps worst of all the humiliation he would put me through before he ended my life. I didn't want to die that way. I chose not to die that way.

I drove to a convenience store where I bought a bottle of sleeping pills and then to another store where I bought another bottle of sleeping pills. I went to a third store and a fourth, buying only one bottle of pills at each so I wouldn't draw any attention to myself. At the last store I also bought two Diet Cokes. By the time I spent my twenty dollars it was nine o'clock. I drove to a park that I knew would be empty that early in the morning.

Ever since my first suicide attempt when I was thirteen, my body would reject pills by gagging, so I used my index finger to shove the pills down my throat one at a time. After I put a pill in my throat, I would quickly take a gulp of liquid to wash the pill down. For four hours I cried and swallowed the pills that would save me from a painful, torturous death. I cried for my kids, wishing I could have given them a better life, knowing that now I was dying they *would* have a better life.

I knew that was true because Greg had told me it was true. Everything Greg had ever said to me was integrated into the person I had become. I thought the words he spoke, I took the actions he told me to take. I was nothing but a slave to him. Greg wasn't a pimp. His business was stealing souls, and somehow he had stolen mine. Maybe he took it when I was sleeping, one of the nights I let him stay in my closet all those years ago. Maybe I even gave it to him when I wasn't thinking straight, my brain blinded by the bright light of his early attention. All I knew was that he had mine.

A person cannot live without her soul. That is why we girls stayed close to him, all of us hoping that maybe someday he would be kind enough to return our souls to us—or that, at some point, maybe when he was sleeping, we could find where he had hidden our souls and we could take them back. But until our souls were returned to us, we were trapped by him, each of us a slave to him and dead to the world.

Around one o'clock I was still taking the pills but starting to feel the effects. I glanced out the car window to see a tall, black, ghostly figure hovering over the ground. Its dark red eyes glared at me, beckoning and impatient as if it were waiting for me.

My heart raced in fear as I quickly rolled up my window and locked the doors. I then saw several more figures standing off in the other direction. Half a dozen of the demon-like creatures started coming closer to my car. I closed my eyes and had nearly convinced myself I was hallucinating when I heard their voices. The high-pitched loud squeaks hurt my ear drums, and goose bumps crawled all over my body. I dropped the few remaining pills as the creatures glided closer to the car, my heart beating faster and the tears streaming down my face. Even the fear fled from my body, ejected by my desperate scream.

"No, *no! Please!* Leave me alone!"

Still they came, until they were so close and their voices so loud that the windows of my car were vibrating. I turned the key in the ignition, put the car into first, and took off as fast as I could, with my eyes closed so as not to see the bloodshed when I ran my car through them. But it was for naught: When I opened my eyes a moment later, they were following me, closing in as fast as I could drive.

I didn't know where to run for help. I needed help from these demons that were waiting for my soul. What would happen when they, too, realized I no longer had my own soul? Could it be worse than dying? I was petrified. I still don't know how, but I drove the five miles to the hospital. Parked outside the emergency room, I didn't even have the strength to open the car door. Every time I tried to raise my fingers to the door knob, my hand would move only an inch before dropping down onto my lap.

A security guard walking past saw me, got me out of the car, and took me inside. The high-pitched squeaks stopped while the doctors and nurses were all around me; but when they would leave the room, I could hear the voices of the demons still waiting for me. I didn't understand why they couldn't see that I didn't have a soul for them to take. Greg had my soul and I would never get it back.

When I woke up a couple of days later, I was embarrassed, scared, overwhelmed, done for. I looked around for God and realized that Greg was right. God didn't want me. God was nowhere to be found, but Greg was there—just as he had sworn he would be. He was there with flowers and I love you's and I'm sorry's. He showered me with hugs, kisses, and the love that I so desperately needed. I was grateful to accept his attention, all the while knowing the price I would end up having to pay. The demons were gone; the Demon was there forever.

Chapter 17
Stayin' Alive

Ah, ha, ha, ha, stayin' alive, stayin' alive
Ah, ha, ha, ha, stayin' alive
Life goin' nowhere. Somebody help me,
yeah.
I'm stayin' alive.
—Barry, Robin, and Maurice Gibb

TRICKIN' AT HOME

We were evicted from the apartment that had briefly given me comfort for too much in-and-out activity and noise. As time went by, we moved around from hotel to hotel, with Greg collecting more girls wherever we lived. We finally found an apartment complex in Federal Way that would accept me as a renter. Nine of us lived in my two-bedroom apartment: Mona, Veronica, Regina, Greg's brother Spencer and his girlfriend Sonya, plus Latasha, Gregory, and Greg and I. Most of them were able to help with expenses, and the girls and I had developed enough regular tricks at the time that we rarely had to work the street. We hung out at home most of the week; on Friday and Saturday nights we would go from location to location for scheduled appointments. Greg ran everything—our stealing and tricking—from his bedroom, where he smoked his crack and gave us drugs and tortured each girl as he pleased.

One trick in particular was a really nice guy who would rent a hotel room and pay me fifty dollars to give me a back rub, without any sex of any kind. He would have me lie naked on the bed, and he would massage my back and only my back. I liked this trick a lot. I called him one day when we needed some quick cash and asked him if he would like to see me. He agreed if I could see him right then because he had an appointment in two hours. I was a little reluctant because Greg was gone with the girls and I was home alone with the kids; but I knew if I didn't make this money, I would have to go out on the dreaded street that evening.

"I have my kids here with me right now and I can't leave them here alone."

"I can go to your house. We can go in the bedroom and the kids can stay in the living room. I'll even give you the money I would have spent on the hotel room."

His suggestion was very enticing. Greg had ordered me to make fifty dollars while he was gone; I knew he would be pleased if I earned more than that. I swallowed my hesitations and gave the trick directions to my house. When he arrived I told the kids that he had come to look at the broken television in the bedroom. I instructed them not to disturb us. They would *have* to stay in the living room and watch cartoons.

Usually I enjoyed the massage, but this time I couldn't relax, nervous that the kids would walk in and uneasy that I was doing a trick in the house while they were home, awake, and in the other room. I was relieved when the trick hurried off to his other appointment. When Greg came home he was so pleased when I handed him the hundred dollars that I felt free to ask for a treat.

"Can I have a five for a pack of cigarettes, please?"

BOOSTING

Regular dates weren't the only way we stayed off the street; some of the girls had other skills. Mona, for example, was really good at boosting—stealing from stores and then returning the items for cash. Greg also wanted me to learn the boosting trade, so when Gregory needed some socks I decided to go with her.

At the Fred Meyer superstore, I selected socks and underwear for Gregory and a cute dress for Latasha. On Mona's cue I put the clothing in my purse. Mona pointed out the cameras and the undercover security personnel. Under her guidance, I felt confident; but I was taken by surprise when a voice shouted as we were walking out of the store.

"Stop! Don't move."

My heart dropped. Mona and I turned around to face the men, who grabbed our arms and held us still.

"Come with us."

The men escorted us to the security room, where they dumped the contents of our purses onto an empty table in the middle of the room and called the police. I looked at Mona for a clue how to act since she had been through this many times before.

"Don't worry, Wendy," said her look. "Everything is going to be alright."

I loved Mona for her ability to calm me down and in a sense take care of me in Greg's absence.

When the police arrived and asked us our names and dates of birth, Mona gave a date that didn't sound right to me. The day was familiar, but she gave a birth year that indicated that she was two years younger than she had told me. I gave her a quizzical look and she responded with a look that said *Sorry I lied to you all this time.* It turned out that Mona was only fourteen years old when she first came around to babysit the kids. That revelation was shocking to me, but too much to absorb at this point. Besides, she was now over eighteen, albeit barely.

When the police arrived they stood on the other side of the room, examining the items on the table and speaking into their walkie-talkies to inquire about warrants out for our arrest. Finally, one of the officers approached us.

"Whose bag is this?" said one policeman, holding the purse that had all the children's clothing.

"It's mine," I muttered, sad that I now would have nothing to bring home to the children.

The police officer looked at Mona.

"You have a warrant for your arrest and you're going to jail."

He then turned to me.

"You'll be getting a ticket and you will have to come to court."

Tears dripped down my face and I began to cry. Again he repeated what he thought would be good news. His words were like a knife being thrust into my heart.

"I said, you're *not* going to jail."

My cries turned to sobs, and I began to grasp for breath.

In exasperation, he looked at Mona.

"What's the matter with her? Doesn't she understand she's not going to jail?"

Mona's explanation was simple and true.

"She wants to go to jail. What she has to go home to is much worse than jail."

I made another gasp for air and tried to speak.

"Mo...o...o....na......wh...at....am....I....go...go...going....to....do? I   ....can't...I   can't..... go....ba...ck...there ....a....lone – I...just can't!"

The officer handcuffed Mona and led her out of the room. I was handed a ticket to appear in court and sent on my way. I walked back to the apartment, still crying and dawdling like a small child who knew she was in serious trouble. There was no question that I would be blamed for this. When I walked into the house without Mona, without money, and without clothes for the kids, Greg knew what had happened.

"You fucking stupid bitch, why the hell did you let her get caught? I told the two of you not to go into that store."

It was true that Greg had told us many weeks before not to go into Fred Meyer, but since then he had sent us into that very store many times. Greg was an expert at looking into the future to identify anything that could happen and making seemingly offhand predictions. Then, *whatever* would happen, he would be right. Even if he said totally contradicting things about the same event, he would remind us of the observation that made him right and, by extension, made us wrong.

"If you had listened to *me*, Mona wouldn't be in jail. Now *you* have to do the boosting until she is out."

When Mona got out of jail, it fell to Sonya to teach us about the big-time shoplifting. No longer would we go into discount stores like Fred Meyer and Wal-Mart to steal and return twenty-dollar items. Sonya taught us about the Gap and Banana Republic. Each of the nicer stores would let us return items without receipts three times a year. Once we graduated to shoplifting on our own, Mona would steal a couple hundred dollars' worth of merchandise, and then I would go into the store and return it for the money. For a while we made so much money during the days doing returns that we didn't even have to see our regular dates. For a few blessed weeks, the nights were our own.

BACK ON THE STREET IN AURORA VILLAGE

Even though we lived in Federal Way in South Seattle, I preferred to drive the car to North Seattle to work. I would park my car at a Kmart for the evening and walk to a 24-hour Safeway about two miles up the road. I liked to go out early so I could make my quota and get home at a decent hour, so I would try to get to the Kmart by eight o'clock. From there, I would walk along the road to the Safeway until I got a customer.

Over the years I had developed my own little techniques to keep myself safe out on the street. I knew places where I felt more comfortable and ways to tell if a guy was harmless. For example, when a guy would pull up beside me and ask me if I needed a ride, I'd say "Yeah, up to the Safeway." During the short trip, I would check out him and his car to determine if he was a cop.

"Can I look in your glove box and under your seats?" I'd inquire.

The tricks would never have any problem with it, but a police officer would almost never allow me to search his vehicle. If the driver complied, I would look in the glove box just to notice if it contained the things a person would typically have: insurance papers, car registration, napkins. Then I'd lean over and push myself between his legs to look under his seat for a gun or badge. I would observe the guy's waist line and pockets for any bulges that could be a gun or badge. After this routine, if I felt okay with him, I would take the encounter to the next level.

"What are you looking for?"

His response usually revealed a lot. If I felt funny or suspicious for any reason about the man, I would remind him that I only needed a ride to Safeway and he'd need to drop me off there.

One evening I started my routine as usual, parking my car at the Kmart and trekking toward the Safeway. I walked for a while, longer than usual, when I felt a car slowing down and pulling close to me. The car stayed behind me instead of pulling up beside me, which meant it was a cop. Cops would always stay behind; tricks would always pull beside. I stopped in my tracks and turned towards the police car, making sure not to make any sudden movements.

I knew the drill. I waited patiently for the police officer to get out of his car and approach me. He was a stocky, short man, only a few inches taller than me. As he got closer, I noticed that he was older than most police officers, maybe fifty-five or sixty. That was my first clue that this encounter with the law might be very different. He walked up to me, getting close enough to be heard over the passing traffic. When he spoke, his voice was almost friendly—not at all like a normal police officer.

"Listen, I know what you are doing out here, and you know what you are doing out here. I'm not going to put you in the position to have to lie to me, so we will bypass that question. I do have one question for you, and I would appreciate your honesty... Are you okay?"

I stood in complete silence. I really didn't know what he meant by the question. I had never been asked that before, at least that I could remember. What stunned me even more was the sound of his voice, the genuine tone in his words. His eyes looked directly into mine with a sincerity that made my heart drop, and I stood there in utter confusion. *He already said that he knows what I am doing out here, that I am a prostitute. Everyone knows prostitutes are the filth of the earth that dirty the city with diseases. He knows what I am, yet he's treating me like a human being.* I couldn't speak, couldn't move. I could only stand there in disbelief.

The police officer broke the silence and brought me back to reality.

"We found a girl up the road and she was murdered. We think it may be the Green River Killer. Do you know about the Green River Killer?"

Words escaped me. It was all I could do to murmur, "Yeah."

"We have a lot of police out here looking for the person who did this, but we haven't found him yet, and it's very dangerous for you to be out here."

I stared at him blankly, not understanding what he was saying. I had heard many times the rough and condescending remarks police would make to girls like us on the street.

"Get off the street and don't come back here."

"If I see you again out here, I'll take you to jail."

"Go find another part of town to work. We don't want you here."

No one had ever told me that it was dangerous and I was not safe. No one had ever cared about my safety. Why would anyone? I knew I wasn't worth anyone caring about me.

"What is your name?"

I knew better than to lie about my name.

"Wendy."

"Where do you live? How did you get out here?"

"I drove," I mumbled.

"Well, where is your car? I'll drive you to it. I really don't want you out here tonight. I don't want to find you dead, too."

I knew I should try to snap myself out of my daze, but I really didn't want to. I didn't know what this strange yet wonderful feeling was, and I didn't want to break the spell. But my better sense prevailed.

"I parked at the Kmart down the street."

"Well get in my car, I'll drive you there," he offered.

This snapped me out of it. Now I understood what this police officer was about. He was just trying to trick me into getting into his car. I knew I couldn't run away from him; he stood too close to me. I didn't have any choice but to get in the police car and be taken to jail. Besides, a night in jail would be a nice break away from all the bullshit that happened at home. I was ready and wanting a break from Greg.

The officer opened the back door to allow me to get in. I slid quickly into the backseat; I didn't want any of the tricks who might pick me up another time to see me. He started down the road.

"So did you make any money tonight?"

"No, I had just got out here."

"Are these your regular stomping grounds?"

"Sometimes it is."

I spoke softly. I was scared and still confused about the feelings I was experiencing. I expected him to turn at the light; that was the way to the police station. Instead, he pulled into the Kmart parking lot.

"Which car is yours?"

There weren't many cars in the parking lot to begin with; mine was in an obscure spot, far away from the store and closer to the street.

"It's the blue car over there," I said as I pointed my finger.

He pulled up right beside it and walked around his car. He opened the door and granted me my freedom. This was just too much to handle, too weird. This was not normal, for a policeman to be kind to me or to treat me with even a modicum of respect or dignity. I got out and went to my car.

"Hey, Wendy," he called out to me. "Try and stay off the street for as long as you can, okay? I'm worried this guy out there is not finished, and I don't want to see you get hurt or killed."

"I'll try. Thank you for the ride."

I went home and told Greg about the policeman telling me to go home because there was a killer out there. But I didn't tell him about how kindly the man talked to me, or the feelings I experienced. I only mentioned that the policeman instructed me not to come back for as long as I could. I embellished the story a little, saying that if I went right back there, he'd put me in jail. My hope was that this little lie would persuade Greg to let me have some time off. He was nice enough to let me stay home for a week without any consequences. When the week was up, Greg's hand of judgment came down.

Greg was a very smart man who knew and understood the laws well. He knew that he could not be convicted of promoting prostitution for using a girl over the age of eighteen, as long as he did not use physical violence in order to make her go out and prostitute. So with us, Greg would find different, more *personal* reasons to make our lives so miserable. That's where the physical abuse came into play. In the end, he would tone down or stop his "non-business" violence and torture, but only if I went out and worked the street to make him money. The more money I would make, the less he would torture me. After the first week, Greg started making me miserable every night that I stayed home. He would stand over me and yell.

"What fucking good are you? All the other girls are out there making money to support your kids. They have more love for your kids than you do. They should be their mom, *not you*, you stupid bitch."

That one always hurt me the worst. Knowing the reality of what a horrible mother I was, allowing my children to be involved with this horrific life of craziness. As the week dragged on, I held strong through the painful nights of humiliation and thousands of interrogation-style questions. But the third week got too much for me. Greg would keep me awake the entire night while he fed me cocaine through a pipe. While I was sleep deprived and drugged, he persistently drilled me for hours and forced me to perform oral sex on him many times.

Finally, I couldn't handle it anymore. I decided that being killed by the Green River Killer was better than living this way, night after night. Almost three full weeks had passed since my encounter with the police officer who had looked out for me. By this time, I had forgotten about the feelings I experienced when he had asked me if I was okay. All I wanted was to go make some money for Greg so he would stop tormenting me, but I also didn't want to run into the policeman. I didn't want him to know I was back out there.

I parked my car in the usual spot at the Kmart and started walking down the street, heading for the Safeway. There weren't many cars cruising by, and when they did the cars were filled with families. I had walked about a mile when I felt a car pull up behind me and slow down. I knew it was a cop. Taking a deep breath and full of disappointment, I turned around to face the police car. Although there were many times I wanted to go to jail, tonight wasn't one of them. I wanted to make my money and go home to my kids.

The door to the police car opened, and I saw that it was the same police officer who had stopped me here before. My heart filled with excitement and I smiled at him, full of joy that it was the kind police officer. I knew I wasn't going to jail, at least not right now with him. As he approached, I started off the conversation.

"Hi, I swear I haven't been out here. I haven't been out here for three whole weeks."

I was looking for the police officer to be proud of me for not coming out. I didn't want him to think that I hadn't listened to him or respected what he had said. I was about to make an attempt at proving to him that I hadn't been out there when he interrupted me.

"I know you haven't been out here. I look for your car every night. I knew you were out here tonight because I went to see if your car was here, and it is." He had slight smile on his face; his voice was soft and sincere.

Again I stood in shock trying to understand what he was saying. He thought of me when I wasn't even around. He went out of his way to see if I was out here. My heart stopped as the thought went through my head, *I exist to him.* He didn't have the same attitude that other police officers had: disgust towards me—a repulsiveness, really. I liked the way I felt when he talked to me. I felt a kind of equality between us. He wasn't condescending. I refreshingly didn't feel like scum.

He went on. "We haven't found the guy who killed that woman yet. In fact we have discovered two more murdered girls all within a few miles of here. You shouldn't be out here, Wendy."

His words echoed through my bewildered mind. *You shouldn't be out here, Wendy...Wendy...Wendy.* He had called me by my name. *He remembered my name.*

In February 1994 she was evicted for being too slow on her rent, and at first she moved in with me. She kept saying she knew she would be breaking up with Greg *sooner or later, but she just didn't know when. We had already decided that the next time she moved in with me, that if and when she moved out, Tasha would stay with me so she wouldn't have to keep switching schools. Wendy moved out of my house after only a month, and was back living with Greg and the mob in motels, staying at each one for a few days up to a couple weeks at a time. Eventually they all found a motel that was more like an apartment, where they could pay by the week, and they ended up staying there for a few months. When Tasha was there on weekends, there would be five adults and two children living there.*

At this point she and everyone else were into a heavy-duty "theft-ring" and using all the money for drugs. She landed in jail a couple times and she was building up lots of fines to pay.

When I called the motel one night to talk to Wendy, I was told they were no longer there. That night when Wendy contacted me, I pretended I didn't know of them moving, and she mentioned it to me. The next day I got nosey and called the motel office and asked if they could tell me anything about them moving, and they told me they were evicted, and that they thought all the girls were so afraid of Greg that they would say or do anything he wanted them to. They also told me they thought Wendy was the only one with a head on her shoulders.

One day Greg drove me and the kids over to my mother's house in Bellevue. There was hardly any traffic on the freeway that day when all of a sudden the car drastically slowed down, making me think there was something wrong with it.

"Greg, what's the matter? Pull over to the side."

"There's nothing wrong."

His tone was stone-cold, and he stared straight ahead. The car continued to slow down until it was only going ten miles an hour, and Greg remained in the fast lane. Even though there were no other cars in sight, it scared me that Greg wouldn't pull over.

"Greg, what are you doing?"

He seemed to be in his own little imaginary world when all of a sudden he looked at me with the weirdest smile.

"I just wanted to know what it felt like to be O. J. Simpson."

After O. J. killed Nicole, that was all Greg would talk about—that he was going to be the next O. J. and he would get away with murdering me.

Chapter 18
Saving Wendy

*If you rescue me from my pipe dreams, I'll
stop smoking fantasies. ¯Munia Khan*

WHEN I WAS TWENTY-FIVE, we were living in Tukwila,
Washington, in a hotel that had rooms that
resembled one-bedroom apartments. My life there
had solidified into a vicious cycle of working the
street and coming home to violent interrogations. The
only friend that could ease my pain was crack. Even
so, I usually greeted the morning with my children,
thinking if I made them breakfast I might at least be a
good mom.

But one morning I couldn't even manage that. I
stumbled out of bed around eleven, and Tasha and
Gregory had been up for hours. I walked into the
living area and watched them as they sat quietly in
front of the television with the volume low so they
wouldn't wake any of the sleeping girls who
surrounded them. I was not in good shape, but I was
sober enough to be filled with disgust at the revolting
scene.

You've smoked crack every day for the past year!!
screamed an inner voice.

I immediately denied this accusation.

*There's no way I would have smoked crack every
single day for the past year.*

No? insisted the intruding voice. *Think about it.*

I began a desperate mental checklist of the previous year, concentrating solely on the special holidays, so I could prove myself innocent. Christmas: I remembered where I was that day and saw myself clearly, the pipe in my mouth. Thanksgiving: I carefully thought about it and realized I had indeed smoked crack. Tasha's birthday: *There's no way I would have done drugs on her birthday!* I struggled to remember that day, and as the events paraded before me, through the day and into the evening, I at last saw the vision: me, smoking crack.

I stood numb, looking at my children and seeing only the reflection of the mother they didn't deserve. I thought back to a time when I had dreams, dreams of having a family and someone to love me, and I went blank—stunned by the realization that my dreams had vanished. There were no dreams to remember, and my future was blank.

I heard Greg waking up and walked back into the bedroom. I stared at the piles of dirty clothes all over the room. Everything in my life, except my two beautiful children, was filth.

"Greg, can you drive me and the kids over to my mom's so we can wash some of our clothes?"

He didn't hesitate.

"Yeah. Get the clothes together. I'll take you now."

I knew he wasn't doing me any favors; he was thinking only about the freedom he would have to do as he pleased with the girls while the kids and I were gone. I scavenged through the piles of dirty clothes trying to find only garments that belonged to me or the kids. I stuffed the clothes into two plastic grocery bags and told the kids, "We're going to Pumpkin Pie Grandma's."

Latasha had given my mom that nickname because she cooked pumpkin pies, which Tasha loved.

When she was small and we talked about "grandma," she would want to know which grandma we were talking about.

"Are we visiting the grandma who makes the pumpkin pies?"

Tasha and Gregory loved going over to Pumpkin Pie Grandma's. There they were free to be children, without chaos, fighting, hiding; and best of all, they never heard anyone say, "Just go to bed and be quiet." They also had playmates there; my mom now had two young children, Danny and Darla. Although they were uncle and aunt to my kids, they were all more like siblings because of the closeness in age.

Greg drove us the fifteen miles from the hotel in Tukwila to my mom's house in Bellevue. The kids jumped out of the car as soon as Greg pulled into the driveway, running into the house to greet Darla and Danny. I grabbed the two bags of dirty clothes, tossed a half-hearted thanks in Greg's direction, and started to close the door behind me.

"Don't even think of doing anything stupid bitch. I will find you and I will fucking kill you."

I stared at him in total confusion, not knowing what he was talking about. At that point, I had no thought in my head of leaving; I had no thoughts at all. I looked at him with disgust, didn't say a word, closed the car door behind me, and walked into my mother's house.

The kids were playing when I walked in the house, and the sight was gratifying. It seemed so right, to be in a loving home where children could play freely. The joy of that moment nurtured the budding idea that Greg had planted. I had no idea who or what was controlling me at that moment. It was as if I were a marionette, manipulated by an invisible puppet master. I walked to the phone and called Richard.

I had known Richard for five years by this time, and I felt pretty comfortable with him. He knew pieces of my life, although not everything. When he answered I heard myself speak, but I had no idea what I was going to say.

"Richard, can you drive me and my kids to Portland, Oregon?"

I had never been to Portland. Perhaps my spirit-controller, knowing that I loved the rain, picked Portland because it was the closest big city with weather patterns similar to Seattle. While I was still on the phone with Richard, I noticed my mother staring at me with a huge, weird smile on her face. When I hung up the phone I gave her a stern look.

"Don't get too happy. I don't even know what I'm doing right now."

Richard arrived two hours later. My kids and I said our good-byes to my mom and put the two grocery bags of now-clean clothes in the trunk of his car. She was very happy that I was doing what I was doing, even though I still didn't know what I was doing.

On Thursday, July 7, 1994, Wendy had Greg drop her off. She called Richard to see if he would be willing to drive her to Portland where she planned to start life all over. Fortunately, Richard was willing to take the next day off from work and drive her and the kids to Portland. She couldn't express to me enough that once Greg realized she wasn't coming back, he was going to be furious, and that I needed to get a restraining order first thing on Friday. She kept assuring me he would be violent and we needed to request police protection. I was not that concerned, but didn't ignore her fears, either. Apparently the straw that broke the camel's back is that Greg had made O. J. Simpson his hero and kept saying he wanted to be just like

O. J., and he was going to do the exact same thing O. J. did. She also kept wondering and wishing if Greg could be retried for pimping so that this time she could tell the truth, and let it be known how he uses either charm or threats to get everyone to lie for him.

When Richard arrived to pick up Wendy I took a picture of them before they left. I was crying because I was so happy.

When I arrived in Portland, I was able to get into a domestic violence shelter. Before he took us to the shelter, Richard played along with my fantasy that this trip was just a little vacation. He rented a hotel room for two days—not the kind of hotel I was used to, but a safe place with nice guests and a swimming pool that the children enjoyed. He rented a DVD player so the kids could watch movies, and he treated us to good meals. He took me to Kmart and bought us the things we would need at the shelter: clothes, hair dryer, underwear. When he dropped us off at the shelter, he gave me some spending money. For a long time, he would send me money weekly so that I could take the children to the zoo.

It was very hard living in unfamiliar territory. Not just the area but the people and a different type of life with organization and schedules. I learned how to take the bus around Portland so Latasha and Gregory and I could visit the zoo and other attractions. I wanted to make this as fun as I could for them. I wanted them to be happy and free to be children.

Soon after we arrived, Gregory started to become violent with me. He would have fits where he would repeatedly hit me as hard as he could. When I tried putting him in time outs, he would act out uncontrollably. I was unsure of my parenting and scared that I would never be able to control his fits. The shelter people directed me to hold him tightly in my lap until he calmed down. When the next fit started, I held him firmly with all of my love, hoping he would calm down. He kicked and screamed until finally, in a burst of rage, he head butted me so hard that my lip split. Blood dripped down my chin and my lip was throbbing. I couldn't hold him any longer, and when I released him, I felt I was giving up on him. Broken-hearted tears flowed into the blood dripping from my face.

The blood and tears frightened Gregory enough that he did calm down. As I cleaned up my wounded lip, one of the shelter counselors approached me.

"Did Gregory ever see Greg hit you?"

I hated the answer I was about to give. I gazed over at Gregory who was now playing with Latasha and softly replied, "Yes."

The counselor continued, "Instinctively when the man of the house is no longer present the son will 'step' into the duties of the man of the house."

I tried to defend myself but even to me my defense was pathetic.

"I tried my hardest not to let either of the kids see it."

Seeing how upset I was, she gently said, "Gregory is stepping into the shoes of the 'man of the house.' Gregory thinks the man of the house is supposed to beat you and disrespect you. He's doing what he thinks is right."

With the counselor's guidance and reassurance, we started play therapy with the children to help them adjust to the situation. I spent another week trying to show Gregory the proper way to act, but the outbursts became more frequent and lasted longer. Because of this, I asked my mom if she could take Gregory for his kindergarten year. I hoped that by then I would have a stable place for him to live and be better suited to handle the problems.

I was lonely without Gregory and missed him a lot. His absence triggered sadness about the other missing pieces of my life, like Greg and the girls. It was hard being away from them. I began to save a little money when I could so I could call him from a pay phone.

It took a long time for me to get enough nerve to make contact with him. I was scared of what he might say and scared of how I would react. One day I called Spencer, who told me how much Greg missed me and the kids. Spencer begged me to call Greg, to at least give him a chance. I called the number Spencer gave me, a hotel where Greg was staying.

Greg's deep voice came through the phone.

"Hello."

I remained silent. I didn't know what to say. His voice was somehow soothing to me though. I wanted to cry, I wanted for him to come and protect me from the uncertainties in the world. I wanted my Prince Charming back, the one I had fallen in love with.

"Wendy? Is this you, Wendy?"

"Yes." My voice was soft, shaky.

"Wendy, I'm so glad you called. I miss you so much; my life isn't the same without you."

I remained silent, feeling my heart beating hard through my chest. I yearned for these words. They obliterated the pain, the disgust, the revulsion of our daily life together. My mind started to reel. *Maybe he could change. Maybe now that I've shown him that I was serious about leaving him, he'll know he has to change in order for me to come back.*

"Wendy, are you okay?" His voice was gentle and sincere. His voice was that of my Prince Charming.

"I'm fine."

"How's Latasha and Gregory?"

"They're fine."

"I miss all you guys and I totally understand why you would leave me. I don't blame you at all for leaving. I would have done the same thing if I were you."

The automatic, recorded operator interrupted the ensuing silence.

"Please deposit another one dollar for an additional three minutes."

I had already used up the phone money.

"Wendy, call me back, please call me back as soon as you can," were the last words I heard as the call went dead.

I stayed in the shelter for a total of forty-five days before moving into a domestic violence transitional housing program. I had my own one-bedroom furnished apartment in a building where no men were allowed. I got a job at the local Greyhound station and began making friends at work and at the mandatory drug and alcohol program for women. Although it was scary and uncomfortable, I continued to pretend I was a normal person, capable of living in a normal world.

Unwittingly, I still followed a lot of the rules Greg had pummeled into me. When I walked down the street, I would stare at the ground. I wouldn't speak to any men unless I had to for work purposes—co-workers and customers—but even then I was evasive and kept the interaction as short as possible. When I wanted to check out at the grocery store, I always went to the line that had a woman cashier.

One time, there were only two open registers, and both of them were attended by men. I stood back for a quarter of an hour, confused, waiting in the hopes that they would open another line with a female cashier. Latasha and Gregory wanted to hurry home to eat the snacks I had purchased and of course didn't understand the delay in going through the line to pay for the groceries. I wanted to please them, but all I could feel was the sensation of Greg watching me. I knew I couldn't pass through the line with the men. Greg's spirit engulfed me, ready to strike if I made the wrong decision.

"Come on kids. We gotta go," I said abruptly.

"Mommy, Mommy, what about the ice cream? Don't leave the groceries!" I pulled the kids by their hands as they continued to tug at me to return to our cart, full of groceries near the cash registers.

"Walk faster, we gotta get home."

I had no clue where these all-consuming feelings came from, but I knew we needed to get home where it was safe. I frantically walked as fast as I could, the children struggling to keep up with me. As we walked the ten blocks, I heard a car in the distance behind me. The radio was playing loud and the bass shook the ground we walked on. I felt the sound getting closer and I realized it was Greg coming after me.

I grabbed at Gregory and Latasha, pulling them into the bushes that lined the street.

"Mommy! What's the matter? You're hurting me, Mommy!"

I forced them to stay down in the bushes with me as I waited for Greg to pass. My heart pounded, fearing that he had seen me jump into the bushes or that one of the kids would escape my grip and stand up as he drove by. I looked at the cars passing and saw the one that was pulsating to the beat of the music filling the streets. But it wasn't Greg's car. I looked hard into the car. The driver was a white man.

"Mommy, what's going on?"

Snapping out of my panic, I straightened up and stepped out the bushes.

"I'm so sorry, baby. I thought someone was after us."

"Can we go back to the store and get the ice cream?"

"No, baby, let's wait for the ice cream. I'll buy something for you from the little store near our house."

That night I filled the bathtub with a nice warm bubble bath. I played my Karen Carpenter tape that always calmed me down and gave me hope for the future. As the songs played, I thought about the events of the day. I clearly saw the insanity of what had happened at the store that day. I wondered if I would always be like that and I wondered if I would ever be "normal." I realized how I had been brainwashed by Greg and how my actions that day stemmed from the thoughts he had repeatedly beat into my head. I started to see how he always got me back by using my weakness and his charm.

I won't let that happen again. I won't, I can't. My kids do not deserve to live in such chaos and insanity. I promise I will never go back. I am making a pact with myself and with God and I promise that I will do everything I can to never go back to that life. With a deep breath, I created a consequence if I broke this promise: *If at any point, I even think or feel in any way that I am slipping back into the state of mind to go back to him, I will kill myself so that my children will be raised by their grandma.*

A New Beginning

As time went on, the counselors were more aware that Wendy's true addiction was to Greg, not to drugs, but since there was no "person addiction" group, she was still expected to continue in [Alcoholics Anonymous and Narcotics Anonymous]. My kids and I made a couple of weekend trips down there, meeting her at the meeting spot, and really enjoying ourselves in Portland. I think both times I'd bring back one child, and the next time I'd switch kids. The shelter counselors nominated Wendy to be interviewed for an 18-month program where she would have her own apartment [in a building] with other people who had escaped domestic violence situations. The people interviewing her just loved her, and before she got back to her shelter, she was already selected. Tasha was very sad about moving, because to her the shelter they were in was "her" big house with 3 floors and lots of stairs. Although the new apartment was on top of a restaurant close to down-town, I was really thrilled that no men were allowed, including brothers and fathers. There was also a priest who lived there, and a man and a woman who were part of the shelter team.

During these 18 months, Wendy was expected to get her head straightened out and her life on track. Her first six months were supposed to be "recuperation" and not try to push herself. Of course, heavy-duty counseling was in the agenda. The second six months was supposed to be job training, and by the third six months, she was supposed to be out supporting herself and off welfare. She came across a stumbling block in Oregon's welfare system, that although they would pay for day-care while she earned money, they would not pay for day-care while getting job training. At the point Wendy went in for an interview with a welfare caseworker about her taking job training, and when she looked at Wendy's file, she told her she did not recommend Wendy taking training yet, as she knew exactly where her head was at, and felt that every time Wendy came across a stumbling block, she would want to just go back to Greg. The caseworker demanded that Wendy first get into some more counseling, which she did. During the next few weeks, Wendy learned a lot about psychology, domestic violence, and herself, but that didn't prevent "Greg withdrawals." She confided in me that she had called him from a pay-phone on occasion, and sometimes they had vicious unfriendly conversations, and other times very friendly conversations. No matter how the conversation went, she had her fix, and afterwards she had no desire to talk to him again. Wendy also went through her mood swings and the counselors all told her it was part of the withdrawal process.

When she came up to Seattle for a week at Christmas time, my worst fear came true that she would not only contact Greg, but make arrangements to see him. At one point she asked me, "Mom, you might as well know, I've already made arrangements to see Greg while I'm here. Should I see him behind your back, or should I make plans to go to Juanita's on Christmas Eve and you and Tom come along so you're right there?" I told her to see Greg at Juanita's. Because her kids were anxious to see their other grandma, and Greg wasn't supposed to show up until 7:00 Christmas Eve, we drove Wendy over there a few hours early, then we planned to go later. Wendy had wanted Mona to come with Greg, as she kind of missed Mona and wanted to see her. When our family got there, [Wendy] and Greg were on friendly terms, and although not with each other every minute, I didn't like them talking outside quite as much as they did. Juanita, who was very concerned about Wendy completely backsliding in a matter of a couple hours, softly said to me, "Sue, get her out of here, quick." She meant that in a very loving way towards Wendy.

In January of 1995 she weakened more often than ever and would call him more often. She always regretted it afterwards, and she always reported it to her counselors.

As I write this, I am not aware of her having contacted Greg anymore in the past month. She has graduated from her 6-month intensive counseling class and is now going through the next step to getting off of welfare. What the future holds, I do not know.

She has been physically away from Greg for 8 months. I am waiting for July 8, 1995—her one year anniversary. I am hoping this is the end to this true saga. If so, it is a happy ending.

Please God, don't let there be another volume to this book!

Chapter 19
Fall from Grace

*She lacks confidence, she craves
admiration insatiably. She lives on the
reflections of herself in the eyes of others.
She does not dare to be herself.*
‾*Anaïs Nin*

MY RESOLUTION TO STAY AWAY FROM GREG didn't last long. Soon I started to miss the other girls. I missed feeling the sense of belonging in this world. I knew how to live as Greg's ho. I knew what to expect in that life, whereas I didn't know what to expect or how to live in the life I was trying to create in Portland.

When my yearning to talk with the other girls and Greg overtook me, I would find a telephone booth to make the call for fear that he would find me if I called from my own phone. Greg's brother had told me they were all living in an apartment in Kent and had given me the telephone number. When I called, I was happy to hear Veronica answer the phone. My heart jumped with excitement to talk to someone who could totally understand.

"Hi, Veronica! How are you doing?"

"Hey, Wendy, I'm good. Where are you?"

There was a cheer in her voice that did not entirely ring true, and with those seven words I immediately knew something was wrong.

"Is he there? Can he hear you?"

"No, he's not here right now."

"What's going on Veronica? Really, what's going on?"

Veronica busted out in sobs; I couldn't understand what she was saying. I stayed on the phone with her as she cried to show her that I cared, and I kept repeating to her, "I understand Veronica. I understand."

Listening to her cry, I remembered the pain and despair I had felt for so long. I started to cry with her, still feeling my own pain as well as sharing in hers. I wanted to be there with her, I wanted to hug her, and I needed a hug from her in return.

I probed again.

"Veronica, what's going on, sweetie?"

"Wendy, I never knew how much he truly loves you."

Her voice was cracking as she continued to speak.

"Wendy, he will never beat you again, I know he won't. He didn't even know how much he loved you and the kids until he lost you."

Something didn't seem right.

"What is going on? Really, what is going on, Veronica?"

"Please don't tell him I told you. You can't tell him."

"I won't, I won't say a thing, just tell me the truth."

"He blames me for you leaving."

I knew what that meant—wisdom borne of pain, since I had been blamed myself for another girl leaving. It meant that Veronica had to pull my weight along with hers. She had to go out and not only make her own money to bring to Greg, but also money that I would have been making. It meant really late nights of turning tricks until way into the morning hours. I hated hearing the pain she was in.

"Veronica, why don't you...?"

I quickly stopped myself from asking her why she didn't leave him. I knew the answer. I knew she would never be able to leave him. The threats he made against her grandmother controlled her. She would stay with Greg out of fear that he may do something to her grandma.

"I just got out of the hospital a week ago."

It was hard to believe she had even worse news to share.

"Why were you in the hospital?"

"I was in the hospital for two weeks with a ruptured spleen. I almost died. It was horrible. I had never felt so much pain in my life."

I had seen the beatings she had received from Greg. I couldn't imagine a person being able to live through that much pain. What could have happened to her that caused her even more pain than that?

"How did your spleen break?"

"He beat me."

"Why? What did you do?"

I couldn't believe I was stupid enough to ask the question. I knew that Greg's beatings had nothing to do with anything we did.

"He started going off on me because you left. I told you: He totally blames me for you leaving. He won't stop beating me until you come back."

Soon after the conversation with Veronica, Greg started making trips to Portland to see the kids and me. I agreed to the visits in part because I hoped they would stop the beatings, but I had other motives as well. I was in severe "Greg withdrawals," and the kids' pleas to see their daddy were tearing at my heart. He was nice and very loving towards us. He brought the other girls with him but kept them at a nearby hotel room, where they could work the streets of Portland during their visits.

Greg had drawn two new girls into the fold soon after I had disappeared: Belle and Miranda. Greg and the girls claimed that the girls were sixteen; later I learned they were only fifteen. Belle was a sweet, beautiful brunette about five foot four with long curly hair; Miranda was a tall, slender, beautiful blonde. Miranda possessed an internal power that the rest of us girls didn't have. Consequently, her beatings were more severe and frequent—Greg was determined to control her, especially because her beauty brought in more money than any of the rest of us could.

Although it wasn't my Prince Charming dream, it wasn't as bad as the way it used to be. In fact, the first few times he came to Portland were wonderful. When I snuck him into the battered women's shelter apartment, he didn't bring any drugs with him. We spent a lovely evening together. He would only stay for a day, long enough to give me the love drug I was so desperate for and to woo the kids into loving him more. Then one night I received a phone call from him.

"Wendy, I'm coming down. Get a babysitter for the kids. I want to take you to a nice hotel room."

I found a neighbor who would babysit the kids for the evening. While I got ready, I imagined our wonderful evening together at a "nice" hotel room. When Greg arrived, I ran outside to meet him for our romantic evening, only to discover the Cadillac was filled with girls, some I had never met before. There were five girls crammed in the backseat and two in the front with Greg.

"I'll be back to pick you up. I'm dropping them off on eighty-second." Eighty-second Avenue was the local "ho stro" where tricks would pick up prostitutes.

When Greg returned to pick me up, he took me to a rundown, roach-infested motel on 82nd Avenue. The hot tub inside the room, which might have been luxurious in another setting, made it even seedier. I had barely made it through the door when Greg took the crack pipe out of his bag and the white rocks from his pocket. He didn't have to entice me; I was so horrified at the sight of the drugs that I needed a hit to ease the pounding in my heart and the heebie-jeebies in my stomach. When he was done taking his hit, he handed the pipe to me, and I gratefully took it.

The next day Greg left with all the girls in tow, heading for California to "clean up."

"I'll see you when I come back," he said as he drove away with the car full of girls. I didn't want him to come back at this point; I wished he would stay gone forever. The events of the night before showed me how easy it was for him to persuade me to start doing drugs again, and I didn't want that in my life. I wondered if there was any way I could get away. He now knew where I lived, and I had nowhere to go. I had already left him, but here I was, back in the same situation. I didn't see an escape; all I could do was beg him to not bring that shit back into my life.

About two weeks later, I got a phone call from Greg.

"Miranda was arrested, and they have her in foster care. She's running away tonight, but she can't stay down here, because the police will pick her up again. Can she please stay with you until I get back? She can watch the kids for you while you work."

During my stay in Portland, I had been working in the snack bar at the local Greyhound station. I enjoyed my job. It gave me a sense of normalcy and responsibility. I wasn't on welfare anymore, and it felt really good to be doing something productive. But the babysitter fees took most of my money every month, so having a few days with a free babysitter sounded really good to me. Plus, I didn't want her out on the street with no place to go. I always liked offering the girls a piece of normalcy, a good breakfast, a home-cooked dinner, and a night of just playing cards or watching movies. I knew how much that meant to me, and I loved being the one who could offer it to them.

Miranda arrived at the Greyhound station the next day. We didn't know each other very well, and the little bit I'd been around her I found her to be unpleasant, but we did share common ground. I understood what she was going through, even though at the time she wasn't willing to admit it. It was nice having company in my apartment, someone who understood the life I used to live, something I could never talk about to anyone else. We kept the conversation sweet, not talking about the things that kept us stuck in the lifestyle, not talking about the violence or the desire to escape. We knew talk like that could get us hurt if Greg ever found out, so we changed the subject whenever the conversation would hint that it was headed in that direction.

Two weeks later Greg returned with only a few of the girls he had taken to California and not even enough money for him to make it back to Seattle. Although I was scared to let them all into my apartment—in part because the rules did not allow it—I wanted so badly to be the savior to all of them. I snuck them in one at a time, being careful that none of them were seen. I fixed a huge dinner to feed them, and I gathered up enough pillows and blankets for them to sleep on the floors and couch. Latasha and Gregory were excited to have Daddy around, and the girls were always so nice to them. Belle would sit and play games with them, laugh with them—things that I didn't even have time for anymore since I worked full-time. The following day the girls went out to make enough money to get back to Seattle, but when they came back Greg ordered them to go buy drugs. As we passed the crack pipe, Greg started the interrogation.

His deep voice verged on angry.

"What have you been doing down here on your own? Who have you been fuckin'?"

The fear started to grow within me. I already knew how this night would end. Trying hard to soothe the situation, I reassured him, "I haven't had sex with anyone. I'm too scared to even talk to men. I work full-time just trying to make a good life for the kids. Please, baby, don't start this." I started to beg, "Please baby, please don't let this happen again." But he turned a deaf ear to my pleas.

"There is no way you have been away from me for seven months and not hooked up with someone."

The entire night I spent pleading with him, trying to convince him that I hadn't been unfaithful, hoping desperately to keep him calm so the physical violence wouldn't start. I knew if it started, the other residents would hear, and I thought we would surely be kicked out. Throughout the night, he would send the girls to get more drugs every time the crack would start to get low. Finally, the money was gone and they had to stay for another night.

I hated that I was in this situation. I knew it was entirely my fault for ever making the first phone call to him. I thought of ways I could escape again, but every plan ended up with me and the kids out on the street with nowhere to go. I would eventually crawl back to Greg, begging for his forgiveness. I felt trapped and disgusted with myself for allowing myself to recreate this nightmare. Envisioning the life my children were in for, I begged Greg the following day to leave us alone.

"Please Greg, I can't take this anymore. I can't take the drugs, or the chaos of the girls, or the prostitution. Your children deserve a better life than that. This is hurting them whether you want to believe it or not."

His evil eyes looked straight into mine and I knew that my plea had angered him.

"You think my kids are better off without me, you fucked up ass stupid bitch? My children love me, and I can give them a better life than you ever can, if you would stop stealing them from me."

Maybe he is right. I saw how happy the kids were when he was around—at least when he was in his good mood. I thought about all the hours I spent at work and how I was always too tired after work to take them to the park. I thought about the day I pulled them into the bushes, driven by a fear that turned out to be imaginary. *Maybe I am crazy… maybe I am a bad mother… maybe I do need Greg in my life.* As the thoughts went through my head he pushed me over the emotional edge.

"You will never make it in this world without me. You don't know how to survive in this world, and the world out there doesn't want you."

Deep down inside, I knew he was right. I was tired and worn out from trying to fit into the real world. I didn't feel I could ever survive out there with the thoughts and emotions that constantly filled my head and heart.

Chapter 20
Hitting Bottom

Death is not the greatest of evils; it is
worse to want to die, and not be able to.
—Sophocles

I WAS SOON ACCEPTED INTO a low-income apartment complex in southeast Portland. Greg was spending most his time in California, giving me the opportunity to concentrate on the kids and trying to find some sort of normalcy in my life. I needed some help moving from the shelter to the apartment, so he sent Miranda and Mona in his low-rider Lincoln Continental with the hydraulics up to Oregon to help me move.

The first night in the apartment was great. It was a three-bedroom, townhouse-style apartment where the kids had their own rooms. Miranda and Mona were staying with us at the townhouse for the time being, too. I liked having Miranda and Mona living with us; it felt like I was part of something, like I had real friends. Since I was still working full-time, Mona and Miranda would move and pack during the day while I was at work; when I got home, we would continue to put stuff away and get pizza and watch movies.

Miranda and Mona were working a little, too; most nights they would leave for an hour or two to turn a couple of tricks and would come home at ten or so, a decent hour. Their tricks didn't contribute much money to our household, since they sent most of the money they made to Greg through Western Union; but they would steal stuff from stores that I needed for the apartment, making it a little bit nicer. It seemed almost like a normal family life.

Soon after we moved, Miranda and Mona came home later than usual one night. I didn't pay much attention; I was busy preparing the home for my children. The following evening, Greg unexpectedly arrived from California while Miranda, Mona, and the kids and I were watching a video. I was happy seeing him walk through the door. I thought his surprise visit was to behold the home I had created for him and our children, and I hoped to hear a bit of praise that I had done a good job. My happiness retreated a moment later when I saw the tension in his eyes.

"Greg," I admonished him, "you promised me you wouldn't bring violence into my home." His demeanor darkened, and my reproach became a desperate plea.

"Don't do anything to fuck up my new home. You promised. *You promised!*"

He quickly looked around the living room to find the phone and followed the phone cord to its outlet. He wrenched the cord out the wall and started thrashing Mona and Miranda. I grabbed the kids, screaming at them, "Quick, get upstairs... Go to your rooms."

Miranda and Mona were running around the living room trying to hide behind each other to avoid the sting of the phone cord. Greg was a madman, violently whipping the cord at them. I jumped in, attempting to stop the attack by grabbing onto Greg's arms from behind, but he was so strong I couldn't hold them still. I screamed at the top of my lungs, "Get out of my house!! You promised you wouldn't be violent here!"

He whirled to face me, locked his evil eyes on mine, and sneered with Satan's voice.

"Bitch, you want me to start on you next?"

All I could do was stand frozen in fear and watch him beat Miranda and Mona with my telephone cord. *Why did I buy such a long telephone cord?* I could see their tortured faces, but I was deaf to the screams. *This is my life.* I remembered the promise I had made in the bathtub at the women's shelter, I remembered the promise I had made to myself and to God and to the Universe. *I have broken every promise.*

Miranda screamed with such agony that it snapped me out of my frozen state.

"Greg, please, *no!* Please stop hitting me! Greg, I didn't mean to. I'm sorry, I'm sorry. *Please* stop hitting me!"

I bolted out of the apartment, not even bothering to close the door. I ran out of the apartment complex and down the street to the mini-mart on the corner. I ran down a road with a gravel sidewalk; when I felt the pebbles tearing at my feet, I realized I wasn't wearing any shoes. Still I ran on. No matter how far I ran, it was not far enough to escape the life I had allowed myself and my children to return to, but I didn't know what else to do.

It seemed like I had run for hours, but only a half mile away I became tired and out of breath, and the bottoms of my feet were starting to bleed. There was an old, gated junkyard off the side of the road, and in the front of it was a large, green garbage can. I raced to hide behind the garbage can. I nestled down behind the can, listening to the barking dog that was penned up behind the gate. My tears obscured the fact that rain was falling, and I didn't even notice that

I was soaking wet. I waited for Greg to come looking for me, hoping that he would be sorry and I would get a ride home instead of having to walk barefooted in the gravel.

My feet were getting cold but not nearly as cold as the dreams of my life—the dreams of ever being normal or being loved. I realized that no one cared about me. I pondered the idea of committing suicide but then I thought of my children, still in the house, upstairs in their rooms, wondering where I was. *This is my life. I allowed this to happen. I walked back into it. I am dead. The only thing left for me is to make the best of it for the children. I will be Greg's ho, I will do as he says no matter what he says in order to prevent the blowups, in order for the kids not to see or know what I have allowed to happen.*

I waited for hours, but Greg didn't come. He didn't care, and I could think of no good reason why he should. I was merely his slave, destined to do as he demanded, whatever he demanded, without asking questions or causing any problems. I was forever his property, his slave forever. I started the painful walk home.

The following day when evening came, Greg said to me, "Wendy, drive the girls to do their rounds. I don't want to take any chances of them getting pulled over."

Veronica had come down from Seattle that day to stay with us. I drove Veronica, Miranda, and Mona first to a local motel room where Greg was hiding Belle, and then drove all of them to a rundown building in northeast Portland where many Mexican men stayed.

Veronica was the last to get out of the car.

"You can come in, Wendy. Besides, the police may get suspicious if they see you sitting out here in the car."

The building was two stories, with a bar on the first floor and fifteen rooms upstairs. Some of the rooms had kitchenettes and separate bedrooms. There were two shared bathrooms, each with two or three stalls. I waited at a tiny kitchen table in the one of the rooms while the other girls went with men to their rooms. Similar to the men in Chinatown, these Mexican men paid cheap, but at least they were quick. Miranda would go into a room with one of the men and come out three minutes later with twenty dollars.

I was lost in my own thoughts when a man who had sat quietly through most of the evening spoke up in a thick accent.

"Hey, baby, how much do you cost?"

Sheepishly, I replied, "I'm not working."

The man continued to pester me.

"I pay you thirty dollars."

Just as he said this, Miranda walked through the door and realized that I was saying "no" to thirty dollars. I didn't think much about it, but a while after I got home, Greg came over to me and started in with a condescending tone.

"What? Do you think you're too good to be turning tricks?" Wrapping his fingers around my neck and slamming me up against the wall he continued his harassment.

"Who the fuck do you think you are? You're no better than anyone else.... If they are out making money, so are you, bitch. Don't ever let me hear again that you turned down a date." Miranda had obviously told Greg what she overheard, and I hated her for telling on me.

The following Friday night Greg again ordered me to take the girls on the rounds. This time, I took a shower and put on my makeup, knowing I would be turning some tricks. The Mexican men always wanted the "new" girl until she was no longer new.

When we walked in the door, the hallways were filled with about twenty-five men, all waiting for us to show up. One man took my arm and politely led me to his room where he handed me a twenty-dollar bill. I removed my clothes and lay on his bed with my legs spread open. I turned off the emotions that were trying to escape as tears, and I gently guided Wendy to the safe place within me.

I made the sex noises on cue, knowing it would make him finish faster. Three minutes later, I was putting my clothes back on and walking out of the room to be presented to my next buyer. This was the ritual for the next forty-five minutes; I earned a hundred dollars by having sex with five different men. Even in my safe place, I couldn't protect myself from the obvious: I was worthless. I felt like shit, and the only cure for this feeling was the crack Greg held in his hand back at the house.

The pattern repeated for several months. On different nights, I would make runs to different apartment complexes, where the Mexican men would wait for our arrival. I no longer had enough dignity to put on my clothes between dates. After the first date, I would lay in the bed naked waiting for the man to get dressed and then tell him as he walked out the door to send in the next one. I would lay there lifeless, except for the few fake sex moans that helped end the night more quickly so I could get home to the drugs that patiently waited to restore me.

No matter how much money we made, it never seemed to be enough. Greg always wanted more—for the drugs he had to feed us to keep us in a zombie state, for the repairs to his three cars, and for his expensive taste in jewelry, stereo systems, and other luxury items. And now he also wanted a WaveRunner, or two or three.

As time went by, Gregory would sleep in Tasha's room so the girls could sleep in Gregory's room. Soon, Greg had all the girls in our room, so I would sleep in Gregory's room to get a moment of peace away from the drama and drugs. I could turn up the radio to drown out the noise of talking and fighting in the next room, and sometimes I would even get some sleep. The long-term plans were for Miranda and Greg to get their own apartment where they would house all of the girls in Greg's stable. The agreement between Greg and me was that as long as he had total control of everything I did, and as long as I would go out and work occasionally (and only with regulars), he would leave me alone to try and live my "normal" life with the kids. I was totally okay with this arrangement; it was better than any other choice I had in front of me—and even if I found another choice, the girls knew where I lived, so there was no hiding or escaping from Greg.

The violence and interrogations became an every-night event; it was only a question of who was getting it tonight. One evening, as it was my turn to cower in the corner, he stood over me with a forty-ounce Olde English 800 bottle, on the verge of hitting me with it.

"Are you ever going to leave me?" he seethed.

My voice quivered, and it took all my effort to expel the words.

"No, Greg, no. I will never leave you. I promise I will never leave you."

I cringed, waiting for the pain from the bottle smashing against my head. With each contention, the evil and the rage escalated.

"I think you're gonna leave me. I think you're sick of me, *aren't you?* You had better *never* leave me, bitch."

How could I reassure him so he wouldn't hit me with the bottle?

"I promise, I promise I won't leave you. I love you too much to leave you."

It wasn't enough. Greg wanted a different promise. He grabbed the Bible from its hiding place in the closet. The Bible had one purpose in our lives and only one purpose. Greg got down on his knees and presented the Bible to me. He put his face right in front of mine, intoning in a deep, gruff voice.

"Make the promise."

I laid my hand on the Bible. I spoke the words that would keep me trapped in this hell but would make the torture stop for the night.

"Greg, I promise you... I swear on my son's life, may he die if I ever leave you."

He looked at me as if I were lying.

"May he die a *horrible, painful* death if you ever leave me."

With my hand still placed on the cover of the Bible that Greg clutched in his hand, I heaved the dreaded words.

"If I should ever leave you, may my son, Gregory, die a horrible, painful death."

The torture inquisitions by Greg became more frequent and longer lasting. Sometimes they would last for weeks. On Greg's orders, the routine was always the same. Whenever we were ready to go home after working the street or making our rounds to our regular clientele, we stopped at a pay phone to call him. He always wanted to know where we were so phone calls home were a constant for us. Most times he would instruct us to go buy drugs. If none of his regular drug dealers had stock, we had to drive to the hood and buy the drugs on the street. After we obtained the drugs, we would call him again to let him know we were on our way home.

When we would get home, he would always be lying on the bed in the room upstairs. All of us girls would march up the stairs into the room, where each of us would hand him the money we had made and the drugs we had purchased. We would all take a seat on the floor and wait for him to split up the crack and hand us our portions. After the crack pipe was passed around, he would count the money and start to ask questions. On this particular night, I was his target.

"Wendy, how many dates did you do tonight?"

I was barely able to talk because my mouth wouldn't move after taking a hit of cocaine. I tried my best to respond with stuttering words.

"I...I...d...d...did...four dates."

He took another hit from the crack pipe and looked at me in disbelief.

"How much did you make off each one?"

All the girls began to stew, waiting for what was to come next. They looked at me with compassion, but I also knew they were relieved. I didn't blame them for being thankful that it was I and not they who was tonight's target, as I knew the feeling well. I, too, had many times experienced that momentary sense of deliverance at the expense of another girl. Still stammering, I tried to respond.

"I made...forty dollars off the first... g..g..guy, thirty dollars on the s...s...second guy, a-a-and the last two...two were thirty-five dollars a p-p-piece."

"Did you fuck them or suck their dicks?"

I hated that question. I hated having to describe what I did to make the money.

"I fucked...three of them...the thirty dollars... was for a....b-b-blow-job."

"Did you use a condom?"

I knew well enough to conceal my discomfort.

"Of course they used condoms."

By now the crack hit was wearing off, and he knew this because my stuttering had stopped. He handed me the crack pipe, a hit already melted and ready for me. I put the fire to the end of the pipe and inhaled the potion—the only comfort that would help me get through this night.

"How do you know they didn't take the condom off while they were fucking you?" The hint of sarcasm further poisoned his sinister voice.

My heart started to pound with the realization that he could continue this line of questioning throughout the night. I knew what he wanted and that was "solid proof" that the men had worn a condom. Trying not to allow him to hear the fear in my voice, I spoke as sternly as I could through the stuttering.

"I...I...I... know...if...some...someone takes...the c-c-condom...off. I would...know...and they *d-d-didn't*...t-t-take it...off."

I could see he was thinking really hard about my answer, wondering how I would know if a trick slipped a condom off while having sex. He asked a few more questions, and each time I had an answer, he became angrier. He got off the bed and started walking toward me. My heart started to pound and I wanted to cry— but I didn't dare cry. Crying always infuriated Greg.

In a deep voice, his evil eyes glaring right at me, he hurled his accusation. "I don't think you're using condoms when you're out there. I think you're lying to me." He stood over me like a gigantic monster. "Prove it."

"Prove what?" I was genuinely confused by his demand.

"Prove to me he wore a condom."

"How do I do that?"

Miranda jumped between us, hoping to deter what was about to happen.

"Greg, Wendy is the most perfect of all of us. What would make you think in a million years that she would do dates without a condom?"

Greg gave Miranda a cold stare, slowly walked over to the closet where he hid his gun. The gun rarely came out, but we all knew that it was there and feared it. Greg stared at the ground while his hand reached up to the top of the closet. We girls knew the gun was coming out tonight, and our hearts dropped as we watched him retrieve the gun and hold it lovingly in his hand. He stood there like a king with all the power of the world.

Suddenly he lunged towards Miranda and grabbed her like she was a puppet doll. He threw her onto the bed and jumped on top of her, shoving the gun into her mouth.

"Bitch!!!! Do you have something to say to me?"

The cold barrel of the gun prevented Miranda from talking. None of us could understand her muffled pleas, but we could imagine what she was trying to say. We sat frozen in terror, crying softly. Our tears only increased Greg's rage. He jumped off of Miranda, threw her back onto the floor, and snarled at me.

"Let me see your pussy."

I looked at the girls who were watching in horror. Almost in unison, they looked to the floor to let me know they would not watch what was about to happen.

"Get on the bed," his voice roared.

I got off the floor and walked to the bed where I took off my jeans and panties. I sat back on the bed and opened my legs so he could look and feel inside me to determine for himself if there was another man's semen inside of me. By this time I had by-passed humiliation and went straight to hatred for him and for myself for coming back to this nightmare. As his fingers dug inside of me, tears started streaming down the sides of my face and onto the bed. I looked at the ceiling in front of me and tried my hardest to pull myself to the safe place within the pit of my stomach.

There was no hiding place any more, and there was nothing of me left to hide—nothing left that was ever truly me. What I was, what I had become, what Greg had turned me into was all that remained of the once dream-filled girl who had fallen in love with her Prince Charming: a ho with no self-respect, no dignity, and no rights as a human being. I was Greg's slave. No fragment of the human being I had been had survived through all these years. The Wendy I had known as a child and even into my early twenties was gone forever.

Chapter 21
The Devil's Tale

"We must have taken a wrong turn
turning somewhere."
"Where, Purgatory?" said Dozy.
"We're in Hell."
— *John Connolly*, The Infernals

IF NOTHING ELSE, we girls did learn from each other and from each other's torture sessions. For a time we would bring Greg the used condoms, presenting them as proof for each trick we had turned. We soon learned that some men ejaculate much more than others and that a condom with "insufficient" discharge served only to inspire more inquisitions and torture. Another shared lesson: Greg could always find a way to undermine our efforts to avoid his abuse.

Each of us had different roles to play to keep us all connected and trapped in our living hell. Some of us were expected to fawn over Greg and prove our undying love for him. All of us were expected to earn money for Greg. The girls who couldn't make much money doing tricks were expected to get money other ways. Mona's expertise, for example, was shoplifting. Veronica didn't have an expertise, but did have a financially well-off grandmother from whom she could steal money. The first time it was easy, but once the theft came to light, it became a little more difficult. Veronica would first have to convince her grandmother that she was a changed person. Each time was a little harder, but grandma was sooner or later always willing to give Veronica another chance.

Greg would send Veronica on the Greyhound bus to Seattle for a few weeks to a month so she could earn her way back into her grandmother's life and steal money to give to Greg. This time, Veronica had been up in Seattle with her grandmother for over a month. I could tell from the phone conversations Greg had with Veronica that she didn't want to steal money from her grandma anymore. I could see that Veronica was tired of living in this crazy life and wanted out. Veronica was older than any of us by several years; she was already twenty-nine when Greg seduced her into the ring.

Miranda and Belle had made a lot of money, giving me a break from working for a little while. Greg had been up in the interrogation room for a couple of days smoking crack. I avoided going anywhere near the room. I would even pee outside in the bushes rather than walk past his room to use the bathroom. A young girl who was still new hung out in the living room waiting for Greg to come downstairs to woo her. I tiptoed around, keeping the kids quiet and hoping Greg would just stay in the room. Miranda and Belle were out, so it was only me, the kids, the young new girl sitting on the couch, and the crack-smoking monster upstairs. Secretly I was hoping that he would smoke himself to death. I smiled when I thought about locking the door to the room and allowing his body to rot into oblivion.

The smile was replaced with jaws clenched in fear when I heard the door open to the room and his footsteps pounding down the steps.

"Drive me to Seattle," he barked in a deep voice raspy from lack of sleep and crack smoke.

"What about the kids?"

He pointed at the girl, who was probably only fourteen years old.

"She can watch them."

Knowing better than to say or do anything other than exactly what he told me to do, I grabbed my car keys and purse and started walking to the car. Irritated with the fact that my three-day vacation from him and his bullshit was over, I threw the car in drive and headed towards Seattle. I knew the drugs were tripping him out and he was acting out some sort of drug illusion that was spurred on from having no sleep in three days. I knew first-hand what was happening to Greg, remembering how he had kept me awake for three days smoking crack. I remember the insane thoughts that went through my head. I was angry that he didn't have someone else drive him to Seattle so I could have more time with the kids and peace and quiet.

Driving north on Interstate 5, I waited until we got out of the city to ask any questions.

"What's going on Greg?" I managed to keep my voice soft and sincere.

He remained silent, looking out the window.

"Greg, I'm worried about you. Can you please tell me what is going on?"

When at last he responded, his voice was quiet and surreal.

"You wouldn't believe me if I told you."

"Please, Greg, tell me what's going on? Why are we driving to Seattle?"

He turned his head from the window to look at me. I had never seen such fear in his eyes.

"I made a deal with the devil."

"*What?!*"

"I made a deal with Satan. I sold my soul to the devil for some information."

He clearly believed what he was saying. I saw how the drugs and lack of sleep had taken over his mind. I was scared. I had to somehow snap him out of this. I was torn between disgust that I had to drive this monster up to Seattle and fear for what was going to happen next.

A wiser head would have stopped asking questions, but I was overtaken by curiosity. *What had Satan revealed to him?* I had to ask.

"What did the devil tell you?"

"He told me that Veronica fucked my dad."

My eyes nearly popped out of my head and my jaw dropped open. Hoping to shock him out of the trance he was in, I raised my voice.

"Are you fucking kidding me? Greg, do you think that this possibly could be the drugs and lack of sleep talking?"

He looked back out the window at the passing scenery.

"No, this is real. This is very real."

I continued to drive north, trying to figure out a way to snap him out of this. I started to wonder what he was possibly going to do with this information revealed to him by the devil.

"What are you planning on doing?"

He seemed uncertain, so I tried to make my question clear.

"What are you going to do when we get to Seattle?"

"I don't know."

With that, he totally zoned into a world that only he knew.

I gave it a little time before pressuring him some more. I was scared for Veronica and what he was going to do to her. I started talking to him in a soft, kind voice, attempting to show him why this was insane and trying to convince him that he hadn't made a deal with the devil—that it was the drugs mixed with sleep deprivation. Nothing I said could rouse Greg from his netherworld.

We had been driving for an hour and a half and were halfway between Portland and Seattle. The pressure was building within me to somehow fix this and protect Veronica from this insanity. I knew she wanted out of this life and she had been doing well. I didn't want Greg to interfere with her progress. She was so close to escaping from him. I knew I didn't have much time; in order to attempt to protect her, I would have to know his plans.

I demanded that he answer my questions.

"Where am I going Greg? You have to tell me where I'm supposed to be driving to!"

"We're going to Veronica's grandma's house," he mumbled.

Perhaps, I thought, sarcasm will pull the information out of him.

"And what are you going to do when we get there?"

The evil voice reemerged.

"I'm going to throw a rock right through that grandma's window."

"*What?*" I screamed. "You *cannot* do that. Her grandma is ninety years old! She may have a heart attack from that."

"I don't fucking care. Veronica is going to pay for this shit. It's Veronica's fault that she is at her grandma's. It will be Veronica's fault if her grandma gets hurt."

Panicking, I started to yell at him.

"You can't hurt the grandma. She didn't do anything wrong." I continued to get more upset and my voice rose even louder.

"Bad, bad things will happen to you if you do anything to her grandma. She is old and doesn't deserve to be hurt. She won't be able to handle the stress of you."

I continued to speak harshly to him, protesting his plans to hurt Veronica's grandmother. My mind was no longer on Veronica. My entire focus was on protecting the innocent grandma. He started to come around to agreeing with me that the grandma should be left alone. Still, he had me drive on.

Seattle was getting closer and I wasn't able to convince him that he was caught in a sick delusion. I wished I could warn Veronica but there was no way I could. I reverted to asking him more questions about the conversation with the devil. When I did, he would remain silent and look out the car window. It was about four in the afternoon on a Saturday when we arrived so there wasn't much traffic. I pulled into the driveway at the grandma's house. The car wasn't even completely stopped when he started to get out.

"Keep the car running. I'll be right back."

A few moments later Veronica came walking out of the house, Greg right behind her. She had a look of confusion and fear on her face. I could only give her the look that said, "I'm sorry, you're the target this time."

The psychic connection that we girls developed with each other was built and maintained by the suffering we endured. One quick glance was worth a thousand words. We spoke with each other through our eyes, sharing small looks that were unnoticeable by Greg or anyone else, but understood clearly between us. Veronica got in the backseat of the car, and I gave her the look that this one was bad. I could tell by her demeanor that she fully understood. Greg jumped into the passenger seat of the car.

"Drive!"

I didn't know where I was supposed to drive and just between you me and the fence post, I am afraid to turn left on any street. It's not as bad when I am at a light with an arrow granting me permission and safety to turn left, but I am unable to make a left turn under any other circumstances. I pulled out the driveway and at the first light I turned right.

Without looking at her, Greg roared at Veronica.

"Do you have something you need to tell me?"

Veronica timidly replied, "No, Greg. What's wrong?"

At the next light I turned right and Greg turned his body to face Veronica.

"You don't have anything you want to tell me?"

Veronica stiffened with fear; she was familiar with the position Greg was now in. She replied sorrowfully.

"Greg, I don't know what you are talking about. I haven't done anything wrong. I promise."

Listening to the two of them and wondering how long this was going to last I turned right again. As we passed Veronica's grandma's house again, Greg looked out the window and discovered that I had only been driving in circles. Taking his attention off of Veronica for a moment, he turned it on me.

"Bitch! Get on the fucking freeway."

Full of frustration I yelled back, "Where am I supposed to go?"

"Back to Portland!"

I looked in the rearview mirror to see Veronica's terror-filled eyes staring back at me. I didn't know what to do. I didn't know how I could stop what was happening. I had no other choice but to do what Greg said. I didn't want to be a part of this kidnapping but I was.

Greg continued his cat-and-mouse game with Veronica. Without giving Veronica any idea of what he was talking about, he asked open-ended questions.

"Do you have something you need to tell me?"

"Have you done anything wrong?"

"Don't you have something you need to confess?"

We had only been driving about thirty minutes when Greg grabbed the empty Olde English malt liquor bottle that sat on the floor of the backseat and started pummeling Veronica. Her screams echoed through the car as Greg turned all the way around in his seat to beat her even harder. Veronica was moving from one side of the backseat to the other, trying to dodge the blows. The car started rocking back and forth to the point that I was swerving in and out of my lane.

"*Stop!*" I screamed at Greg. "I can't drive the car if you keep hitting her."

Something wet splattered on the side of my face when I turned towards Greg. I thought it was spit until I saw the blood scattered on the windshield. I quickly pulled onto the shoulder, hoping I could somehow stop Greg from hitting her.

When Greg realized that I was trying to stop the car, he sat back in his seat. For a split second, I thought he was going to stop beating Veronica. In the next moment, my head smashed into the driver-side window. Pain surged through my head from Greg's hand hitting one side of my head and my head hitting the window on the other side. My vision blurred and even though his voice was muffled I could hear his angry ultimatum.

"If you stop this car again I will fucking kill you."

Scared to death, I pressed my foot on the accelerator and tried hard to focus on the blurry road ahead of me. Greg returned his attention to Veronica, goading her with more revealing questions.

"Do you have something to tell me about my dad?"

"About your dad? What do you mean?"

Finally Greg tired of his game, he finally made his Satan-inspired accusation.

"Have you ever fucked my dad?"

Veronica shrieked in response. "What are you talking about? *No!* I have never fucked your dad."

Greg didn't believe her and repeated his question again and again. Soon I could tell that Greg was madder that she might be lying about having sex with his father than he would be if she had actually done it. He started hitting her again, even harder than before. Blood splattered on the ceiling of the car. I numbed to her screams, knowing all the times she had been beaten this viciously on my behalf.

Halfway to Portland the fuel gage indicated we'd soon run out of gas.

"Can I stop for gas at the next exit?"

He double checked the gas gage.

"Yeah."

At the gas station I got out of the car and started pumping the gas. Veronica opened the back door to throw up on the ground. Our eyes met, and for a split second the tiny fragments that were left of our souls connected. I was able to tell her to just tell Greg that she had indeed had sex with his father so he could feel that he was right and the beating would stop. I knew Greg well enough to know that if she didn't admit what he wanted her to admit, he would continue to beat her.

With a full tank of gas and another hour to get to Portland, Greg started in on Veronica again. Veronica pleaded with Greg, begging him to believe her. That only would enrage Greg further, and he would turn around in his seat and beat her more. After another five minutes of accusations and blows, she finally yelled out, "*Fine!* You want me to say it? *Yes!* I fucked your dad. We had a *great* time. He fucked me *real* good! Are you happy now?"

As Veronica cried in the backseat, I could feel Greg's pride swell to know that he was right.

"I want to know all the details. Tell me everything that happened," Greg demanded.

"What do you want me to say Greg? Tell me some of the details so I can tell you what happened."

Greg turned in his seat and punched Veronica right in her face. Again blood splattered throughout the car as Veronica screamed in pain. I looked in the rearview mirror and saw that her eye was bleeding and was quickly swelling. She started making up the story of how she and Greg's dad ended up having sex, telling all the dirty details that we both hoped would satisfy Greg.

"It was about a year ago when we were living at the hotel in Renton."

Greg badgered her with questions: How big was his dad's penis? How long did the sexual act last? When she told Greg that she had not given his dad a blowjob, Greg demanded she tell him the truth. Veronica repeatedly denied the accusation, but the more she denied it, the more agitated Greg became. She finally admitted to giving his dad a blowjob. Veronica continued to fill in kinky details all the way to the apartment, and Greg felt vindicated that he had discovered the truth.

When we got to the apartment, Greg took Veronica up to the room. I was too afraid to follow them. Over the next two days Greg would occasionally come downstairs to get something to eat and then return to the room. Occasional screams would vibrate the house and I would freeze in my tracks, but most of the time, it was quiet. The kids and I, along with the new girl all stayed downstairs and watched television.

I was worried about Veronica and really wanted to check on her. On the third day, I waited for Greg to come downstairs to get something to eat and I went upstairs to use the bathroom. The bedroom door was open so I looked in as I walked by. I saw Veronica sitting on the bed, looking totally drained. Her eyes were black and swollen. I walked to her and put my hand on her shoulder. Trying to comfort her, I said, "That was really smart of you to just tell Greg what he wanted to hear. He would have killed you otherwise."

Veronica looked up at me with her pathetic eyes. "Wendy," she whispered. "I really did have sex with Greg's dad. It wasn't a story...It really did happen."

There was only one way Greg could have known that. He really had sold his soul to the devil.

Chapter 22
Family Trip

When I am not desperate, I am worthless.
—Ivo Andric

WEEKS SLOWLY TURNED INTO MONTHS. Sometimes the Mexicans would move, and our only recourse to make money for Greg was to walk 82nd Avenue. Greg had us put our earnings into money orders so he wouldn't buy drugs; even he realized that once we took our first hit, all self-control went out the window and he could easily spend all of our money in one night on drugs. Sometimes he had us bring the money to the store to make payments on his WaveRunners.

Greg and Miranda finally got their own apartment, and I was relieved of the interrogations and the constant drug use. The children and I had my apartment more or less to ourselves, since all the other girls stayed at Greg's and Miranda's apartment, which Greg had fixed up with expensive, Egyptian-style furnishings. Miranda started working the escort services and money was coming in, keeping Greg happy and me somewhat free, since it meant that I wouldn't have to go out for weeks at a time. I got a job at a local Dairy Queen in order to get off of welfare and have another attempt at normal life.

For a few months, I was reasonably happy. Now and then, there were even some good times. Greg would come over and treat me like a princess. He would take us all to the lake for the day to hang out, ride his WaveRunner, and have a barbecue. We would laugh and swim and the kids would play with all the girls. He still supervised the kids and me, but he did this from a distance. Even though I no longer shared a household with Greg, I always called him when I would leave the house to let him know where I was going. Directly upon my return, I would call him again to tell him I had returned.

I felt as normal as I could, given that I was still under Greg's control; but I guess I started to feel a little too free. One day, I called him to tell him I was going to the store, but I forgot to call him when I returned. When the phone started ringing a few hours later, I realized my mistake. I'd been so good for so long. This was my first fuck-up in quite some time—surely he would let me slide on this one.

"Bitch! Where the fuck have you been? Why haven't you called me?"

I was unapologetic.

"I got busy putting the groceries away and doing things with the kids." Continuing to dig my own grave, I added, "You should know by now you have me totally trained. I'm a fucking expert at being your bitch, and I know what I am and am *not* allowed to do. Quit being fucking paranoid."

Feeling the thrill of unfounded emotional power, I hung up the phone. I immediately realized the error of my ways.

Oh, fuck! Shit! Damn! I'm fucking dead now.

I was getting sick of this fucking shit, sick of being under his control without any of the benefits of being "his woman" and the kicks that went with it. No wonder I wasn't thinking straight. I wasn't "free"; I was in withdrawals. He hadn't come over to see me and woo me with his charm in weeks. He had deprived me of the love drug, my greatest addiction and the one that only he could feed. Realizing my huge mistake I quickly called him back.

Miranda answered the phone.

"What the fuck did you do, Wendy?"

"I hung up on him."

"*Oh my God! No! You didn't!* Wendy, are you *nuts?*"

Realizing the dire situation at hand, I shouted into the phone as I hung it up, "I gotta go!"

I dashed to the door and locked it, while yelling at the kids, "Tasha! Gregory! Go to your rooms quickly, and be quiet."

Sad to say, Tasha and Gregory were very familiar with these drills. Without hesitating or asking any questions, they ran upstairs. I stayed by the front door, now dead-bolted and locked, wondering what to do. With the strong-headed delusion that I could talk him down, I watched out the peephole and waited for him.

It had only taken him about five minutes to drive the three miles to my house, and he charged up to the front door like a bull on steroids. Still looking through the peephole, I could swear I saw smoke coming out of his ears. He looked furious, and I realized I was not going to be able to talk him down from this one.

Banging on the door with full force, he screamed, "Open the fucking door, you bitch. No one *ever* hangs up on me."

Pleading through the still-bolted door, I started my "I'm sorry" routine, which sometimes, occasionally, very seldom worked—but it was the only hope I had at that point.

"Greg, I'm sorry, I didn't mean to. I thought we were done talking, and I was just real..."

"Open the fucking door you bitch. I'm going to teach you a lesson you will never forget, and you will never hang up on me again."

I wasn't in the mood for getting hit, and the apartment was so clean and orderly; if I let him in he would tear the place to pieces, breaking everything inside while throwing it at me. Envisioning the damage Greg would do, I stood facing the door, looking at the floor, not knowing what to do. Suddenly there was a force against the door so strong that the entire door slammed down flat on top of me, trapping me underneath. I was able to see, but the events were surreal, as if I were watching a comical movie on television. Greg stood on the door, jumping up and down to expel the disobedience in me. I watched in amazement at the scene unfolding in front of me, and then the screen went black.

Dairy Queen had withheld income tax from my paycheck, so the following March I received my tax refund. Along with the Earned Income Credit, my check was over three thousand dollars. For quite some time I had wanted to take the kids on a family trip to Disneyland, and this seemed like the right time. Greg wooed me into letting him bring the girls along to make money while we were in California, promising me that I wouldn't have to work with them during our trip.

"It's our family vacation, Wendy. I'll make it perfect for you, I promise."

I hadn't yet realized how many girls he had gathered at Miranda's house. There was another new addition to the family: Rob, our own pimp assistant. With one minivan and two Cadillacs, Greg transported his harem of eight slaves—each under the same delusion that she was the one Greg really loved while the others were only there to make money for him. Along with Rob and me, his "wife," we all drove with the children down to Southern California for *my* trip to Disneyland.

The first couple of days were really fun. I bought three-day passes to Disneyland for four people. One day Greg went with the kids and me, another day Belle went with us, and the next day I let Rob and Miranda take the kids while I rested. The girls had one hotel room, and the kids and I had another. In theory, my room was also Greg's room, but he never spent the night with us. Some nights, one or two of the girls would stay with the kids and me. Regina came and stayed with me one night when she started fighting with Greg, and we just hung out, ordered pizza, and watched movies. We all would swim in the pool and just have lots of fun.

On the fourth night, five of the girls were detained by the police; the adults were sent to jail and the under-age girls to juvie. The only girls left at the hotel were Miranda, Mona, Veronica, and me. Miranda could bring in pretty good money, but Mona and Veronica weren't able to make enough to comply with Greg's standards. The next evening, Greg approached me after our fun in the pool was over.

"Wendy, can you just go out for one night? You'll make bank real quick down here."

"You promised I wouldn't have to work on our family vacation, Greg."

"I spent all the money on fixing the cars up and we're not going to have enough to get back."

Between the cost of the hotel room, gas driving down, Disneyland tickets, and food, my three thousand dollars was gone. I was depending on Greg to get us home. Continuing to entice me into doing this with a happy face, he added the charm.

"You're going to out-bank these girls in a second. You go show them how to make some money."

It was so easy for him to turn me around. Greg had manipulated his girls into a paradox: We were a synchronized unit, and we were also very competitive for his approval. When he complimented me like that, it almost made me want to go work for him. I was happy enough with praise to agree.

Rob drove the four of us girls to a donut shop known for its tricks on Harbor Boulevard in Santa Ana. There wasn't much going on there, so we started walking the street. I did one for forty dollars while Miranda got the same, and then it was dead. Miranda with her bright ideas spoke up.

"Why don't we go out to Sunset Boulevard in Hollywood? I'm sure we can make lots of money there."

We drove back to the hotel room where Rob switched places with Greg and watched the kids while Greg drove us up to Hollywood. I threw on a sexy, cute dress that made me look like a prostitute. I was ready to experience what Hollywood was really about, but I wasn't expecting the scene we found on the Boulevard. Girls were in negligees, prancing around the streets half naked. Pimps who looked like the pimps in the movies, with flashy suits and big hats with feathers, strutted along the Boulevard as if they owned it.

I looked at what I was wearing.

"I don't look like a Hollywood prostitute. I'll never get picked up."

We drove a few blocks away from where all the activity was going on, but I was still nervous. I followed Miranda; she had been there before, and I hoped she would set me up with a date. We had been standing on the street for over forty-five minutes without one car stopping; my hopes were dashed that I would make any money at all that night. I was worrying about how disappointed Greg was going to be in me and how he would order me to go out again the next night to make up for it, when a man pulled over in a Porsche and offered me two hundred dollars for two hours. I looked at Miranda, who was standing next to me, and she gave me a shrug, which meant, "You don't really have a choice. It's the best offer either one of us has had so far."

The man drove for five minutes up a long winding hill to a huge house where he rented a mother-in-law apartment downstairs and to the side. He ushered me in to his room, handed me two hundred dollars, got undressed, and lay on his bed. I took off my clothes, tucking the money into my shoe, and, taking out a condom, I sat down beside him on the bed.

"I don't want to wear a condom. All I want is a blowjob."

"Sorry, I won't do anything without a condom... too many diseases running around."

"I'll pay you an extra hundred dollars."

"Nope."

"Two hundred."

I shook my head.

"Three hundred extra dollars. Come on, I don't like to wear condoms, and it's only a blowjob."

This was getting mighty enticing, but didn't know at what point I was supposed to say "yes." Greg had never told me if there was an amount of money that would make it worth it for me not to use a condom, especially when it was just a blowjob.

"Four hundred dollars. My final offer," adding in a begging voice, "Come on, please?"

I started doing the math in my head. I would come back with six hundred dollars. I was sure Greg would be very happy with that. I hesitatingly accepted the extra four hundred, not sure what Greg would say and wondering if he would be mad or happy with me.

I knew he'd be pleased about the money but I wasn't sure what he'd say about my not using a condom.

The man was on some sort of drug that I did not recognize. He couldn't get an erection no matter how hard I tried. An hour and a half went by and I told him I needed to leave.

The young man pleaded, "Please stay for just fifteen more minutes. I'll pay you another twenty dollars." I took the twenty and continued the fruitless job at hand. Ten minutes later I stopped what I was doing.

"I really need to get back now. My friends are going to be worried about me."

Again he pleaded, "Please stay just fifteen more minutes. I'll pay you another twenty dollars."

He went to the closet where he took out another twenty dollar bill, handed it to me, and then went to the kitchen to snort some white powder that lay on the counter. He returned to the bed and I continued my job. Five minutes later I was tired and badly wanted to leave.

"I really should go now."

And the man's response was the same: going to the closet with the stash full of money and handing me another twenty dollar bill. I realized that he was not paying attention to the time and every time I said that I wanted to go, he would pay me another twenty dollars. I used this to my advantage. An hour later I had twelve hundred dollars packed away in my shoe.

I started getting scared that this man was going to kill me, for who in his right mind would pay someone twelve hundred dollars?

"I've been gone for over three hours now. My friends are going to call the police if I don't get back soon."

"I'll give you five hundred dollars if you come back for an hour more." He sounded desperate.

He drove me to where he had picked me up. The girls were still scattered at different intersections on Sunset Boulevard. I looked for Greg but couldn't find him so I ran up to Veronica and in a panic asked her, "Where's Greg, I have to find Greg."

Hearing the fear in my voice, Veronica responded, "What's wrong? Are you okay?"

"I don't know. I have to talk to Greg."

We walked around the corner where Greg was sitting in the car listening to music. When he saw us walking towards him he got out of the car.

"Where have you been? What took you so long?"

In my anxiety, I attempted to put the blame on him so he wouldn't be angry with me for not using a condom.

"You never told me what to do? I didn't know what to do in this situation. You can't get mad at me because you never told me what to do."

In a comforting voice he responded, "Wendy, calm down, what happened?"

Very timidly I asked, "At what amount of money should I agree to not use a condom while giving a blowjob?"

I could see the anger building in his eyes. "How much did you get?"

"Twelve hundred dollars," I softly said, waiting for him to start yelling at me and calling me a slut.

The look in his eyes quickly changed from anger to joy.

"You have twelve hundred dollars?"

Extremely pleased to see the joy in his eyes, I added, "He wants me to go with him again for another hour for five hundred more."

"Well, go with him. What's the matter?"

"I don't want to Greg. I got a funny feeling about the guy. Please don't make me go back with him. He's really high on some sort of weird drug and I'm scared to get back in the car with him."

"Baby, you can't give up five hundred dollars. You know we need the money. Come on, it's only one hour. It's an easy five hundred."

Easy? Easy?! Sucking on a limp dick for an hour is not at all easy.

I knew I had no choice. I looked at the ground, which was the proper position for any ho, and I gave the required response.

"Okay."

I walked slowly back to the man's car, wondering if I would ever see my children again, hoping they had enjoyed our last vacation together.

Chapter 23
The Fire

Experience: that most brutal of teachers.
But you learn, my God do you learn.
—C. S. Lewis

SOON AFTER WE GOT BACK from California, Miranda found out that she was pregnant with Greg's baby. Most women in this situation would probably feel jealousy towards each other, and even though there may have been some, I felt more of a relief that someone else in this world would be in the same position as me—forever linked to Greg by her own child, being trapped in the chaos of trying to be a good mother while being under his control.

A month later I discovered that I was also pregnant with our third child. The craziness, the insanity of the situation did not escape me. I was one of two women having a child by the same man, and this commonality drew us closer together. We both wanted out of the game, out of the craziness that surrounded us, but neither of us could see a way out. It seemed there was no choice but to continue living like slaves forever, trying to make the best of the situation. Both of us were too scared to ever testify against him in court. There was no opportunity for even a glimmer of courage; he often told us that his brother Gary, who was now living with us after ten years in prison, would kill us if we ever contacted the police. Besides, with so many other girls surrounding Greg and loving him, they would do the same thing I had done when I was seventeen: lie on the witness stand to protect Greg.

Miranda and I did tricks throughout our pregnancies, but we weren't able to make as much money as we normally could. Greg started collecting his next batch of young girls, using his time-proven routine: He would first proclaim his love to them, and then trap them forever in hell. Miranda would come over to my house for days at a time, trying to escape from the drugs and Greg's crazy-making.

Greg was skilled at identifying girls who would be susceptible to his manipulation, and he soon had a whole new harem. He worked a few of these girls in quickly, regaling them with tales of the fun and money they could have by coming and working with us. Greg ordered Miranda to teach the few girls who didn't need much grooming how to work the streets.

One girl insisted to me that she was sixteen years old, but I knew she wasn't. She had no business on the street; both Greg and I could plainly see this. Greg should have sent her away, but I knew he didn't care how young she was. He would continue to groom her until he decided she was ready.

One day this child was sitting on the couch with Latasha, who was then twelve years old. They sat together watching cartoons on television, laughing and talking while they huddled close to one another as if they were best friends. I couldn't stand what I saw, this girl so close in age to my own daughter, knowing what Greg had in store for her. *What if this were to happen to Latasha? What if she ended up with a guy like Greg and there was a woman in the house like me? How would I want that woman to act?*

I played it out in my head and I knew I would want that woman to protect my child and tell her to go home. The next day, Greg was outside cleaning his car while Candace and I were in the house alone. I cautiously approached her.

"Can I talk to you, Candace?"

Even her voice was twelve.

"Yeah, sure."

I didn't really know where to begin. The question just popped out of my mouth without even thinking.

"Do you know and understand what is going on here?"

She looked at me as if she didn't understand the question, even though I was pretty sure she did. I pressed on.

"You do realize that Greg is a pimp and we are all his hos? That we have to go out and have sex with men for money in order to keep from being beaten by him?"

She continued to stare at me without emotion. Her blank eyes suggested she totally understood the situation and wasn't surprised by my news. I continued to plead with her.

"Candace, I have lived my life like this and it's not fun, it's not worth it. I understand that right now you probably think that Greg loves you a lot and you probably think he is going to leave all of us once we make enough money for the two of you, but that's not going to happen. You may be having fun right now, but you don't know what it's like. You don't want to end up like me, Candace. You have a mother who loves you and cares about you. Even though you may be having problems with her right now, those problems are nothing compared to the nightmares you will suffer if you stay here."

Her vacant stare filled with anger. She turned to walk outside; as she got close to the door, I entreated,

"Please don't tell Greg. Please don't tell him what I said."

Candace walked through the door and shut it behind her. I started cleaning up the house, acting as if I had done nothing wrong, hoping and praying she wouldn't tell.

A few minutes later, Greg stormed through the door.

"What the fuck are you telling this girl?" I could see Candace standing in the doorway, watching and listening to everything.

"Greg, she's too young, she's too young for this. Can't you see that?"

He didn't yield for even a moment. His yelling escalated, calling me all kinds of names, telling me I was a piece of shit, and warning me to never scare her again. He sang Candace's praises, exclaiming that she was a real woman who cared about him. He ranted on, alternating his praise for Candace and his disgust for me.

I knew exactly what he was doing. I had been through it a billion times before, and I had seen it too many times to even be affected by it anymore. Candace stood in the doorway feeling better and better about herself, seeing how much Greg loved and cared for her that he would cuss me out and say all these horrible things about me and good things about her. Before my eyes, Candace emotionally evolved into his Princess and he into her Prince Charming. She was hooked.

Greg set Candace up with her first date, which she did in my house, in Latasha's room to be exact. I wanted to care—the person I had once been would have cared, but that person was gone, replaced by a broken spirit.

One day I was walking down the stairs and heard Candace ask Miranda, "Why doesn't Greg beat Wendy?"

The question kind of stunned me, both that she would ask such a question and also because it made me realize it had been a very long time since Greg had physically hit me.

Miranda answered, "He doesn't have to. The fear has been permanently beaten into her. She does what he says. She doesn't ask questions. He doesn't need to beat her anymore. He has total control over her and has had it for quite some time now."

I stood at the bottom of the stairs listening to Miranda's explanation and knowing she was right...and, honestly...I felt nothing. I walked into the kitchen to get something to eat to feed the hungry child growing under what had once been my heart.

In the fall of 1998, I was about seven months pregnant and Miranda was about eight months along. All of us had gone up to Seattle to see Greg's mom for Thanksgiving. Driving back to Portland, I drove Miranda, Latasha, and Gregory in one car, and Greg drove all the other girls in another. In the middle of nowhere, Miranda started to talk about the realities of our pathetic lives and how horrible it was for our children. Both Miranda and I were done. Our lives were nothing like we had ever thought they would be. We were tired, pregnant, and hopeless enough to give words to our pain.

"Is this the way you thought it would be?"

"Never. It wasn't supposed to be like this... It was never supposed to be like this."

"How did this happen? How did we end up like this?"

"I don't know, but what can we possibly do? We're stuck."

"We can escape right now, Wendy."

"What? How?"

"Just start driving slowly and he'll pass you, when he gets far enough ahead just get off on the exit. By the time he realizes we aren't behind him and he comes looking for us we'll be gone."

"Where will we go?"

"My uncle has a place in Yakima. He'll let you and the kids stay for a while."

"Are you sure?"

"I'm pretty sure. He's not going to let you stay out on the street, not while you're pregnant....and he loves kids. He'd love Tasha and Gregory."

I looked in the rearview mirror at Tasha and Gregory and wondered how they would be affected by this.

"What about the apartment and all our stuff?"

"Forget all our stuff... It never lasts anyways."

I wanted to leave so badly. I slowed down so Greg would pass us and he did. I lagged further and further behind until finally the lights on his car were only a speck in the distance. I saw the exit up ahead and knew this was our chance.

"Take this exit, Wendy."

Consumed with fear, I tried my hardest to turn the steering wheel in the direction of the off ramp, our opportunity for freedom. I started to cry.

"I'm too scared, Miranda. I can't. I'm sorry, I'm sorry, Miranda."

"It's okay Wendy, I understand. It's okay."

Later that evening after we had arrived home, Miranda and I were watching television with the kids when Greg stormed through the front door.

"*Get in the car!*"

Neither Miranda nor I said a word; we just did as we were told, leaving Tasha and Gregory to watch the Simpsons by themselves. I got into the front passenger seat, Miranda got in the backseat. As soon as we got in the car, I could smell a strong, repulsive odor that hurt my stomach, but I couldn't figure out what it was. Greg got in and started to drive.

Miranda spoke up. "What is that horrible smell?"

"Greg," I added, "we're pregnant. We can't be around smells like this."

Greg maintained an eerie silence.

"Where are we going?" I demanded to know, but there was no response. "What's going on?" I looked at Miranda in the backseat for some sort of clue; she clearly did not know what was going on.

"Greg, I don't have any shoes on. Where are we going?"

"You'll see." His abrupt response cut like a switchblade through his mysterious silence.

As the smell became stronger, Miranda and I could feel each other's increasing unease about what was happening. After Greg had driven us about two miles, we came to a street lined with fire trucks. As we got closer we could see a house on fire, and police had the area cordoned off. Greg pulled up right behind one of the police cars, giving us a clear view of the house, flames leaping out of its windows. I was frantic.

"Greg, why are you stopping here?"

He put the car into park and turned directly to me. His cruel eyes stared straight into mine. Terror silenced me completely. He then looked at Miranda, who was also frozen in fear. He again turned his gaze at me. His voice was calm but his eyes burned like fire arrows.

"If either of you bitches ever even *thinks* about leaving me again, this is what I will do to your parents' houses." As Greg pointed to the burning house, Miranda and I both realized what we smelled in the car: gasoline. Arson's fuel.

He looked at Miranda but his message was for both of us. "Never forget, I know what you talk about and know what you think. I'm inside you and you will never be free of me.... I own you."

Neither of us girls spoke as he sat back into his seat, put the car into drive, and drove us back to the apartment. Only the poor devils in hell could hear our silent, anguished screams.

Chapter 24
Sentenced to
Freedom

Long enough have you dream'd
contemptible dreams,
Now I wash the gum from your eyes,
You must habit yourself to the dazzle of
the light
and of every moment of your life.
¯Walt Whitman, Leaves of Grass

IN EARLY 1999, MIRANDA HAD HER BABY and I had Mikey. Both of us had been evicted from our apartments because of the loud fighting with Greg, and we had all moved in together into a house right off of 82nd Avenue in Portland. Our lives soon took a dramatic turn.

FEBRUARY 4, 1999: THE RESCUE

The day began peacefully. At two o'clock in the afternoon, the house was quiet. My new baby was asleep in the living room, on the couch next to his father, who was playing a video game. I was in the kitchen making macaroni and cheese, gazing absentmindedly out the window. My two older children would soon be home from school. It was the kind of day that could easily lull me into the fantasy that I was living the life of a contented homemaker with three beautiful children—except that Fawn, Greg's current favorite, was also there, asleep in the back room.

A sudden movement at the front of the house caught my eye. I glanced out the window to see a team of police officers, all in SWAT attire, surge towards the house. "Protecting Greg" had been literally beaten into each of us, and I knew what I was supposed to do: immediately warn Greg so he could run out the back or hide. I had been schooled so many times that my reaction should have been automatic. I certainly knew better than to ever open the door for the police.

All the training sessions, all the drills were for naught, ambushed in a split second—not by my fear or memory lapse, but by a glimmer of humanity. A police officer was looking right into my eyes, his gaze freezing me in my tracks with kindness. It had been so long since anyone had looked at me directly in the eye. In that moment, I was filled with the hope that I could someday be recognized as a human being. The officer motioned with his hand, and I could read his lips as he mouthed *Open the door.*

In a trancelike state, I walked to the front door and turned the knob. Fear had vanished. I looked at Greg and informed him in a very calm voice, "The police are here."

I hadn't even finished the sentence before the SWAT officers barged through the open door. I watched in silence as they threw Greg on the floor in front of me and handcuffed him. And then, in an instant, he was gone. Even in the turmoil, a dream began to unfold in my heart: I would soon be free. Free from this monster, free from this life. The police were there to rescue me.

My sense of relief was short-lived. One of the officers gently pulled my arms behind my back and handcuffed my wrists. A movement down the hallway caught my eye, and I saw a police officer walking Gregory and Fawn from the bedroom. I hadn't even realized my son was home; had he snuck in during all the commotion?

Baby Mikey was still lying on the couch; no longer asleep, he started to cry. One of the officers came over to me and said, "I'm going to put the handcuffs on in front so that you can hold your baby. Sit on the couch with your baby and don't move."

It was very difficult to hold Mikey while I was handcuffed, but I was grateful for the continued kindness. Another officer told my son Gregory to sit by me. I sat as still as I could, comforted that my sons were close. My mind and my body began to grow numb as I watched the police ransack the house. I kept wondering, hoping that this was indeed my rescue; but I couldn't ignore the cold reality of the handcuffs around my wrists and the police tearing everything apart, just as my life had been torn apart for the last fourteen years.

Emotions seesawed between hope and resignation. Could this be my liberation? I was tired. I wished I was dead. I was disoriented in a whirl of thoughts when the sound of my mother's voice lifted my mind from its haze.

"What's going on now?"

As casually as I could, I replied with a question of my own.

"Mom, what are you doing down here?"

Mom would usually tell me when she was coming to Portland. I had always tried to present her with a picture that my life was good with Greg. I would prepare the house, which mainly meant that I would send the other girls away. Had she told me she was planning to visit? I couldn't remember. Still, I wasn't ashamed or embarrassed. I didn't care anymore if she knew the truth about my life—I was Greg's ho, nothing more. Besides, who was I kidding? Hell...I had never been able to admit the truth to myself, but my mother had always known.

Mom's marriage to Tom had crumbled and he had moved to California with their two children. She told me she was driving from Seattle to California to start her new life and to be close to the kids. I was shocked to see her, but I was also glad she was there. I knew she would love me and help me no matter what. In the midst of all the commotion, we sat on the couch—she with gentle hands folded in her lap, I still in handcuffs—and had a pleasant mother-daughter conversation. I didn't know what was going to happen, but I knew she would not hesitate if I asked her to stay a few days and help me with the baby while I cleaned up the disaster that the police were making of the house. The thought calmed me. I knew that Grandma would bring happiness to the kids while I tried to pick up the pieces of my battered life.

At some point Latasha came home and saw the police rummaging through all of her belongings. She was too old to be having to go through this. We were all too old to be going through this. It had to end this time—this had to be it. Someone had handed me a bottle of warm milk, and, still in handcuffs, I was trying to feed Mikey. Gregory and my mother sat with us on the couch. No one said a word.

The silence was broken by a gentle, sweet voice.

"We need to take you down to the station to ask you some questions."

I looked at my mom. "Can you watch the kids for a little while?"

Before she could answer, the police officer added, "I don't think it will take very long. We just need to ask her some questions."

I handed Mikey to my mother. The officer removed the handcuffs from my wrists—not, as it seemed, to free me but only to pull my arms behind my back and relock the cuffs. I was placed into a police car and driven to the Multnomah County Sheriff's Office in downtown Portland, where I soon found myself in a small concrete cell all by myself, my hands still bound behind my back.

RESCUE DENIED

I thought about the questions they would ask me. I remembered the words Greg had beaten into me many years before: "If the police ever question you, you had better not say a word. Don't even open your mouth to them or I will kill you. Remember, I'm too smart for the police. They will never be able to keep me down. Whoever betrays me will never outlive the pain I will cause them."

I started rocking back and forth trying to keep myself calm, torn between my two options: keep silent, or tell the truth. I couldn't be sure what would happen if I kept silent. I'd probably spend some time in jail, only to be released to return to the nightmare that had become my life. I knew full well what consequences I would face if I exposed Greg and he tracked me down. Tears streamed down my face as I reflected on my life.

My entire life had been wasted. I thought about the suffering my children had been through, the suffering that I had allowed every time I didn't call the police for help. My head overflowed with thoughts and questions, confusing me more. For brief moments at a time, my thinking was clear. I could see reality. I knew I had jeopardized my children. I knew other minors were being victimized by Greg. I had not only done nothing to stop it, I had helped him. I envisioned the times that I had driven the girls to the track to turn tricks with me. I started to wonder if I would be charged also.

With that startling revelation, my thoughts turned to the other girls. What would they say or not say? They hadn't been around as long as I had. They hadn't been conditioned the way I was. Maybe they wouldn't be as scared as I was. Dare I hope that the other girls would be brave enough to tell the truth?

For hours I rocked back and forth, tears falling down my face, whimpers escaping my lips. For hours I wondered what was happening and what Greg would do to punish me when I got home. As time passed, hope waned. I became convinced Greg would never be caught. Just as he always said—he was smarter than the police, and his girls would protect him. For any girl who accused him, there would always be ten other girls to testify on his behalf, calling the accuser a jealous, scorned, lying woman—just like I had done myself so many years before.

After several hours a woman opened the cell door. I figured she was a police officer, although she wasn't dressed in a uniform. When she saw that my hands were still handcuffed behind my back and that snot and tears were dripping down my face, she ran to get a Kleenex and the keys to the handcuffs. Her kind, sympathetic voice renewed my hope.

"Let's get those things off of you, Wendy."

As soon as my hands were free, I grabbed the Kleenex; but as I tried to wipe my face, I started to cry all over again.

Gently holding onto my arm and speaking softly, the woman escorted me out of the concrete cell.

"Greg wants to talk to you."

I couldn't believe what I had heard. I didn't understand why they would let me talk to Greg. I thought Greg, once again, had manipulated his way through these people. I thought that maybe Greg was pretending to have a heart attack, which he did every time he was arrested. He did this so the officers would feel sorry for him and possibly not arrest him. If they did go through with the arrest, he would be taken to the hospital where he would have the opportunity to escape.

The lady took me to a very small room with a table and four chairs. She pulled one of the chairs out for me. In resignation, I sat and waited to see Greg. He would tell me what I was supposed to do, instructions I would certainly follow.

As the time passed, there was no sign of Greg. Two male police officers in plain clothes walked into the tiny room and sat down in the two chairs across the table from me. To my enormous relief, the Greg who wanted to talk with me was the officer in charge, Greg Davis. My relief was short-lived when the woman police officer walked out of the room, closing the door behind her and leaving me alone with the two men.

I looked down into my lap and stared at my knees, just as my Greg had taught me to do. One of the men started to speak to me, but I knew I wasn't allowed to answer. I started to think of the consequences if I were to look at them. My mind brimmed with floating demons—one of them Greg, filling the room with his presence. I continued to stare at my knees, biting hard on my tongue. If I could only make my tongue bleed—that would prove to Greg that I didn't speak to the men!

I hated being alone in the room with the two men. They didn't understand what they were causing, the punishment and torture I would go through because they were in the room with me. As my thoughts floated between the room of punishment with Greg and the tiny room I was trapped in, I heard one of them ask, "You have three children with Greg, don't you?"

That was such a simple question. Surely I could answer that one.

"Yes," I whispered. The next question came quickly.

"How long have you and Greg been together?" Greg's demon glared at me, and I retreated into my head, where I answered only to myself.

Since I was fifteen years old.

The men, the room, even demon Greg faded as I pondered my life. Where had the years gone? I was twenty-nine years old... I would turn thirty in a few days. I didn't feel twenty-nine. I looked hard at my hands, folded in my lap—did they reveal anything about the years that had passed? Years of torture, pain—interspersed with occasional interludes when I felt like a princess—flashed through my head. I was tired. I wanted it to end. For a moment I imagined myself telling them everything. How it would sound to them? How they would react to my story?

The room re-emerged from the haze, but a cloud of fear and confusion muffled the police officers' voices. I needed a cigarette, but smoking was not permitted anywhere in the police station or jail. The cloud started to lift, and I heard one of them say, "Would you like an attorney?"

I blurted out, "Yes." In my mind an attorney would be a female. I could talk to a woman; she would understand. I could tell her everything and ask her for help. If I could tell her, she could explain it to the men for me.

The men rose from their chairs. The gentle kindness was gone, replaced with an angry voice.

"If that's the way you want it, that's fine. I hope you are ready to go to jail for a really long time."

They escorted me down the hall to the elevators, where we waited in silence for the elevator to arrive. I was confused and frightened by the sudden turn in the interview.

"Can I ask you something?" I inquired sheepishly.

"Sure. What?" His voice was still tinged with anger.

"What am I being charged with?"

There was no hesitation in his response, as if he had memorized his lines for a play—just another act in my life's drama.

"Thirteen counts of promoting prostitution and thirteen counts of compelling prostitution."

I stood quiet for only a moment while I tried to figure out on my own what the word "compelling" might mean. I didn't want to ask, but I could hear the elevator coming to rest at our floor and I needed to know.

"What does compelling mean?" I asked him, hoping he could hear the sincerity and respect in my voice.

His voice didn't soften, but he did answer my question.

"It means you forced the girls to prostitute."

I was relieved. I knew there was no way I would ever be convicted of that. I had never forced the girls to prostitute, and I was confident the girls would tell the police that much of the truth. Still, I was scared. I was uncertain of my future. I couldn't wait to get to a cell so I could let my welling tears flow. The police escorted me to the booking center, where I began the intake process. I was going to be staying in jail.

As dim as the ray of hope was at that point, it had not died. I was thankful that my mom was at the house to watch the children. I knew I wouldn't be in jail for more than a couple of days. How could I be? The other girls would tell the police the truth and I would be released, and my new life could begin.

COMFORT

For five months I sat in the county jail cell wondering what was going to happen to me. One day my lawyer would call and tell me I was looking at ten years, and then the next week she would call and tell me I would get off with probation. I was stuck in a world of uncertainty regarding everything in my life, including my children and where they were going to end up.

The day I was arrested, the police had called Children's Service to have the kids taken to foster care. My mom had just rented out her house in Bellevue to move to California. She believed I would be released soon and would be able to get the kids back on my own; but in any event, not even knowing where she was going to be living, she was unable to take the kids.

I could easily have fallen into complete despair if it had not been for two loving women. One was my mother, who made sure I got at least three or four letters a week from her—many weeks her letters arrived daily. Sometimes she had nothing to say, so she would send me jokes she found on the Internet or inspirational stories. Every word she sent was a lifeline to my dream of a better life.

The other woman was Miranda, who, as luck would have it, was also being held in the county jail. The jailors purposely kept us separated so we could not compare stories, but we were permitted to write to each other. Every prisoner was given two free stamped envelopes each week, and Miranda and I used them to comfort each other as much as we could.

One day an envelope came from her, a short letter:

To Wendy Barnes

I'll always remember why we became friends because a female will be there for you even when Greg isn't. I love you with all of my heart and I'll always be there for you. Pray for Stacey, Tina, and Candace all the time because otherwise we would still be doing this every day.

I love you always,
You're my best friend for life.
Love, Miranda

Miranda had also written a poem, which she enclosed with the letter. "Our Life with the Devil" captured everything there was to say about our lives—the horrors of being Greg's property, the destructive comfort we had found in crack cocaine, the girls' futile struggles to protect each other, the desperate efforts to break free, the salvation we may have found through our arrests.

I love you always. Best friend for life. Her poem was powerful, honest. Perhaps these were only words, but I felt anchored by the love that women share when they've experienced hell together. I held the letter close to my heart, where my dream struggled to survive. These words, this love just might be enough to free us from our demons, to make the dream come true.

JULY 23, 1999: THE DAY OF SENTENCING

I was awakened from my sleep by the sound of my cell door lock being repeatedly unlocked and locked. This was the typical way inmates were summoned to get up. I jumped down from my bunk, trying not to wake my new cellmate, and quickly brushed my teeth and combed my hair. I wanted to look at least halfway decent when I stood in front of the judge, but with no makeup or proper hair care products, the attempt was futile. I couldn't even wash properly for the court appearance; showers were scheduled for later that afternoon.

I was transported from the Multnomah County Jail to the courthouse in handcuffs and shackles. About ten girls in orange or blue jail suits stood in the sally port—a secure holding cell with two locked doors. The guard chained us together, and we were led, stumbling, into the transport van, trying to be careful not to fall or affect the person to whom we were chained. When we arrived at the courthouse, guards removed the handcuffs, chains, and shackles; and we were put into a cell with about twenty other female inmates.

"Wendy."

My heart skipped a beat when I saw Miranda walking towards me. We embraced each other. I hadn't seen Miranda in five months and I had missed her so much. She was my best friend because she understood everything: what I was going through, what had happened in the past, our hopes for the future. We spoke at the same time, asking each other the same questions.

"What do you think is going to happen? What did your lawyer say?"

Miranda's tone was reassuring.

"Wendy, they are not going to give us any time. They understand the truth of what happened. I can't imagine the judge locking us up any longer, especially since we both have children. Where are Tasha, Gregory, and Mikey?"

"They are still in foster care, but I think they will be going to Juanita soon."

Miranda's face contorted with alarm.

"Wendy, you can't let the kids go there. You have to stop it somehow. You know she will be on Greg's side and not let you see the kids."

I knew this was a possibility, but I also believed it was better for Greg's mother to have custody of my children than to have them sent to an unknown foster home. I knew that Juanita would not physically hurt the kids in any way, and with foster care there was too much of a chance the kids could be harmed.

"It's complicated, Miranda. I don't have much choice right now."

As we sat down on the concrete benches in the cell, I asked the ultimate question. The answer would determine if we had a chance to be free or if this was just a bump in the road.

"Has Greg been sentenced yet? Do you know what's happening to him?"

"I don't know. I haven't talked to my lawyer in a couple of days. I think Greg went to sentencing a few days ago," Miranda speculated.

My mind started to reel. What had happened to Greg? How long did I have until this monster would come after me again? Did he blame me for his incarceration? If he did, what would the beating and torture be like when he was released and found me?

The steel door to the cell opened. "*Barnes!*"

Miranda turned and embraced me. "Good luck, Wendy. Be strong. Everything will be okay."

I tried hard to hide how scared I was as the guard again locked me in handcuffs and shackles. I kept my eyes to the ground as we made our way through the open hallways of the courthouse. I knew people were staring at me, and I was embarrassed, ashamed. The guard took me to the front of the courtroom, where my court-appointed defense attorney sat at a big desk.

"The judge wants to talk to us alone in her chambers," my attorney informed me. I was happy to hear it was a woman judge. I was more comfortable speaking with females.

"Do you have any idea of what is going to happen? Do you know how much time they are trying to give me?" I anxiously inquired.

Without a hint of emotion the lawyer replied, "The district attorney is recommending thirty-six months, but I strongly believe the judge sees the truth of what happened, and you won't get that much time."

"Is there any chance at all that I will be able to get out soon, that I won't have to go to prison?"

The lawyer's terse reply did nothing to comfort me. "Anything is possible."

In the judge's chambers, my attorney and I sat in chairs on the opposite side of the judge's huge desk, which was filled with papers, folders, and case files. She was an older lady, maybe in her early fifties. The judicial black robe draped over her slender body, emanating an air of crisp professionalism and authority. My heart was pounding and I felt ashamed to be facing her in this way. The handcuffs made noise every time I moved my chained hands, reminding me that I was not only a defendant in her court but that I was still trapped under Greg's jurisdiction.

The judge was compassionate, but she also saw the big picture—how I had allowed Greg to victimize young girls for many years. I had done nothing to stop him, and even helped transport them, and for this, the judge said, I needed to be punished. Still, she was clearly considering my future and my family. She recognized that I had three children and I was thirty years old. She wanted me to be released from jail when I was still young enough to build a new life and have a meaningful relationship with my kids. With that, she felt that a sentence of twenty-three months would be appropriate. She punched some numbers into a calculator.

"You will only serve nineteen months. Since you have already served five months, you only have a little over a year left to serve."

It was an offer I could not refuse. I felt I had no real choice in the matter, and I was relieved the sentence wasn't longer. I agreed to the plea bargain. The judge instructed me to return to the courtroom, where she would conduct the formalities that would close the deal.

Back in the courtroom, I was comforted to see Miranda and her family waiting for her turn to go into the judge's chambers. With my lawyer at my side, I stood stone-faced in front of the bench as the judge hammered her gavel to indicate that she was about to render the final judgment for my case. She started reading words that I didn't understand, a full description of my crime and the number and letter citations for the laws I had broken. As she spoke, something she read inspired my lawyer to lean over and whisper in my ear.

"Wendy, I forgot to tell you. Promoting prostitution is a sex crime. You will have to register as a sex offender for the rest of your life. Really, it's no big deal. You just have to go to the police station once a year and register with them."

Register as a sex offender for the rest of my life. The words were a knife to my heart. *No big deal.* I choked on the thought. A sex offender is my stepfather...a sex offender is a horrible person who does horrible things to helpless children. I felt hopeless, knowing that I would be labeled a monster and knowing I couldn't do anything about it. It was the price I had to pay to get out of there. All I wanted was to wake up from this horrifying nightmare.

The judge finished her statement, and it was over. Even handcuffed and shackled, I started to breathe a little more freely. It was faint, but I could hear the freedom dream whisper in my heart.

LEAVES OF GRASS

During the very long waits before and after my sentencing, a few of the girls who had been there before explained what I could expect if I were to be sent to prison. These were the experts; some of them had been to prison many times.

"The food is so much better than this county shit they feed us now. It's prepared by the inmates for the inmates, and they don't feed you crap."

The food critic was trying to be helpful, but dinner was not my biggest worry. I had seen the prison movies where women would gang up on one girl and rape her with a broom, making her their sex slave forever. As much as I wanted to know, I didn't want to come straight out and ask, so I started with an easier question.

"What prison will they send me to?"

A girl I had seen many times during my five-month stay in the county jail spoke up.

"At first everyone is sent to Oregon Women's Correctional Center, OWCC—it is a maximum security facility that houses the worst offenders."

My eyes started to bug out of my head thinking of the evil women who would soon enslave me.

"OWCC," my jail mate continued, "is the place where they take everyone to determine what kind of facility you need. Once you spend thirty to forty-five days there, they will send you to the facility where you will spend the rest of your time, either a max-, medium-, or minimum-security prison."

During the few days between our sentencing and our transfer to OWCC, we learned that Greg had been sentenced to ten years in prison—which meant that, with good behavior, he would be out in seven years. We also wondered about the other girls who were over eighteen. Even though they were not at the house when Greg and I were arrested, I was confused why the police had not taken them into custody and charged them. Most of the older girls had been interviewed by the police, but they were never charged. Mona had even told the police that I was much less involved than she had been in taking the younger girls out to work the streets. These girls were my family, so I was thankful that they weren't charged—and I was grateful that they had stood up for me in their reports to the police. Still, I was confused to be the one going to prison when the other girls had had been more involved with working the younger girls than I ever was. I never learned the answer to that question, but I did learn through the grapevine that some of the girls had used Greg's arrest as an opportunity to try to escape from his grip.

OWCC was in Salem, Oregon, normally a forty-five minute drive south of Multnomah County Jail. Because we had to make stops at other jails to pick up other women, the trip took hours. This slow, tedious process required that we be escorted off the van and into a holding cell at each jail. Each time we were returned to the van, we were strip searched.

Each jail had its own process for this. Sometimes we girls would have to stand together in a line and remove all of our clothes. The female guard would then shout, "Raise your breasts!" Every girl would lift her breasts, being sure her fingers were spread open so the guard could see she wasn't hiding anything in her hands. The guard would walk down the line, observing each of us carefully before she shouted, "Turn around, bend over, and spread your cheeks!" Like a chorus line, the girls in unison would bend over in the most demeaning positions, waiting to be inspected by the fully clothed authority figure.

The first few times I had to go through this, my spirit would die from the humiliation. I felt lower than shit, the same way Greg made me feel about myself. I would secretly cry, trying hard not to let the officer see my tears, knowing weakness was dangerous. But as I stood upright after the cattle inspection, the tears would stream down my face. After ten of these inspections, I no longer cried. My reaction by then was worse than crying. I had been dehumanized to the point that I no longer felt embarrassed. I was a robot that did everything they asked with no emotion, leaning over with my butt cheeks spread.

The one saving grace that day was that Miranda and I were being transported to OWCC together. Although I knew that we would end up being sent to different prisons because we had been sentenced to different amounts of time, I was still thrilled that we would have our first experience of prison together and yearned that we would be put in the same cell while we were housed at OWCC. Maybe then I wouldn't be raped by the evil women who filled every prison.

When we finally arrived, we were immediately taken to the lunch room where two very friendly inmates greeted us.

"I bet you're hungry for some good food, huh? How long have you been in county?"

Miranda answered for the two of us. "Five months."

"Oh, you are going to love this then, just sit down here."

We sat down on the round, hard plastic seats at a table that seated four. The two girls brought us each a plastic tray with five compartments: one filled with fresh fruit, the others with crisp, hot, green beans, a hot piece of bread, and some kind of food product that looked like mush.

"What would you like to drink? We have real soda-pop here."

I hadn't tasted a Coke or Pepsi in what seemed like a million years.

"Coke, please," Miranda and I answered at the same time. We sat and ate our meals, which didn't look so great but, as the experts had promised, tasted wonderful compared to the county jail food.

Around one o'clock, the nice inmate girls who had fed us told us to go to the clothing room to change into our uniforms. With great pleasure, I put on the jeans and blue t-shirt with the big orange Oregon State Inmate logo on the front and back. I hadn't worn jeans in a long time, and it almost made me feel human again to be in jeans and old, worn-out tennis shoes instead of the orange flip flops I had worn for five months at county.

While I was changing into my jeans, Miranda disappeared. My joy at the "new" clothes dissipated, and I was again consumed by the fear of being alone. The movie scenes raced through my head, accompanied by the repeating mantra: *This is not where I belong. Only bad girls go to prison.* It had to be a mistake that Miranda and I had been sent to this evil place intended for really bad people... Yes, I was certain. This was a mistake.

The guard's voice broke my meditation.

"Follow the orange line," she commanded as she handed me sheets and a wool blanket. I followed the orange line through the quiet hallway, lined with cell doors on both sides. The orange line disappeared under a door leading outside, and I started to wonder if maybe I had misunderstood what the guard had said. Where was this orange line leading me?

I walked through the door and out into a small courtyard. The orange line ran to a large dormitory room, filled on all sides with bunk beds against the walls. A guard sat at a desk at the front, surrounded by many smaller tables and chairs. I dutifully continued to follow the orange line, straight to the officer's desk. She seemed to ignore me as I stood before her at the end of the orange line.

A few moments later she tersely acknowledged me.

"Fourth bottom bunk back, on the right-hand side."

I turned around to see all the bunks filled with women, all lying down as if they were on time out. Some were napping, some writing letters or reading books. As I walked to the designated bunk, my eyes searched the lines of bunks for Miranda. She wasn't anywhere to be seen.

A large, mean-looking woman was assigned to the fifth bottom bunk, right next to me. The front of her hair was a short crew cut and the back hung in a long, stringy salt and pepper mop. As I got closer, my head nearly exploded with the idea that this woman would be my new Greg. She would make me her property, would beat me and humiliate me whenever the guard turned her back. I wanted to cry but knew that I couldn't show the fear. Tears would show I was weak, would send a message that I was really a bitch to be fucked with, controlled, and turned into a sex slave. I tried hard not to make any eye contact with her, concentrating more on the task at hand: making my bed and laying down for time out like the other women.

After I carefully made my bunk, trying not to disturb the woman in the top bunk, I nonchalantly lay down, acting as if I had been there before and knew the drill. I lay on my stomach with my head in the opposite direction of the biker bitch who, I knew, would soon be my master. I did not have a clue how long we all would be in this time out, or where I would go once released from it. Again, I fought the tears that were starting to well in my eyes. I thought about my children, wondering where they were and what they were thinking and feeling. I hoped they were at least having a little fun wherever they were. I hoped beyond hope that their lives were now better than the life I had given them.

My daydreams turned to the day I would be released. Calculating how old I would be when I would be free, I started wondering about Greg. *Does he know where I am? Does he realize I'm in prison? Does he feel bad that I'm in prison and our children are in foster care? Does he care at all about me, or was our life really just a game to him? Did my love mean anything to him, or did he really not love me at all?*

I was shaken from my self-interrogation by the sounds of grunting and groaning coming from the direction of my evil master, who was still sitting in the bunk beside me. At first the sounds were infrequent, and I didn't really know what they were; but as the horrifying sounds of the animal growling next to me got stronger, my mind turned again to the prison movie memories. *She's making a shank to cut me with. She will use it when we are released from our time out.* I could almost feel the sharp blade of paper against my neck. I could envision her pinning me against the wall, her free hand fondling my breasts. I could almost hear her telling me I was hers.

As the grunts and groans grew louder and more frequent, I realized the inevitable would soon happen. I needed to make a plan, find a way to escape my new master. The guard was writing at her desk, totally ignoring the noises. I realized my only hope was to keep the guard in my peripheral vision so I could run in her direction when my nemesis made her move. I nonchalantly turned my head to the other side, being very careful not to make any eye contact. I could see that she was still sitting up in her bed, making small movements. I was now even more certain she was making the paper knife as quickly as she could.

Suddenly the noises changed in tone, just enough to make me glance briefly in her direction. I realized that the noises I thought were grunts and groans were really sobs and moans. She was crying uncontrollably, trying hard to stop the pulsating cries and quick breaths. I set aside my nightmare that she wanted to make me her bitch. My heart filled with compassion for this woman who was plainly suffering. *She can beat me up later.*

Softly and filled with fear, I gathered the words, "Are you okay?"

The tears were streaming down her face as she looked at me and wept, still gasping for air.

"I...c-c-can't....do....this.... I...don't...belong....here."

Her thoughts were my thoughts. She was just like me.

Between the sobs, she told me her story. Four years ago, she met a woman and had fallen in love. They were very happy together, each working every day at their individual jobs that supported a comfortable life. One day they were invited to a party, where they were introduced to methamphetamines. They decided to try it, just this one time. One time became two, and then ten, and before they knew it, neither of them could live without it.

In short order, they had both lost their jobs. They discovered how to make money forging checks and stealing identities. She went into detail about how checks could be altered; I could see that even now it was just as fascinating to her as it was to me that hairspray and fingernail polish remover could be used to erase ink off of checks. Everything went well for a while after they learned the check game scam, but their desperation to acquire the drugs continued to get worse. Their addiction took over their lives and turned the check game into an everyday affair.

When they found out that the feds were watching them, the two made a deal. Instead of both of them going to prison, one of them would take the full blame so the other could be free to keep the house in order. She loved her girlfriend so much! She couldn't stand the thought of her beloved going to prison. She volunteered to take the fall alone, with the commitment that her lifelong mate would stand by her side, keep their home in order, and send her money to get through her time in prison. The woman's sobs became stronger as she told the devastating blow that ended the story.

"She left me for another woman. She sold everything in our house and ran off with another woman and I don't know what to do."

I felt her sadness, for I, too, knew what it was like to be alone and unloved. I now saw this woman for what she really was: kind, sweet, somewhat naïve and innocent, hurting and scared. I pondered her story. I personally understood the power that drugs can have on a person and knew that her story could have easily been mine. I quickly came to the conclusion that she didn't belong in there either. The court system had made a horrible mistake in sending us, two good people who had made some bad choices, to a place full of evil, rotten, bad people.

The loud speaker in the dorm room roared "*Yard!*" I didn't know what this meant, but knew enough to learn by example. All the other women jumped from their beds and straightened the lumps from their blankets, so I did the same. I joined the herd of women, not knowing where I was headed but trying to stay in the middle because I knew that the cows on the outside of the herd would be attacked by the other dangerous animals of the wild. As we charged through the hallway, some women would veer off, entering small rooms in the hallways that were not inmate cells. I wasn't entirely certain what to do, but I continued to follow the pack, hoping I wasn't headed for the guillotine.

As we moved along, I relentlessly scanned my surroundings looking for Miranda. *Where could she be? Is she in the same herd that I'm in?* The throng started to bottleneck at a green door that led outside. I waited my turn to walk through the door. All the women looked so comfortable there, all knowing what they were doing and talking amongst themselves. It seemed that I was the only one who didn't know anyone else, and I felt so alone. Even my new friend was nowhere in sight. A small paved area with three picnic tables opened to a larger space, where a dirt trail circled a large grassy yard with a volleyball net. A covered section of the yard had eight pay phones and a basketball hoop. Fences surrounded every section of the yard.

Some of the women ran to form lines at the phones, which were already all in use. Other women started walking the circular dirt path within the fences. The outside space was huge—larger than any other place I had been in the past five months—so the fences locking me in didn't even faze me. At last, I spotted Miranda sitting in the grass on the back end of the yard. My heart filled with joy as I raced towards her. Finally, I knew someone! I was no longer totally alone.

I got close enough for her to hear and see me.

"Where did they take you?"

As she started to answer me, I stretched my arms out and bent down to sit in the grass. When my fingers touched the thick, green grass, Miranda's words faded into the distance. The grass was so soft and felt so luxurious. I plopped my butt down and realized how much I had missed the feeling of sitting on luscious grass. My mind drifted to my childhood— to visions of little Wendy lying in the grass, looking up at the blue sky, the clouds floating through her daydreams.

My eyes slowly made their way to the bright blue sky. A few billowy clouds lingered in the distance, and I felt a sense of comfort I did not recognize. I took a deep breath. The blue sky and billowy clouds gave me a sense of hope for the future. Miranda and I sat quietly, absorbing the warm sunshine, both knowing the other was also enjoying this unfamiliar but wonderful feeling, a feeling powerful enough to last even when Miranda broke the silence.

"It's so beautiful out here."

I gently ran my fingers through the grass.

"I love the feeling of the grass," I shared, adding, "I think I had forgotten the feel of grass."

We looked out to the horizon, the shining sun warming our bodies and offering us release from our grim situation. Even the tall barbwire fence couldn't block out the beauty of the sky.

Without a word being spoken, we each knew that both of us were experiencing the same mysterious feeling of grace washing over us. The feeling tickled our hearts, and we couldn't help but start to laugh slightly. We smiled at each other in a way we had never smiled before. Together, we continued to smile—relishing our mutual confusion and our mutual delight.

"Oh, my God. We're fucking free, Miranda! We're *free!*"

We both lay down in the grass, laughing hysterically from the wonderful, exhilarating feeling of freedom, a feeling neither of us had ever felt before, at least never like this.

"I'm never going back to him again, never," Miranda vowed. "Greg will stay locked up for a long time after each of us gets out. We'll have time to get our lives together and go into hiding where he will never be able to find us."

We shared our dreams and stories— how we planned our lives without him, without the torture, without the drugs. The joy continued to grow into more hope for the future and the reality of real freedom at last. *"Oh, my God! Is this what it feels like to be free?!"*

Chapter 25
Recreating Wendy

We're going to have to let truth scream louder to our souls than the lies that have infected us. ⁻Beth Moore, So Long, Insecurity: You've Been A Bad Friend to Us

THE FORTY-FIVE DAYS AT OWCC WERE FUN for us. We would sit and play cards until lights out, comparing stories from the past, revealing truths we weren't before allowed to share, and laughing hysterically at the insanity of our lives.

Other girls would walk by us and ask, "What the hell are you two so happy about?"

Our reply was always the same, and always with a smile.

"You don't know what our lives were like before this. You would be happy, too."

Prison was easy for me as I already knew how to follow the rules that controlled me. I did what I was told to do without asking questions and remained quiet when I was supposed to. During those forty-five days, I met other women who were good people with great hearts who didn't belong in prison with all the evil, mean people. At that point, I thought prison was only for "bad people," and it seemed to me that none of the women I met really belonged there. Every story had the same general plot: When she had no choices, she had made poor choices that turned into awful events that sooner or later involved the police. Our society locked these women away for being "bad people," not knowing they were really good people who had made bad choices. Of course, it was up to each person whether she chose to use it as a turning point for herself—but maybe there was a better way to accomplish that?

When the forty-five days were up, I only had one year and one week left in my sentence. I knew I would be sent to the Columbia River Correctional Institute—CRCI, the minimum-security unit in northeast Portland. This was the "releasing" facility that every woman prisoner went to once she had only one year of her sentence remaining. Miranda would be sent to a medium-security facility in eastern Oregon because she still had three years left to serve on her sentence.

I signed up for Turning Point, a voluntary drug and alcohol treatment program that was available at CRCI. In spite of my obvious appreciation for my soothing friend cocaine, I didn't really think I was a drug addict; but I thought the program would include the counseling I knew I needed. I figured the inmates involved with the program were on a journey of change; and since I, too, was on a journey of change, I would fit in.

I arrived at the prison that would be my home for the next year of my life. I went through the same strip search I had been through many times before, was handed sheets and a wool blanket, and was then directed to "Follow the green line." The green line led me to an area of the prison that had a guard station, huge dining and living room areas, a small kitchen, and seven different dorm rooms, all connecting throughout the living room and kitchen. The rooms accommodated fifty women. Two rooms were intake rooms with twelve beds each. Four of the rooms had six beds, and one room had two beds. The guard instructed me to go into Room 3, which was the room with twelve single beds. I was relieved to find I would not have to share a bunk bed.

All the women were in their time out period, which I had early on learned was called "count time" because all the inmates are to sit on their beds and be counted by the guards to be sure no one had escaped. This happened routinely four times a day. I walked into the room with eleven women sitting on their beds, all staring at me as I made my bed.

I had managed to hold myself together during the intake, but when I sat down on the bed I could no longer control my emotions. Tears flooded my eyes and I started to weep uncontrollably. I lay down on the bed and buried my face in the pillow. I cried for my children, I cried for the loneliness I felt, I cried because I missed Miranda, and I cried because I saw how completely I had fucked up my life.

The girl next to me would occasionally console me gently.

"It's okay to cry. Go ahead and let it out."

It was kind of her to try to reassure me, but I didn't agree and would constantly try to stop. The more I tried to stop, the more I cried, and then I cried more because I couldn't stop crying. I was a mess. The sadness consumed me, and the future that Miranda and I had been dreaming about just weeks before was no longer even a glimmer in my thoughts. All I could see ahead of me was uncertainty, and my spirit began to fill with the fear of the unknown.

Turning Point consisted of fifty women at different stages of recovery and with different release dates. There were different types of classes throughout the day: anger management, relationships, self-control, drug addiction. Each woman was also assigned a job detail that depended on her stage in the program and her release date. I was assigned, along with a dozen others, to garbage pickup. During the first three months, we would get up at five in the morning and get in the van that would take us to collect garbage along the side of the roads and at the airport runways.

I liked going to the airport and watching the planes take off. I would imagine that I was in the plane going to a faraway place; the thunderous roar of the airplanes taking off so close to me gave my daydreams an aura of possibility.

The Turning Point program amenities included an activity room with a ping pong table and a large cupboard stocked with games and other diversions. The cupboard was always locked; I didn't know exactly what was in it or how to get the keys to get in it. One day while I was playing ping pong, the guard opened the cupboard to retrieve a game for a few of the girls, and I caught a glimpse of a keyboard. An electric piano about four feet long stood upright in the cupboard! My heart began to pound and I felt my soul soaring with the idea that maybe, just possibly, I would be able to play it.

I was so excited I stopped playing ping pong in the middle of the game to find my counselor, hoping and praying she would allow me to play the keyboard.

"I saw a piano in the game closet. Could I play it?"

Her response was typical and understandable. "I'm sorry Wendy, but we don't want people banging on that thing. It makes too much noise."

I was in eighth grade all over again.

"But I know how to play it. I won't bang on it, I promise. I know how to play music."

She seemed a little suspicious, but she did reach into her pocket to pull out the keys.

"Show me."

By this time the room was empty. She removed the piano from the cupboard and put it on the ping pong table. I plugged it in and sat down in front of it. My fingers touched the keys that would, like magic, create a beautiful song. My counselor stood in amazement, watching me play. I closed my eyes and felt the music move through my body and lift my soul to the heavens. A tear slowly fell down my face as my thoughts filled with images of my children and I together again. The piano gave me hope for the future.

I finished my song and looked up at my counselor, now surrounded by a few guards and other counselors. They all applauded.

"Anytime she wants to play the piano," my counselor told the guard, "she is allowed to."

All of the women were required to go through psychological testing. For my exam I was taken to a quiet room where I was given a dull pencil and a bunch of pages with lots of questions. The questions were hard for me to answer—statements that I had to rate very true, true, neutral, untrue, or very untrue. I had no idea what those categories even meant to the psychologists. Wasn't something either true or untrue? I tried to assess each statement based on how I had felt over the past couple of days; even with those boundaries, the answers would range from the two extremes and anywhere in between. Simple statements that might be easy for others to answer just baffled me.

I like myself.
I love myself.
I hate my actions.
I feel happy.
I am lonely.

After I finished the test, I was taken into another room with a lady who asked me a few more questions. Our conversation didn't go very far; she wasn't interested in my story or me. She was just there to do a job: evaluate the answers I had given to the few questions on the written test.

About a week later I was called into the nurse's office and was handed a bottle of medication.

"What are these for?"

Without even looking at me, the nurse glanced at my chart and said, "It's for your depression."

I was curious what else was on the paper she was looking at. I thought it was strange that they could identify that I had depression without ever really talking with me. I didn't feel depressed... I felt confused, scared, and lost. Still, I trusted that they must know what they were doing. I agreed that I was depressed.

"Is this based on the test I took last week?"

"Yes." She handed me a pill and a small cup of water.

"Does it say anything else? Am I crazy?"

Without any reaction, she looked at the file again.

"You have borderline personality disorder, bipolar tendencies, and depression."

"Borderline personality what? What does that mean?"

"You'll have to talk to your counselor about it." She handed me a piece of paper that gave me the freedom to walk back to my dorm without a guard escort.

On my long walk back to the dorm I kept repeating the name of the disease that controlled me. *Everything now makes sense. I am crazy. I stayed with a manipulative, horrible person because I am crazy. There is*

something horribly wrong with me—I had no control over
my actions and decisions.

Tears pooled in my eyes as I realized the horrible truth: If borderline personality disorder was the reason I allowed myself to end up in that life, I would never be out of that life because I could not control it. *It was all my fault. Even if Greg hadn't gotten to me, I still would have ended up living a horrible life making bad decisions because I am crazy. My 'disorder' will prevent me from ever making good decisions with my life.*

I got back to my dorm and found my counselor. When she saw how upset I was, she dropped what she was doing to take me into a private room.

"Wendy, what's wrong?"

My tears fell freely as I explained to her the conversation with the nurse and the fact that I was crazy and I would never be able to be normal or be able to make good choices.

"What if I keep going back to Greg because I have this disorder?"

"Let me guess, they said you have borderline personality disorder?"

"Is it that obvious?!" I cried out.

With an empathetic chuckle she explained.

"Wendy, calm down, you are not crazy. Borderline personality disorder is a name that is given to anyone who does not fit within the 'norms' of society. Society says that a woman—and especially a woman with children—should not be in prison. You do not fit within society's definition of normal. A woman who is an astronaut would get the same diagnosis. A man who stays at home taking care of the kids while his wife works outside the home would be diagnosed as having borderline personality disorder. Wendy, you are *not* crazy, you have *total* control over your life, and you *never* have to go back to

Greg or any life like the one you were living unless you *choose* to do so."

This was puzzling to me but also calmed me down. She handed me the keys to the locker that held my comfort and escape. I went into the quiet room, unlocked the cupboard, and took out the small electric piano that could make my pain float away. I started to play, and I again began to breathe—and for that moment, all my problems did disappear.

The fate of my children was partly based on my sentence. In the state of Oregon, if a parent is not able to take care of his or her child for eighteen consecutive months, the state automatically puts the children up for adoption. Even though I was still in prison, I was permitted to be at the hearing that would determine their future; I was transferred to Multnomah County in order to appear before the children's court judge.

Handcuffed and shackled in my blue jumpsuit, I was ashamed of myself and heartbroken for my children. The judge's voice and disgust in her eyes cut through my heart as she berated me for allowing my three children to suffer the fallout of my life and the choices I had made—all the more agonizing because I knew she was right. I had been a horrible mother to my children. It didn't matter that this wasn't what I had planned or wanted, or that I felt I had no other choices. I had exposed them to hell.

The judge awarded guardianship to Greg's mom. I had been expecting this; my attorney had discussed it with me. To add to my heartbreak, it was not an option for my mother to have custody of my children; her marriage had broken up and she was struggling with custody issues related to her own children. The irony of Greg's mother having custody had not escaped me, but I also knew Juanita loved the children, and I preferred that my kids be with family than with some stranger—even though I worried that Greg might someday get control of them again.

I still had a dim hope that someday, if I did good things with my life, I could get them back and make it up to them. When the judge slammed down her gavel, even that hope was extinguished. She stripped away forever my rights as a mother, with the added condition that I could never appeal her decision. She made it crystal clear that I would never be a mother to my children again.

It was too painful even to imagine, not being a mother to my children. I wept for days, wishing I had made different choices, wishing I had never let Greg into my life. I would never even have a chance to know my youngest child; even if I was allowed to visit Mikey when I got out of prison, he would never consider me to be his mother. I knew that to Latasha and Gregory I would always be their mother. No court order could ever take away the relationship that we had. Still, the fact that I was considered an unfit mother and the consequences my children would pay were devastating.

Fall turned to winter with each day pretty much the same as the last. Even in the cold wind and rain, we would go out in raincoats to pick up other people's garbage from the sides of the road. It was not cheery work. As I would walk through the ditches swollen with high grass, I would sometimes imagine finding one of the girls from the past lying dead in the ditch.

Once a prisoner proved that she would not run away, she was assigned to work at the local food bank. I was relieved when I got that transfer in January, along with about fifteen other girls. The prison van dropped us off at seven each morning to work various warehouse jobs. Half the girls would go back to the prison at noon for mandatory classes, while the girls who were closer to their release dates would stay until four o'clock.

"Run if you want. We'll find you again," were the guards parting words every morning as we exited the van. We were free to run, but none of us did because it was too close to the time of our release.

My mother would write me letters almost every other day while I was in prison. I also got letters from my dad and, much to my surprise, from my cousin, who I thought had never really liked me. I eagerly awaited mail call days, for those were the days that I felt I was somehow connected to the world. It was those days that I felt that I existed.

During our counseling sessions, we often had writing exercises. One was to list out all of your own personal characteristics—the qualities within yourself that make you who you are. I sat with my blank piece of paper, my equally blank mind failing to grasp onto anything. I visualized experiences in my life that would reveal some sort of characteristic that was me. I saw myself turning tricks and giving the money to Greg. I saw myself stealing from stores in order to return the stolen items for money. I saw myself with a crack pipe in my mouth. I saw a horrible mother to my children, who deserved so much better.

"Think harder, Wendy," said the counselor in charge of this activity. "Start with thinking about the things that you like to do or things that you like to eat. What do you like to do, Wendy?"

I tried my hardest to think of something that I liked to do.

"I like spending time with my kids."

"But what do *you* like to do? Do you enjoy painting or reading, do you have any hobbies?"

Her response angered me. She continued to list ideas, but her suggestions had nothing to do with me. I didn't have *hobbies*. I had been a ho, a thief, a drug addict—but I had also been a mother, and that is what I best liked to "do." I became sadder and more filled with hopelessness. I thought of my children and how I wanted to play with them and take them to the zoo. I wanted to sit and watch cartoons with them. I also thought of all the things I didn't do with them that I now wished I had. *Could I possibly ever be a mother to my kids again?*

A fellow prisoner, Lisa, looked over at my empty piece of paper.

"When you're nothing, you're free to create who you want to be."

At first her comment confused me, but then she asked, "What is an attribute that you highly respect in other people?"

I thought for a moment.

"I don't know."

She continued on her probe.

"Who is a person that you like?" I looked around the room and saw Stacey filling her paper with her own great characteristics and I pointed at her.

"What do you like about her?"

I thought about why I liked Stacey. She was nice to me and always kind to everyone around her, but there was something about Stacey that I respected even more and that was her ability to be honest in a very kind way. We had many talks where sometimes she hurt my feelings, but the hurt feelings quickly subsided when I realized the gentle truth in what she was saying.

With excitement that my paper would not be totally empty, I wrote in large letters on my no longer blank paper:

HONESTY

I practiced being honest and realized I needed some sort of waiver that would give me permission to lie in appropriate situations. I continued to write.

I have the right to not answer any question.

I have the right to beat around the bush enough to make someone think I answered the questions when in fact I didn't.

The "honesty" on my paper had quickly turned into "no lying," and I was okay with this.

After about three months in the program, I received a letter from Greg. My heart pounded when I saw his handwriting on the paper, and I was scared to see what it said. Even before I read the letter, I could tell by the writing that it was a nice letter without anger or threats. He apologized to me and told me how much he loved me for not telling on him. He had filled the paper with positive comments about who I was and how much he missed what we used to have when we were young. He described what our lives would be like when we were both free, how we would go to work and raise the kids and of course be happily in love with each other, keeping each other close.

All the counseling, all the medications, all the time in prison, and I had made no progress at all. I hadn't even finished the letter before the smile formed on my face and the image of Prince Charming and Princess Wendy Living Happily Ever After danced in my head. A nirvana of emotions immediately blossomed within me. I ran around showing my closest friends the letter from Greg, gushing, "He loves me, he loves me, oh my God, he loves me!"

I was high on the drug of love—the same drug young girls are fed when they watch Disney movies like *Sleeping Beauty*, *Snow White*, and *Cinderella*. I danced around in my imaginary world that filled me with complete happiness and ecstasy until finally one of the girls stopped me.

"Wendy, don't you remember what this guy did to you?"

I showed her the letter, still clutched in my hand.

"But look! He's sorry and he loves me."

Her disgust was palpable.

"There's something seriously wrong with you, Wendy. This man has some sort of weird effect on you. You look and act like you are on drugs right now. You are acting like the two of you have had some sort of wonderful life and you're living in some sort of fantasy." She turned to walk away, forcefully adding, "You need to snap the fuck out of this."

In my gut I knew she was right, but it felt so good, to be in love! and to be loved! I didn't want to lose the happiness I was feeling. Angry at the woman who had tried to throw ice on my happiness, I sat down to write a love letter back to Greg. In my letter, I handed all my worries and fears to him, relieving myself of any and all responsibility I had for my life and what it turned out to be. My letter reflected the characteristic I said I wanted to be: honest.

I anxiously waited for his response. My love drug high was wearing off, and I needed another hit. A week and a half later, when a letter finally arrived, it was not the fix I wanted but it was without a doubt the fix that I needed.

"You fucking stupid bitch, why did you talk to the police? It's entirely your fault your kids were taken away from you and you deserve to be where you are." After a page filled with humiliation and an emotional beating, his tone changed somewhat.

"You're lucky you're getting back together with me and not leaving me forever. If it weren't for me your life would end up miserable and awful forever.

No man will ever love you like I can. No man will ever be able to handle your bullshit and craziness like I can. Believe me when I tell you, you will *never* find a man that will love you the way I do."

It wasn't enough. I was cold sober, collapsing into the first stages of withdrawal. My body heaved with sobs as I saw clearly the reality of my life. I was sitting in prison, all three of my kids had been legally taken from me, and I was yearning to be with the person who had been the root cause of it all. I ripped up the letter and let the debilitating and healing pain wash over me.

Chapter 26
Release

Was it too much to expect a future?
—*Alan Gibbons,* The Dark Beneath

AFTER MY SENTENCING, the only thing that kept me going was the anticipation of seeing my children on the day I was released. I hoped that Juanita would allow me to live with her so I could be close to my children. About six months into my stay at Turning Point, during one of the many processing groups, I shared my enthusiasm for my plans. The counselor, knowing my case well, spoke up.

"Wendy, you can't live with Juanita when you are released. Your children are there and the law will not allow you to be around *any* children because you are a sex offender."

I was certain that this counselor was unaware of my special circumstances. I wasn't a sex offender. A sex offender is a person who molests children and rapes women. That wasn't me, and I wouldn't be forbidden from seeing my children. The sentencing judge plainly stated during our plea agreement conversation that the reason she was not giving me more time was so that my children and I could reunite and build our relationship. Admittedly, not as a parent figure, but it was clear she intended for me to see my kids.

"No, nobody has ever told me that I wouldn't be able to be around children," I insisted. "My lawyer plainly told me that it was a simple procedure where I would have to go down to the police station once a year and register with them. My case is different; I'm not considered a real sex offender."

I continued to mentally argue with the counselor's contention. I thought back to the few times my mother had brought the kids to the prison to see me. *If I were a sex offender who was a threat to children, there would be no way that the prison would have allowed me to have contact visits with my children.*

I made an appointment with my official prison release counselor. These people weren't really counselors in the traditional sense; they were prison staff who could officially tell me my release date and approve my post-release living arrangements. When my appointment time finally arrived, I walked into her office with the intent of setting things straight. I needed her assurance, and I was confident that she would confirm that I was *not* a sex offender and that I would be able to see and live with my children when I was released.

I was wrong, very wrong.

"Mrs. Dorothy told me that I will not be able to see or live with my children when I am released. Can you please tell her that she is wrong?"

The release counselor revealed no emotion as she looked through my file.

"You are a sex offender. Sex offenders are not allowed to have contact with any children."

"My lawyer told me that the only thing I would have to do is go to the police station once a year and register," I protested. Then, trying to point out the injustice and mistake she was making, I added, "The judge decided how long my sentence would be based on the fact that she wanted me and my children to build our relationship together."

"When you are released, your parole officer will make the final decision about you being able to see your children." She made no effort to soften the blow. "There are very strict rules that surround your release, and these rules are that you will not have any contact with children. If your parole officer feels that you deserve to see your kids and you are not a threat to them, it will be up to him to change the rules regarding your specific case."

I was devastated. I couldn't believe that on the day of my release from this prison, I would not be hugging my children. I wouldn't be taking them out to the park to play or to the zoo, or share any of the many other activities with them that I had been planning for the past year. I would be walking out of the prison alone, with nowhere to go.

I cried for days, desperately hoping my tears would wash away this reality. My children were my life, the only thing I had to live for, the only value that I still had in this world. I had so much to make up to them, so many good times we all deserved to have together.

Both my excitement and anxiety grew. I would try to visualize what my life would be like free from Greg and living in the "real" world, but I wasn't able to form the picture in my head. An inner voice taunted me with the self-image he had beaten into me. *You'll never make it in the real world. You're nothing without me. Everything you touch you will destroy.*

Even a week before my release, I had no idea where I would be going. Because I was a sex offender, the prison was having a hard time finding a halfway house that would accept me. The counseling staff discussed the situation with me, telling me that I would have no choice but to be sent to a special halfway house in downtown Portland that housed only sex offenders. The expressions on their faces as they spoke of this told me this was a horrible idea. One of the counselors stood up for me.

"There is no way I will allow Wendy to be sent to live with male sex offenders. She will immediately be victimized by dangerous predators. We have to find another option."

Finally, two days before my release, I was called into the counselor's office to go over the plans for my release.

"We found a place that will accept you because of your special circumstances. The YWCA downtown has a women's shelter that also serves as a halfway house for women being released from jails and prisons." Opening up the file sitting in front of her she continued, "You must check in with your parole officer within four hours of your release."

She looked up from the paper she was reading to see the fearful look on my face. In my mind, a parole officer was a man sent to further punish me, degrade me, and emotionally rape me—just like all the other men in the world had done.

Allaying my fears she added, "It's a female parole officer whom I have known for a very long time, and she is going to help you greatly along your way. She's very nice and understanding."

For six months I had been told that only my parole officer could give me authorization and permission to see my children.

"Did you ask her if I could see my children when I get out?"

"That will not be decided until she meets you and sees how you are doing out in the community. You are not allowed to have contact with any minor child or to go anywhere near children, any park where minors may be...." On and on the list went of all the places I could not go because I was a registered sex offender.

"Am I allowed to go to church?"

"Do children go to church?"

I couldn't quite believe what I was hearing. "I guess so."

Her moment of kindness expended, her response was cold and sarcastic.

"Well, then, I guess not."

I couldn't believe that I was seen as a threat to children as if I had molested or hurt children in any way. I still was not able to fully understand the effect I had had when I was with Greg, not only on my own children but also on the many children whom I had helped him victimize by not standing up for what was right. I still didn't understand that doing nothing was a choice and an action in itself and that my "action" of doing nothing to protect the girls had hurt many children over the years. The fact that I had been one of those children was not a mitigating factor in the jurisprudence system.

I was scheduled to be released at six o'clock in the morning. I woke up around four and packed up my belongings. Most of the things I had owned before going to jail were gone; of the remaining items, there were very few I wanted to carry into my new life. I threw many things away or gave them to other inmates.

In cases like mine—that is, when a person is a "good" inmate— the prisoner is escorted by a guard a few days before her release to a second-hand store and given up to ten dollars' worth of clothing. I dressed in my ill-fitting charity outfit and prepared to leave my prison room for the last time. I looked and felt like a homeless person, embarrassed by the rags I wore and where I was coming from.

The good news was that I wouldn't be alone. My dad and his wife met me at the prison gates, along with my Aunt Janice and her daughter, Julie, the cousin who had exchanged letters with me while I'd been in prison. We drove to a local Wal-Mart, where Aunt Janice bought me some new clothes to start my new life. It felt strange that someone would do something like that for me—someone who really didn't know me and probably thought I was a disgrace to society, not to mention her family. Her kindness reminded me of my sweet grandma who had by that time passed away—my grandma who loved me for who I was and cared for me unconditionally. In fact, I knew my grandma's spirit was in my Aunt Janice that day, sending her blessings through my aunt's generosity.

My dad and stepmother drove me downtown to check in with my parole officer within the required time. We walked to the front desk; I told the receptionist my name and asked for the parole officer I was assigned to. After a few minutes of looking in the computer database, she casually—as if it wasn't going to devastate my life—said, "Your parole officer is Dominic Torno. Go to the second floor and wait in the lobby."

Knowing she was wrong, I demurred. "I was told that my parole officer is Sara McGregor, and Sara is expecting me."

"Sara McGregor is no longer working in the sex offender unit. Your parole officer is Dominic Torno."

I dropped my head in shame. It seemed everywhere I went, everyone knew that I was a sex offender. Yet they didn't know the story, they didn't know the truth of what happened. I was sure they saw me as a child molester who hurt little children. I hated myself for what they thought of me.

I was thankful that my dad was with me. I knew he would strike up a conversation with this man about the weather or birds, which was his favorite subject. I hoped that maybe, just possibly, I could be invisible. Knots started developing in my stomach as we took the elevator upstairs to the second floor. Not wanting my dad to see me cry, I unobtrusively wiped the tears from my eyes. Once again a man was going to be in charge of my life—a man who would not care about me and would surely use me and degrade me like all the others. *I will never be free.*

I didn't look at the parole officer when he opened the door to the adjoining hallways and summoned my dad and me to follow him. My father, as I suspected he would, stepped up to Dominic and said with a firm handshake, "Hello, sir, I'm Floyd Barnes. I'm Wendy's father. May I come back with her?"

I kept my eyes to the ground. I knew I wasn't supposed to look at men unless they were tricks and this man was not, at least not yet, a trick to me. I remained quiet as Dominic escorted us into his office, grabbing an extra chair along the way so all three of us could sit down. My dad, right on cue and just as I had hoped, started the conversation.

"So how's the weather been down here?"

The two of them continued to talk for about five minutes and to my delight they even talked about birds—a topic, as it turned out, that also interested Dominic.

A condition of my parole was that my parole officer would have to know my whereabouts at all times, so my father asked, "Can you give permission for Wendy to stay with us at a local hotel for the weekend so we can spend time with her?"

Dominic leafed through the thick file on his desk.

"I don't see any problem with that. She will need to check in at the YWCA and I will need to know the name and address of the hotel you will be staying at."

I was so happy that I would be able to spend the weekend with my family, a small escape from my life, a break before I would have to begin the long journey of repairing my life. I heard Dominic continue, "Wendy, I'm scheduling you to come in next Wednesday for another appointment and we'll discuss more then."

Still careful not to look at him, I whispered, "Okay."

I checked in at the YWCA and deposited my few belongings in my room. My family drove me to the hotel where we would be together for the weekend. I put on my new bathing suit and went directly to the hotel pool. I jumped in the cool refreshing water, allowing my entire body to relax as it released the frustrations that had accumulated for fifteen years. I loved to swim, and I hadn't been swimming in a long time. I dunked myself back under the water and heard the sweet sound of silence. I stayed underneath the water for as long as I could, holding my breath and feeling the calm. I was free. For this one moment, I was free. It didn't matter that I had a male parole officer who would control my every move for the next four years—for in this one moment, I was out of prison and able to take action to create my new life and discover the person I wanted to be.

On Monday morning my father dropped me off at the YWCA and we said our good-byes. It felt weird, realizing that I had a father who cared about me. I had never felt that before, even when I visited him as a child. Even though it felt weird, it was really nice in a strange sort of way. Still, I held on to the belief that his love was conditional: He would support me and love me only insomuch as I did the things he wanted me to do.

I went to the office to check in and then had a meeting with the woman who would be my counselor while I lived at the halfway house. We went over the rules I needed to follow and the goals I needed to achieve while I was there.

"So, Wendy, what are your plans? What is on your agenda?"

I didn't know what to say for I really had no idea. The week before, I didn't even know where I was going to be living, and my only "plan" at the time was not to stress out about that.

"I guess I'll try to find a job," was the only thing I could think of. *Who's going to hire a person with a felony—worse yet, who's going to hire a sex offender?* My future looked so bleak. I would think about the thousands of jobs one might find in Portland, only to realize that they all presented barriers to me: either children would be present or the company would not hire a sex offender. The best I might hope for was to become a street sweeper.

I was assigned to a small bedroom that I would be sharing with another woman who had been in jail for the previous five months. It did not take long for me to learn that her goals were not similar to mine at all. She was constantly preoccupied with contacting her boyfriend, who also was recently released from jail, and finding a place to live with him. Even though I didn't actually have any goals, I knew whatever goals I would someday be making would not be in line with hers. I didn't want anything to do with men; in fact, I wanted to stay as far away from them as I possibly could. In my life, men were nothing but trouble.

Chapter 27
Stepping in the
Right Direction

*I don't fit into that life anymore, yet I
don't fit into this life either—and I don't
know where I belong. —Wendy Barnes*

I SPENT THE NEXT DAY WALKING around the city trying
to figure out what I was going to do with my life. In
the middle of the afternoon, it started to rain; I
continued to walk, unprotected, observing other
people hiding under their umbrellas. Didn't they
realize how healing this rain was? When the rain got
heavier, I laughed at the people who started running
to their destinations; and when the rain started to
pour down on me, I leaned my head back to catch the
raindrops on my face. I stretched my arms out wide,
welcoming the refreshing raindrops that offered me
hope for the future. This time I didn't cry, but smiled
and laughed because I was at last free to dream. I was
totally soaked and I didn't mind at all.

When the rain turned to a light drizzle, my hope
diminished along with it. I started thinking about my
children. I wondered where they were right at that
moment. I wondered if they missed me. I missed my

children so much and I wanted so badly to be with them.

I knew I needed to find a job, but I was afraid and lost on where to go. I knew the question that awaited me on every job application: Have you ever been convicted of a felony? I didn't know how to explain to a total stranger what had happened, even if I got a chance to try. I wanted to set my life straight; how could I do that if I couldn't get a job?

I at last came up with an idea that would be a meaningful step forward and simultaneously give me a good excuse to not look for work for at least one more day. I decided that the following day I would take the bus to the local community college to find out how much it would cost to enroll in a math class. I still to this day do not know where that idea came from or why I wanted to know anything about math. Perhaps the rain inspired some clarity in my thinking. I mostly just wanted to do something that would take the entire day to accomplish so I could keep my mind off the overwhelming task ahead of me: repairing my life. I also wanted to learn and get comfortable with the bus system and I thought the forty-minute bus ride to the college would be a good first destination.

The trip the next morning was just the right ticket. I enjoyed the scenery and the fact that I was doing something that wasn't bad. Since I had made so many bad choices in my life without realizing it most of the time, I knew I needed to scrutinize every choice now. Would it lead my life in the right direction or the wrong direction? It may have been a small step and nothing may come of it, but I decided that my taking the bus to the college to find out the cost of a math class was, at least, not taking my life in the wrong direction— which to me meant it must be the right direction.

When I arrived at the huge college campus, I wandered around looking for an information booth where someone might be able to answer my question. I walked slowly through the campus, looking at all the people, relishing that they didn't know my secrets. They didn't know I was a bad person who had just been released from prison. I was no one among all these people, and for once it felt good to be so invisible.

When I finally did reach the information desk, I was directed to the counselors' office. I found it so strange that so many people were called counselors. I had learned the hard way that most of the counselors in prison weren't counselors at all. Except for the Turning Point counselors, my fellow prisoners gave me better guidance than the counselors had. Now I was being directed to see a counselor just to find out the cost of a math class. It was a pretty good bet that they weren't real counselors, either.

I took a number and waited to be called. I sat in this unfamiliar world and realized I had better get used to being in a lot of strange circumstances in my new life. To me "normal" was strange. I wanted to be normal more than anything. I wanted to learn to fit into this world, and I wanted my children to have a normal mommy. *Will I ever feel normal? Or at the very least will I ever stop feeling like I am living in a strange land?*

A petite Asian man came out a door and called my number. I didn't feel as weird around him as other males; he was just one of the fast tricks who wouldn't beat me up or try to take my money. I followed him into his office where he offered me a seat.

"How can I help you?"

"How much does a math class cost?"

It was a simple question, and I just wanted a simple answer, but it was not forthcoming. He asked me a few more questions:

"What was your grade point average in high school?"

"Have you ever taken any college courses?"

"Do you have a GED?"

Being very careful not to reveal any part of my life, I answered him as best I could. He then took out a pamphlet and started talking to me in what seemed to be half English and half whatever his native language was.

I didn't want to let on that his English was so bad I couldn't understand him, so I nodded my head, all the while wishing he would stop talking so I could leave. I started to regret coming to the college. It was a huge mistake for me to ask such a silly question, especially when I knew I wasn't going to actually take a class. I just didn't know what else to do with my day. Of the many things I could have done, this had seemed like the best way to start my "right" way of living.

I could understand every few of the words the counselor said, and that is how I knew he was getting ready to let me go. As I stood up to leave, I realized that I hadn't even gotten the answer I had come for. I felt like crying. *How am I going to survive in this life if I'm not even capable of getting an answer to a simple question? Maybe Greg was right. Maybe I won't make it in the real world. Maybe I am too stupid to survive and I will always have to go back to him in order to live.*

As we reached the door, the counselor handed me a three-by-five card.

"You need to go to this tonight. It's at seven thirty and I think you really need to go to it."

I took the card from him, but that wasn't enough for him. He wanted a commitment.

"Go to the class," he said firmly. "It's free, it will help you. Just go to the class."

Walking back to the bus stop I read what was on the card and found that it was a workshop for women returning to college. Why would I need to go? I wasn't returning to college. I counted the time it would take me to return downtown to the YWCA, eat some dinner, and take the long bus ride back to the school. Since I didn't have anything else to do and I could plainly see that it wouldn't be a bad choice that would lead me in the wrong direction, I decided to attend the workshop.

I arrived early to make sure I would be able to find the correct classroom and not be late. As I lingered around the campus, I experienced an unfamiliar sense of power. It was invigorating to know that I could be somebody else, that I could pretend I was normal. The other students were oblivious to my story; nobody would look at me twice to discover I wasn't normal.

While other women took their seats in the classroom, I pretended that I knew what I was doing and that I really belonged there. The teacher came in and introduced herself, gave a small opening speech, and told us she would like to know why we were attending the workshop. My heart sank. I didn't know what I was doing there, and I wasn't prepared to answer any questions, especially in front of the other eighteen women present. The teacher pointed at the lady sitting closest to her.

'What are you doing here?"

"I'm here to get my nursing degree," said the pretty woman who looked about twenty-six years old. She obviously belonged there.

"Great." Then looking to the next person, "And you?"

"I'm here to get a certificate in accounting."

Again the teacher responded, "Great."

Around the circle they went, with each woman having a direct answer that specifically answered the teacher's question.

"I'm here to get my Oregon Transfer Degree to go to Portland State."

"I'm here to take art classes."

More than a few women were going for their nursing degrees and I wondered if I should just say the same so as not to look as stupid as I felt. My heart pounded harder and harder as the question got closer and closer to me. I didn't know what I was going to say, and I totally regretted coming to this stupid class. The teacher looked at me and I could only look back at her like a deer stuck in the headlights. She repeated the question.

"What are you doing here?"

My answer slipped out, unaccompanied by any conscious thought on my part.

"I don't know." And I sat there looking as stupid as my answer was.

With a smile, the teacher said, "Great."

During the class, the idea of actually going to college floated through my head. The teacher talked about how to register and what the college had to offer and I wished I *could* go to college. I wanted to go to college, but since I was only pretending I was supposed to be there I knew I wouldn't actually be able to go.

When the class ended, I knew the women would start chatting with each other. I wanted to hurry and leave so I wouldn't risk anyone asking me any more questions. I was almost to the door when the teacher called out to me.

"Wendy, wait. I'd like to speak to you."

At first I thought I was in trouble. As I turned around, I saw her approaching me.

"Wendy, I loved your answer tonight. It was so honest and sincere. I work in the Women's Resource Center and would love to talk with you more about starting college."

Starting college? I can't go to college... I just got out of prison. I'm a registered sex offender. I'm a high school drop out with a GED that I only obtained through sheer luck, guessing the correct answers on the test. I can't go to college. I'm way too stupid to go to college.

"Can we meet tomorrow morning?" she asked.

Except to see Dominic the next afternoon, I didn't have any plans. I thought about the long bus ride up to the college and how much time I would be able to kill not doing something wrong.

"Sure, I can come in."

The next morning, I met with the teacher in the Women's Resource Center. She brought up financial aid that might help pay for some of my classes and books; to assess whether I qualified, she needed to know how much money I made last year.

The thought of going to college was making me happy—happy enough that I was compelled to tell her the unthinkable. If she knew who I truly was and still told me I could go to college, it might actually be something I could do. I took a deep breath and let the words tumble out before I had a chance to reconsider.

"I've been in prison for the past nineteen months. I didn't make any money at all last year. I don't know what I'm doing here. I only came here to see how much a math class costs. All this college stuff sounds really good. Can people like me still go to college?"

She looked at me with warm, compassionate eyes.

"Of course you can go to college. I think college would be perfect for you."

She brought out brochures about different classes, programs, and financial aid. The more she talked, the more she started using the same language the Asian man had used during my meeting with him. From listening to her in class the night before, I knew she wouldn't be speaking broken English, so I stopped her in mid-sentence.

"What are you talking about? I don't understand the words you are using."

This woman had already shown her ability to care and she knew where I was coming from, so even though I felt a small amount of shame, I was willing to ask. She didn't laugh or even hesitate; I got the impression that other people may have asked her the same question. She started explaining the words I didn't understand: curriculum, syllabus, syllabi. I started to laugh at myself for thinking the Asian man was speaking his native language. I told her why I was laughing and we shared the laugh together.

"Wendy, anytime you do not understand something, please come and ask me. There are no stupid questions. The more questions you ask, the more educated you will be... And I will never laugh at your questions."

After I took a few tests that I thought revealed how stupid I truly was, she sent me on my way. She told me to return the following day for the results and to apply for financial aid. On the bus ride back into Portland, I imagined myself with lots of books and being really smart. I started going down the list of all the things I wanted to be. Racing back into the memories of my childhood before Greg stole my soul, I remembered how I wanted to be a lawyer. I couldn't remember why I wanted to be a lawyer, but "a lawyer" had a nice ring to it.

Chapter 28
Growth
Opportunities

The world was an awfully large place and
it wasn't easy to find a person who'd gone
missing sixty years earlier, even if that
person was oneself.
¯*Kate Morton,* The Forgotten Garden

I MADE IT TO THE APPOINTMENT with my parole officer and sat in the lobby with butterflies in my stomach. This time my dad wasn't there to keep up the conversation, and I knew I would be forced to talk to Dominic. I kept my eyes to the ground because that is what I was trained to do. In the corner of my eye, I could see Dominic's figure in the doorway.

"Wendy, come with me."

I got up and followed the backs of his shoes into his office where I took the nearest chair. He sat quietly for a few minutes, which made me very uncomfortable. I found the coffee stain in the carpet that probably no one else realized was there, and that was where I stared during the entire meeting. We both spoke softly.

"So how is the YWCA?"

"Fine."

"Do you have any plans yet of what you're going to do?"

I was afraid to let him know about my ridiculous plan to go to college. I knew he would laugh at me if I told him about it and he would put me down and tell me I wouldn't be able to survive there and would surely inform me that people like me don't belong in a place like that. But with nothing else to say, no real plans for my future, I chose to reveal the ridiculous instead of nothing at all.

"I was thinking maybe I would go to college."

"Really?" The sound of his voice suggested he had a smile on his face or a twinkle in his eye. It wasn't a sarcastic tone, either—the one I had heard from other advisors so many times before. In fact, he sounded curious.

"Have you made any plans to go check out the college campus?"

Proud of the answer to that question, I replied, "I've already been up there three times, twice on Tuesday and once today."

Dominic remained silent; I wasn't sure what he was doing or thinking, so I continued on.

"There is a lady there who thinks it would be a good idea for me to go to college, and she thinks I would be a good student. I took some tests this morning, and tomorrow I go back to find out the results."

I waited for his condescending remarks, but there were none.

"I also think that's a great idea, Wendy. Keep me informed of how it goes."

I was surprised to hear him give me his approval. He wasn't going to force me to go out and find a job as a street sweeper. For a brief moment, I felt happy and confident—but Dominic swept those feelings aside with his next topic.

"You know you need to go down to the police station and register as a sex offender."

He handed me a list of all the places I could not go and a list of all the times I would have to re-register with the police. Any time I moved, every year on my birthday, any time I changed jobs. Without hesitation he added, "You also need to start sex offender treatment."

I wanted to shout at him. *I am not a sex offender! Have you even read my file? I have never touched a child inappropriately, I am not a monster!* But I couldn't find my voice.

"Let's meet next Monday around two o'clock," he added before releasing me from his office.

To get it over with, I went straight to the police station to register as a sex offender. I walked into the lobby, where three other people sat on plastic chairs waiting their turns. Two police officers sat at a counter behind the glass wall with only a small speak hole. I knew I would have to announce that I was there to register as a sex offender, and I didn't want the strangers in the room to hear me. I sat down on one of the chairs and waited for the lobby to be empty of people; but as soon as one person would leave, two more would arrive.

Hours went by. Occasionally I cried. One of the police officers had noticed that I had been sitting in the lobby for a long time and shouted through the glass, "Can I help you? Are you waiting for someone?"

With a tear-stained face and eyes still full of tears, I slowly walked up to the glass and whispered into the hole.

"I'm here to register as a sex offender."

He looked at me, irritated, and spoke loudly through the hole.

"What did you say?"

I looked behind me; the other people in the waiting area were all staring at me. I was mortified. I would rather die than be seen as a sex offender.

"I'm sorry, never mind," I said to the man behind the speak hole. I turned and left the police station, walking as fast as I could without actually running.

On August 24, I had been out of prison and recreating my life for one full week. On my second attempt, I had managed to register as a sex offender without bolting out of the police station; and I had completed all the steps to sign up for college, which started on September 25. With that step in the right direction, I had also given myself permission to dream, and with that dream I was filled with hope. Although I was still scared, I continued to put one foot in front of the other, doing all of the things I was required to do.

Before school started I was accepted into Multnomah County Women's Transitional Housing Unit, a halfway house that served women who were either in the process of trying to get their kids back or keeping their kids while on parole or probation. Although my kids had been officially taken away from me, the case was still open, so I qualified to live at the halfway house. The counselors there were very compassionate and understanding of my situation. They had a lot of influence on the children's court judges, and they gave me a slight hope that I could get my kids back if I did really well in the program. They were also supportive of my going to college.

Even though I had just registered the month before, I had to again visit the police station when I changed my address. I knew I needed someone to help me navigate through the humiliating process, and I turned to Officer Greg Davis. Although he had been hard on me at my arrest interrogation, we had recently had an opportunity to establish a better relationship; and I knew he was now committed to my success.

While I was in prison, Latasha had informed me that during the raid, the police had taken all of our photo albums, pictures and baby books, and other memorabilia. I gathered up enough nerve to write a letter to Officer Davis to ask him if I could retrieve our personal belongings when I got out of prison. In the letter, I explained that the items had sentimental value. I had also explained my behavior the day of my arrest.

"Just so you know, for future reference, the reason I did not talk to you during the interview was because I was not allowed to talk to men unless they were tricks. If a female police officer had talked to me instead, I probably would have told her everything."

A few weeks later I had received a letter from Greg Davis. He said that when I got out of prison, he would be happy to release baby pictures and any photos that did not have anything to do directly with the crime. He would not be able to give me pictures that included the underage girls. He also added in the letter that he wished he had known the reason I had not talked to him. He acknowledged that the police did not have a good understanding about "that life" and that it would benefit the police greatly if I would be willing to speak with him openly, with a female police officer present and with the guarantee that there would be no additional charges.

A couple weeks after I had been released, I had been very anxious to get my personal photos back. I contacted Officer Davis, and he arranged for us to talk with a female police officer, Officer Heart. The interview lasted four hours. They asked lots of questions and I told them everything. They were stunned. They admitted that they had no idea of what was happening behind the scenes. They recorded the entire interview, which they planned to use to train police officers on the reality of human trafficking.

So I was confident Officer Davis would be willing to help me get through the second registration. When I called him he offered to meet me at the station and stay with me through the entire process. It was so much easier with him at my side. The following February he again accompanied me through my birthday registration. He was very considerate of my feelings; whenever we met to talk, he always included Officer Heart so I would feel comfortable.

The day I moved from the YWCA to the Multnomah County Women's Transitional Housing Unit was also my first day of college. I selected four classes, spread throughout the day from seven-thirty in the morning to three in the afternoon: Basic Math, remedial English Composition, Basic Computer Skills, and a "how to go to college" class. I scheduled the classes with breaks between each one so that I could work on the homework between classes while the information was still fresh in my head.

The breaks also allowed me time to wander invisibly through the campus. I loved being there. I watched the students of different ages and races walking across the campus or sitting and doing their homework. *Do they have secrets like mine? Do they feel like they don't belong here?*

Twice a week I rushed downtown for my meeting with Dominic. It was becoming increasingly comfortable for me to talk with him, although I still wouldn't look at him. I would wait in the lobby until the door opened and he called my name. Staring at his shoes, I would follow them to his office where I would take my seat and we would talk. He would ask me questions about my day and how I was doing. He seemed genuinely interested in me as a human being, not as a prostitute or a parolee. He would ask about how I was feeling, about the struggles I was facing. He would offer me advice—not in a demanding way, but in a way that suggested it was okay for me to make my own decisions. As positive as Dominic was, though, we couldn't avoid the unpleasant topics, the ones relating to my parole and probation.

"Wendy, as part of being a sex offender, you are required to take a full disclosure polygraph test."

"What's that?"

After a short pause he replied, "We'll talk about that later, don't worry about it for now. You just keep doing what you're doing and if you ever need me, Wendy... You can call me, we can talk. I'm here to help you."

College was proving to be a struggle. A month into my classes, I sat in my English Composition class where most of my classmates were teenagers, fresh out of high school. The students were taking turns reading their stories to the class when, suddenly, I felt like crying. I didn't know why. I tried to fight the tears that welled up in my eyes, but before I knew it, the tears were flowing down my face. All I could do was run out of the classroom, hoping no one would notice. I found a place in the hallway where I could somewhat hide. I was scared because I didn't know why I was so overwhelmed or why the tears kept streaming down my face.

What if I never stop crying? What should I do? Who could I call? I miss my friends so much. I want to talk to Miranda or Mona or Veronica, or Belle. Any of them would surely understand. They would comfort me. Greg was right. Maybe it's his demon powers that are provoking me to cry uncontrollably.

I remembered Dominic's words. "If you ever need to talk, if you ever feel you are in trouble, you can call me and I will help you." I walked down the halls to the pay phone, hoping he would be in his office. By the time he answered, I could only gasp for air through my sobs. I tried to spit out the word "Dominic" but it only came out in syllables between the gasps of breath.

"Wendy, is that you?"

"Yeah," I whimpered.

"Where are you?" His voice was full of kindness and concern.

"At the college."

"Can you come into the office?"

"Yes."

"I'll see you in a little bit."

I caught the next bus back into the city. I had no idea what I was going to say to Dominic. I felt so stupid for crying. I pulled myself together some on the bus, but still the teardrops freely flowed down my face. I waited in the lobby for Dominic's shoes to appear in the doorway and for him to say my name. He guided me into his office.

I told him I didn't know why I was crying and that I was really overwhelmed but I didn't know why either. He asked how school was going and I told him all about the classes I was taking and the time I spent at the campus doing my homework and watching the other people. I confided in him my fears that I would fail my classes because there were so many big words that I didn't understand, but I also showed him the paper that had earned me an A.

Dominic was pleased. It felt so good for someone to be proud of me, not for how much money I made on tricks, but for doing something good. This guy was different, and the way he made me feel about myself was different. I wanted to see what he looked like; I wanted to see this person who could make me feel good about myself. I started to raise my eyes, but the fear of looking at a man other than Greg froze my head in place.

Over the next few months, I visited Dominic more often. I really liked him a lot. He wasn't like the other men who had been in my life. Each time I saw him, I revealed more about my fears and frustrations. He would always help me get over the obstacles that I would encounter, even helping me with some of my school work. I was also perplexed by Dominic, mainly because he *did* believe in me. I didn't understand, I couldn't understand why anyone would believe in me when over and over again in my life I had proven I am not worthy of another's confidence. I could also tell that Dominic wasn't stupid, and that confused me even more—because only a really stupid person would ever believe in me.

Finally, after three months, the urge to see what he looked like overcame me. He was so kind and his voice was always so soft, I needed to know what this man looked like. I was familiar with every pair of shoes he wore and what he looked like from behind, but I had never looked him in the eyes. I sat in the chair looking down at the floor trying to get up the nerve to look at his face. We kept talking as we always did, about life and how I was doing.

I first looked at something behind him so I could see him in my blurred peripheral vision. My spirit's blurred vision saw Greg, standing over me with the forty-ounce Olde English bottle, but hope continued to stave off the fear. I needed to look at Dominic, this wonderful, kind man who didn't abuse me and genuinely cared about me as a human being. He saw me for the person I was, not the crime I did or the money I made. He accepted me with all my faults and insecurities and fears and encouraged me to be the best I could be. I no longer cared that Greg was going to beat me. To see Dominic would be worth the beating. I turned my face directly toward his.

It is very hard to explain what I saw when I looked at Dominic. What I saw was not a man in human form, but a soul, the most beautiful soul that shined with radiant, soft colors.

With Dominic's guidance and support, I continued to make steps in the right direction. Soon I was allowed to see my children. I would visit them in Seattle at Juanita's house as often as I could, and occasionally my mother would come up from California and bring them to see me. The short visits filled my heart with joy, but they were also bittersweet. I could see that my kids had created lives of their own. I had been out of their lives for so long that it seemed I wasn't even a part of them anymore. We did have fun when we were together, going to the zoo and doing other activities—just as I dreamed we would when I was in prison.

I also continued to go to college, with success that I could never have imagined when I was in prison: I qualified for the honor roll and president's list three times, and a paper I wrote earned me a fifteen hundred-dollar scholarship. I also continued to develop my musical abilities after I discovered the practice pianos in the basement of the college music hall. I would spend hours and hours in the piano room, and I even spent some of my meager income on sheet music. Playing the piano again, I could escape deep into a world of safety and comfort as my emotions floated on the notes of the beautiful music.

The Women's Transitional Housing program and its counselors gave me lots of support and guidance. The counselors would help me with my homework when needed and teach me day-to-day living skills. Because of my stealing before I went to prison, I had been permanently banned from shopping at Fred Meyer. The counselors encouraged me to write a letter to the department store to request that they waive the ban in consideration of the changes I had made in my life, and they all wrote letters on my behalf to support my claims. One day, I received a letter from Fred Meyer; they told me how proud they were of me and they welcomed me back as a customer. That was a major accomplishment in my life—it made me feel so good about myself. It may seem like a small thing to most people, but it was *huge* for me.

Still, I struggled with my emotional progress. Many factors can cause a person to stop growing emotionally: childhood abuse, a struggle to survive financially, addiction. I had struggled with low self-esteem all of my life, feeling friendless and bullied as a child, succumbing to the first guy who seemed to like me, selling my body to feed my child and to please my man, and having no sense of who I was without Greg. Although I was now building a life I could call my own, and was even spreading my wings intellectually, I felt emotionally stunted. At thirty-one years old, my self-confidence and sense of worth was stuck at seventeen.

Other people could see that, too—but I resisted their attempts to help me. When my correctional counselor gave me a special assignment, I balked, believing it to be ridiculous and pointless.

"Wendy, you need to start self-affirmations."

She handed me a box of cards with sayings on them: I am special. I love myself. I am unique. I have a purpose. I hated this assignment because it required me to violate the one characteristic that I had established for myself—honesty. As far as I was concerned, my assignment was to lie to myself, and I hated to lie.

Each day, I sat in my room with the affirmation cards and read them out loud, as I had been told to do.

"I am special."

"I am unique."

"I am worthy of love."

"I am loveable." That one made me laugh out loud.

"I can do anything I put my mind to."

I did the assignment daily as required, but I didn't see any change in my life or my attitude. After a few weeks, I put the cards in my drawer, rarely taking them out.

Another challenge to my emotional growth was that I could not trust my judgment about other people. In the sex offender treatment sessions, I sat with women who, I thought, were truly nice people—until I discovered that they had done horrible things to children. I couldn't reconcile the things I heard, my conviction that child molesters were monsters, and my initial impression that these were nice women.

Even though I could not yet trust my own judgment, I had learned to trust the judgment of my correctional counselors. I did nothing without first running the idea by them to make sure I was doing the right thing. Over time, they started putting the decisions back on me. "Do you think it's the right thing?" After I answered their questions and explained my point of view, they would either send me on my way, or ask me to think harder about it—thus giving me the tools to start trusting my own judgment.

I also struggled with my self-identity. What role did I play in my own life, much less in society? It seemed no matter how hard I tried to fit in, I just didn't. For example, while I was in prison, I couldn't wait for the day I could start going to a real church—but when I did, I was completely out of place, the odd duckling. I didn't know how to speak to other people, so I would keep my eyes to the ground. The only thing

I could see was a large red neon arrow pointing down at me in the middle of the sanctuary. Every Sunday the arrow was there, pointing at me, the sinner, the sex offender, the person who didn't belong there. Even though I knew the arrow wasn't real, I blamed it for my misery. Because of the arrow, no one would ever like me or talk to me. I found no comfort at church, and I would run out as soon as the service ended, wishing I had never gone.

The weekends seemed the hardest for me, so I joined Habitat for Humanity to keep myself busy on Saturdays. People would come in groups to help build a home while I would arrive all alone. Even there, where we had a common cause, I couldn't connect with the other people.

On Sundays, I was usually alone in the house. I'd spend the day cleaning my room and mulling over my future. *Will I ever have a purpose? What am I supposed to be doing?* My father had given me a journal, and I thought writing might help me sort out my life.

Saturday I stayed home instead of going to Habitat for Humanity. My room has been a wreck for quite some time, kind of like my life. When I clean up my room it symbolizes me cleaning up my life. Well, so I try and think. I went through my drawers looking at all the useless items it was full of. I found coins from Alcoholics Anonymous, symbolizing my dates of sobriety. Why do I need these? I threw them away with the belief and hope that I would be throwing away the fact that I was an alcoholic. The same process happened with my Narcotics Anonymous key chain tags, I threw them in the garbage saying good-bye to the fact that I was a drug addict, or am I still? Digging deeper into the drawer and into my life, I found papers from prison. Papers that I no longer needed or wanted to remember. Into the trash they went, as I felt the satisfaction that I was erasing that from my life. The garbage bags got fuller and so did the idea in my head that I was taking action to change my past into something it wasn't. Then came the court papers that I was instructed to hold onto forever. Court papers regarding my children and the fact that I was losing my identity as a mother. As the tears started collecting in the corner of my eyes, I put the papers in the trash along with the fact that I would never be a mother to my children again. I sat and cried, totally overwhelmed with the way my life had turned out. If only I had made different choices, how would my life be different? I took a four-hour nap that afternoon, where in my dreams I was able to see Greg and the other girls. We did our drugs and sucked Greg's dick, just like it used to be. It actually felt good to be somewhere familiar. I knew Greg was getting ready to start trippin', I knew what I was going to have to go through. Though my future was bleak, it was okay because I was prepared for what was to come. My hopes did not rise above the outcome of what was to happen. There were no dreams in my heart. When there are no dreams, there are no disappointments. Sometimes disappointments hurt more than being pushed down a flight of stairs. Unfulfilled dreams can tear through your heart stronger than Greg's words and anger. As I woke up the next day I was filled with sadness as I looked around and saw that I had not changed my past. The fallout of that destructive life was still scattered around me. I could feel the aftershocks of the devastating earthquake I had created with the choices I had made. Forever I will feel the aftershocks, forever I will see the fallout. I cannot run or hide from me. I don't know how to

live with me. I don't know how to live with my past.
I don't know how to live without Greg.

I only made that one entry in the journal. Would I ever be able to see a way to make a life for myself without Greg?

Chapter 29
Losing Dominic

Hard is trying to rebuild yourself, piece by piece, with no instruction book, and no clue as to where all the important bits are supposed to go.
− *Nick Hornby,* A Long Way Down

ALTHOUGH I WAS STILL ALLOWED to see my children, the children's court had determined I would never get them back, and my case was officially closed. I stayed at the Women's Transitional Housing Unit for another year and a half, taking college classes and fulfilling my many parole requirements. When things got tough and I could see that I was close to giving up, I would grasp onto the belief that Dominic had in me and I would use that as my strength to continue to move forward in my life.

I moved into a small studio apartment in a low-income apartment complex across the street from the college. Although I was scared the first night I stayed there, I learned to love it. I steered away from men as much as I could. I didn't want anything to do with them and was mostly uncomfortable and scared of them. My mind was set that all men were either pimps, tricks, or gay, and that the only good man is a gay man—but every now and then I did have an encounter with a man who didn't fit into any of my categories. One was a neighbor who would say hello from time to time. When he did, I didn't feel threatened—his voice was soft and he was so overweight that I figured I could easily outrun him if he did try to attack me.

Our occasional hello's in passing were comfortable, and I was willing to accept when after a time he invited me to his place for dinner. He was an excellent cook and it didn't take long for me to ask him if I could come over for dinner again. He was sweet and kind and I grew to feel safe with him. He accepted me for the messed up person I was and I loved him for that. Occasionally, I would spend the night with him, and, without any sex, we could cuddle with each other. Mark was my warm-blooded teddy bear and the first man, outside of the correctional department, to make me wonder if there just might be another type of man besides pimp, trick, or gay. Although it perplexed me, I was not yet ready to dig deeper to understand it.

Another man I met and befriended in the apartment building was Damen, a guy who was visibly gay, meaning to me he was safe. Our relationship was unusual—especially since I had developed a crush on him, ignited by his being gay and therefore unavailable—but it was fun and safe. There were a lot of single men in the building who would flirt with me and it was difficult for me to turn them down, so Damen volunteered to become my "boyfriend," telling everyone that I had turned him straight. Only Mark knew the truth.

Damen and I grew to love each other very much. We decided to move in together, still paying the affordable rent on both of our apartments so we could move from one to the other whenever we felt like it. We acted just like a married couple except for the sex: We slept in the same bed, argued, went everywhere together, co-mingled our finances. We would talk for hours about my life. He would encourage me whenever I was down, and I would do the same for him. Damen would accompany me on my humiliating birthday treks to the police department. As I shouted "I'm here to register as a sex offender" into the little hole in the glass, he would stand by me, his eyes shooting knives at anyone who glared in my direction. With the support of Damen, Dominic, and my correctional counselors, I began to feel I could get over all the rough patches.

Then a piece of the sky fell: Dominic was transferred from the unit that supervised me. I was devastated that he would no longer be my parole officer. In his gentle voice he reassured me that my new parole officer was going to be a woman. He told me her name and informed me that she was a very kind woman who would surely understand my situation. He was so certain, I was almost convinced; but when I arrived for my appointment to meet my new parole officer, I was not surprised to discover that Dominic was mistaken. I had again been assigned to a male parole officer.

The woman behind the glass at the County Corrections Office was not sympathetic. She was uninterested in my concerns and not willing to listen to the information Dominic had given me. Her personality was as parched as her words.

"Your parole officer's name is Russell Brown. Go up to the second floor and wait for him to call you."

I was familiar with this process—I had done it a thousand times before. As unhappy as I was, I knew what to do; but my confidence faltered when a black man called my name and introduced himself as Russell Brown. Even with my hesitation, I knew there was nothing I could do to change this, and I looked at the situation as a learning opportunity. *I can't keep basing my attitudes and beliefs about black men solely on Greg. I have to be opened-minded and calm about this situation.*

My composure was short-lived. It became clear as we talked that Russell Brown was all business, focused solely on the rules that controlled me—the rules that Dominic had appropriately and compassionately bent. His voice was deep, filled with authority.

"You are not allowed to be in contact with any minor child."

"I'm allowed to see my children. It has been determined that I am not a threat to minors, and I have been freely seeing my children for the past year."

He was not interested in the special circumstances surrounding my situation.

"Promoting prostitution is a sex crime. You are a registered sex offender. As a sex offender you are not allowed to be close to any minor."

He then asked me, "What are you doing for work?"

Hoping that he would see that I was doing well in my life, I proudly responded, "I go to college. I've been taking college classes since I first got out of prison. I'm now in my second year."

His face filled with concern. "Are there any minors in your classes?"

"It's college. People are adults there."

"Not necessarily. Some high school students take college classes and many people graduate from high school early and go straight into college when they are seventeen."

I stared at this man as if he were crazy. *He can't be saying that I won't be able to go to college!*

"Are you saying I can't go to college because I am a sex offender?"

He didn't even acknowledge my fear and confusion.

"I'm saying that if there are any minors, anyone under eighteen years of age in any of your classes, you are in violation of your parole and probation and you may go back to prison."

I'm sure the look on my face was very similar to the one I had the day I met the man with the cucumber fantasy. I couldn't believe that I was working my butt off in school and doing the right thing to educate myself, that I was trying my hardest to be a good person—and succeeding in nearly everyone's opinion—and that now this man who was supposed to be committed to my success was telling me that I would have to drop out of school.

I then realized why so many people fail parole and probation; I understood why the recidivism rates were so high. Yesterday, my life was going well, I had total freedom to see my children as much as I wanted, I was supported in going to college, and everyone around me—including everyone I dealt with in the Department of Corrections—believed in me, was proud of me and liked me. Today, in the blink of an eye, in one conversation with one person, everything is turned upside down. I am not allowed to have any contact with my children and I have to drop out of school.

I tried one more time to convince this man that I wasn't what he thought I was—that I wasn't the crime listed on the piece of paper in front of him.

"Please, will you at least talk to Dominic? Will you talk to the police officer who arrested me? Will you talk to the Department of Corrections counselors who have seen and interacted with me every day for over the past year?" If he didn't believe me because of the name of the crime that defined me, maybe he would believe his professional colleagues.

"Sure, I'll talk to them, but they can't say anything to change my mind. I follow the rules very strictly."

The situation was crystal clear: Russell Brown was an autocrat. He had no intention of getting to know me or to support my efforts to succeed.

I walked out of the parole office with tears streaming down my face. I lingered at the Burnside Bridge, about a half mile away from the parole office and looked down into the dirty water that flowed below. *Will my life forever be defined by the name of my crime? Will I ever be able to do enough good things to make my past disappear?* For a moment, I thought how wonderful the water would feel if I were to jump in. I wondered if I would drown. *Maybe that would be the best solution.*

At home, Mark listened to my dilemma and wiped my tears. With his encouragement, I called all the people in the Department of Corrections who knew me well. I called the state social workers who had fully endorsed my visits with my kids, and I contacted the judge who had heard my case. They all talked to Russell and told him that I deserved special consideration, but he was true to his word: Nothing they said could change his mind. I was a sex offender. It didn't matter that I had passed a full-disclosure polygraph test that proved that I had never crossed any sexual lines with a minor. The name of my crime defined the outcome, not the circumstances that surrounded the crime or even the specifics of the crime itself. It was the name of the crime that now controlled my life.

Chapter 30
Tough Love

*We have to confront ourselves. Do we like
what we see in the mirror? And, according
to our light, according to our
understanding, according to our courage,
we will have to say yea or nay—and rise!*
—Maya Angelou

SINCE RUSSELL DIDN'T EXPLICITLY TELL ME I couldn't go
to college, I continued to attend my classes. I became
even more reclusive, keeping an eye out for other
students who looked like they might be under
eighteen. There were a few people who I thought were
questionable, so I steered far away from them. I
continued to put one foot in front of the other,
concentrating on doing the next right thing. I had lost
Dominic, but not all had been lost. Officer Davis was
still my ally, as were my correctional counselors; and
they supported me through all of this.

One day Greg Davis called me.

"Hey, Wendy! How are you doing?"

"Okay, I guess." He already knew my
circumstances, and I had no news to share.

"I want to know if you would consider speaking
to a small class of graduating police officers about
your story."

It struck me as an odd request, and at first I didn't know how to respond. He continued, "It's important that police officers understand the situation you found yourself in. If the new police officers hear your story, they will know how to approach other girls."

Once I understood what he was asking me to do, I felt honored and happy to share my story in the hopes that it would help other girls like me. So it was that a month later I found myself standing in front of eighteen graduating police officers. I told them how I had been affected by most police officers over the years, that the way they had treated me usually reinforced the message Greg had beaten into us. I also was sure to tell the story of the kind police officer—the man who had treated me as if I were a human being. I shared how I felt and emphasized that the world needed more police officers like him.

I had been very nervous before the talk, but the graduating officers were warm and encouraging. I was especially gratified to read some of their comments, summarized in a letter from the police captain:

City of Portland, Oregon Bureau of Police
June 25, 2003

Dear Ms. Barnes,

Thank you for your exceptional presentation to the Portland Police Advanced Academy class on June 13, 2003. A group of rookie police officers might be intimidating to some people, but you were able to relate to them within a matter of minutes. The officers were leaning forward in their seats, focused on you and hearing every word. The experiences which you shared with the class were intense and heartfelt and will not be forgotten when these officers are out on the street working.

All academy classes are evaluated and comments on your class included:

"Wendy's presentation was the most beneficial."

"The presentation by Wendy really gave some insight...."

"I would recommend having Wendy come speak at all classes."

We appreciate you donating your time to address the academy class and hope you will be willing to return to teach another class. We believe your class will have far-reaching benefits to the Police Bureau and the community.

Sincerely, Cliff Madison, Captain

After three months of weekly meetings with Russell, working harder to succeed than any other felon he had ever managed, he began to see why other people had encouraged him to see me as a special circumstance. He could see that I was determined to build my life into something good. He saw that I had a good heart with great intentions and that I had integrity and honesty.

"Wendy, I think it will be okay for you to see your kids. I've seen enough for me to know that you deserve it and you are not a threat to them."

I immediately made arrangements to go up to Seattle and see my children. Later that year, they visited me in my small studio apartment for Christmas. We had wonderful times together—but once again the joy was fleeting.

Three months later, Russell was transferred to another department. Once again, the new parole officer ripped me away from my kids. Not only did he prohibit me from seeing my children, I was not even able to talk to them.

This time, I took it much better, for I knew that once he got to know me, he would have a change of heart. I continued to do my best, and sure enough, within three months I was again allowed to see my children. I would take the bus to Seattle every six weeks or so, and they visited me on a few occasions during the two years I lived in the small studio apartment. I was thrilled, even though the visits were infrequent and painfully short.

Convincing the revolving door of parole officers that I was worthy wasn't my only challenge with the system. Changes in the state sex offender treatment program required that I be transferred to another program. Because I was the only woman in the new program, I was assigned to a female counselor who was in training. I explained my life story to her, the things Greg had done to control his girls and the torture we had experienced. I explained how I had come to believe that calling the police would further endanger the children he was victimizing.

When I finished telling her my story, she looked at me with disgust.

"You really like making excuses for your actions, don't you?"

I didn't quite understand what she was saying. I wasn't making excuses; I was telling her the facts. She continued to speak to me as if I were the worst person in the world.

"You're not here to make excuses for the things you did." Her eyes were stern and her voice felt like a rock hitting me.

"You're here to take ownership and responsibility for the crimes you committed. You are a sex offender and a felon because of your actions."

Again I was told that a condition of my treatment was that I would not be allowed to be around any minors. I began to explain to her the special circumstances around my case and that my parole officer had said it was okay for me to see my children.

She barked at me in mid-sentence. "You like to manipulate people, huh? Well, you cannot manipulate me like you have your parole officer. Do you understand that the only way you will ever get off parole is to complete sex offender treatment? A condition of your treatment is that you cannot have any contact with minors."

I tried to stay centered, but I could feel myself filling with hate—for the counselor and for myself. I walked home crying my eyes out. I felt like the worst person in the world. I felt like a pedophile who deserved to be punished. I repeated her words to myself, over and over. *Am I really a sex offender who would harm children?*

I called my parole officer and correctional counselors and asked if they would contact the treatment counselor on my behalf. I also called the state social workers and Greg Davis, hoping the more people who spoke to her, the more likely it would be that she would believe me.

The treatment center supervisor participated in my next meeting with the treatment counselor. Although my heart skipped a beat when I saw that the supervisor was a black man, I thought the phone calls from the other officials had convinced them of the truth and they were going to tell me that I could see my kids. The supervisor spoke first.

"What makes you think that you are special in any way? We are the experts in this field and we make the rules, *not you!*"

I started to get scared realizing I was in trouble because I had made him mad.

"Just because you can manipulate everyone else around you doesn't mean you can manipulate us. I have dealt with your kind too many times, offenders who think for some reason their case is different and they should be treated different."

It was painful seeing myself through his eyes. In my mind's eye, his resemblance to Greg grew as he spoke.

"We do not want any more phone calls about you or you seeing your children. If we receive one more phone call, we will consider it a violation of your treatment. My best advice to you, Wendy, is for you to get on board and engage in your treatment instead of trying to change it and fight it."

I had only been trying to help them to understand my story. I wasn't trying to fight them or make problems; but I could see my only hope was to, as the supervisor said, "engage" in treatment and conform to their view. Over time, I spent every session repeating the counselor's prompts.

"It's my fault those girls were turned out."

"Hundreds of children will forever be devastated because of my actions."

"I hurt many young children."

The counselor also challenged my inaction in every session.

"Why didn't you call the police? Why didn't you stop him?"

It didn't take long for me to learn that if I gave the real answer, I would be attacked.

"You are making excuses for your actions. Taking no action is an action. Not doing anything, sitting by and watching what was happening is a crime against humanity and a crime against those children."

The statements slowly integrated into my self-image. I came to believe they were true, and they became my mantra on my long walk home.

I know now that this may be a stretch for other people to understand, but please try. Walk with me as I share my thinking process with you.

I am a sex offender.

The world would be a better place if there were no sex offenders.

A good person tries to make the world a better place.

I would be a good person if I took sex offenders off the planet.

In order for me to be a good person, I have to kill myself.

I wanted to be a good person. I looked through the apartment for some way to accomplish being a good person, some way to rid the world of me, a sex offender. I didn't have any pills to swallow but I had a kitchen knife. Through tears I started cutting my wrists but soon realized the knife wasn't sharp enough even to cut the skin.

I went into the bathroom and found a disposable razor. I ripped it apart to get the razor blade and started cutting into my wrists, waiting for the blood to spill out, ending my life and making me a good person. I wasn't brave or strong enough to cut through the vein, but I discovered the feeling of relief that the deep bleeding wounds offered me. It was relief from the world I lived in, a secret that gave me power and self-punishment that I felt I deserved. Maybe the punishment would be sufficient to make me a good person.

I continued the sex offender treatment, allowing the people with power to turn me into the person they wanted me to be—just as I had allowed Greg to turn me into a sex offender. I also continued the secret cutting to relieve the torturous truth I was being forced to see every week during our session. The longer I went through the agony of taking full responsibility for not only myself but the horrors in the world around me, the more I believed what they told me. I integrated "no excuses, no reason" into my daily life. My intentions, my heart, my values didn't matter. The only thing that mattered was my actions, whether my actions were right or wrong as defined by my counselors.

The silver lining in the cloud was that the more responsibility I took for my actions and inactions, the more they would allow me to talk to my kids. After about six months, I was allowed to start seeing them again.

Chapter 31
Claiming Gregory

*Once you choose hope, anything is
possible. —Christopher Reeve*

I WAS IN MY FOURTH YEAR OF COLLEGE, still trying to earn my Associate of Arts degree. I had become comfortable in the learning environment and more open to interacting with other students. Occasionally, I would get to know one of them well enough that I would give her a small glimpse of my life, but I mostly kept it a secret.

In January I got a phone call from my son Gregory.

"Mommy, I can't live with Grandma anymore. I want to come live with you."

I tried to calm him down, telling him that he couldn't live with me because the court order stated that I could not ever again have custody of my children. The judge had made it very clear that she would never allow me to be in the parenting role to my children again. While I was talking to Gregory, my call waiting beeped. I switched to the second caller, Gregory's grandmother Juanita, who was angry and upset.

"Wendy, you have to take Gregory. I'm putting him on the bus right now. It's time that you take responsibility for him and take him."

Knowing she was too upset to listen to reason, I didn't bother to question her motives. I had permission for Gregory to come down for visits, so I chalked it up as a visit and told her to send him down.

It was so wonderful having Gregory back with me. The day after he arrived, I bought a real bed, not a mattress on the floor in the corner. To make sure there were no misunderstandings with the authorities, I called my parole officer and the state Children's Services to tell them what was happening.

Gregory was nine years old when I had been arrested. He was now fourteen years old but to me he was still nine. I babied him and treated him as if he were nine, and inadvertently, he acted as if he were nine at times. I loved having my son back and being a mother to him—the kind of mother he deserved to have. I knew I had worked hard over the past three and a half years since being released from prison. I had overcome numerous obstacles during that time, and I was ready to overcome the one created by the court's custody decision.

Although the court ordered that neither Greg nor I could ever appeal or open the case, the decision kept open the option for any of my kids to re-open the case. I made the decision that I was going to get custody of my son. I was going to work at this until it happened and not give up until he was mine. I explained to Gregory that if he wanted to live with me, he would have to write a letter to the judge requesting she re-open the case. We sat down together with pen and paper and wrote.

Dear Judge,
I want to live with my mom. I am requesting that you open this case back up so I can have a chance to live with my mom.
Gregory Hightower II

Soon, we had a date to stand before the same judge who had taken away my rights as a mother. The court date was a few months away, so I began getting letters from all my past parole officers, correctional counselors, teachers from school, and the police officers with whom I had developed supportive relationships over the years. I continued to go to school and I got Gregory started in school.

I knew I needed help being the best mom I could be, and Gregory did have behavior challenges that had precipitated Juanita's decision to send him to me. The ironic thing was that when I went to Children's Services to ask for help, they asked me if I beat him. When I told them I did not, they told me they could not help me. I spoke to many people about this, and my former correctional counselor suggested that I have my parole officer contact Children's Services to report concerns that a child was living with a sex offender. It was only then that Children's Services stepped in. As part of their investigation, they offered to provide counseling for Gregory and me.

Gregory and I were building our relationship. No longer was either of us the same person we had been before I went to prison. For one thing, I had recently realized the benefit of affirmations—an approach I had dismissed a few years earlier as dishonest. I had seen how Greg had brainwashed me, and I also began to understand how the sex offender counselors used language to integrate their thinking into me. I could see that I was becoming what they, and I, wanted me to be—a person who takes responsibility for her actions. I realized how easy it was to "become" what I was told to be. I wondered if I could brainwash myself with the self-affirmation cards. I once again took them out of the drawer and started reading them, and I again felt like I was lying to myself—but this time I changed what they said to statements that rang true for me.

"I want to be good."

"I am kind to others."

"I will love myself."

"I will allow others to love me."

"I care about others."

"I will care about myself."

"There is beauty within me."

There is love within me

I could believe these affirmations, and I had started repeating them to myself... continually. The more I said them, the more I believed them, and then I became them.

The state counseling was also helping Gregory and me grow into the people we wanted to be. I learned how to parent better, and Gregory learned how to follow the rules of the house, which we created together during one of the sessions. We were also building a home together. We only had to stay in the studio apartment for another month. The manager liked me and made an extra effort to arrange to move us into a one-bedroom apartment. I had made a decision to get custody of Gregory and knew I would do anything in my power to make it happen. I worked hard to stand up for what was right and to show Gregory how to do the same.

When the court date finally arrived, my assigned lawyer took me into a little room on the courthouse.

"Wendy, I have never had a client make my job so easy. You have impressed everyone in this case. There is not one person or agency that is not in favor of you getting Gregory back."

The state had completed its investigation and created a report on the findings, which raved about my going to school and accomplishing all of my parole and probation requirements. It described how

I had reached out to Children's Services for assistance with counseling for Gregory and me and when I didn't get it, I continued to fight until I found a way to get the services we needed.

I would soon be off of parole and probation and be free to leave the state. My plan was to move to California with my mother to start a new life. Now, I only had to convince the judge that the positive reports were deserved. Gregory and I walked into the courtroom with our attorneys. Following behind us were Officer Davis and Officer Heart. My current and past parole officers were also in the court room, along with my correctional counselors from the halfway house. My mom, who drove up to visit me at least once a year, planned one of her trips so she could also attend the court date with me.

They allowed Greg to attend by phone from prison. One by one, the judge asked each person his or her thoughts and reports on this matter. After all the officials had spoken, she addressed Gregory.

"Gregory, how are you doing living with your mom?"

Gregory sounded nervous but was confident about his answer.

"I'm doing good. I want to keep living with her."

She looked at me.

"Why should I give Gregory back to you?"

I summoned up all the courage I had; I was so scared to speak to this lady. I remembered how she spoke to me the last time I had stood in her courtroom wearing my blue jumpsuit, handcuffed and shackled. I remembered the things she said to me the last time and I was afraid she wouldn't see how I had changed.

"Your Honor, I have worked very hard to learn to live a healthy, productive life. I have done everything asked of me by Parole and Probation and then some. I see now how my actions, including not taking action, created devastating consequences for my children. I look very closely at the choices I make every day and I ask myself if I am headed in the right or the wrong direction. I take responsibility for my life and the consequences of my actions. I am not the same person I was before. I would love the opportunity to show my son the things I have learned over the past few years and for him to see who I am now."

At first she was quiet and gave me a look that made me feel very uncomfortable. I didn't get the feeling that she believed what I was saying. She then spoke into the air.

"Mr. Hightower, do you have anything to say about all of this?"

Could she, as I did, hear the evil in Greg's voice? His words came through the phone and filled the air with assurance, as if he were the one in control of the situation.

"I don't believe Wendy is in a position to take Gregory. Even though there are some problems with him living with my mother right now, I strongly feel he needs to go back, work the problems out, and live with her." His concern for Gregory seemed to grow as he continued to talk. "I have knowledge of Wendy still using drugs and being promiscuous with men. She would be a very bad influence on Gregory and she is not a good mother."

With every criticism he advanced about me, the judge's demeanor became more incredulous. When Greg declared, "I am not okay with Wendy having Gregory," I could almost see the decision on her face. I honestly believe that Greg's demand was the straw that broke the camel's back, the ultimate deciding factor for the judge. He had essentially threatened the judge, and in return I was granted sole parental rights to Gregory.

That court case happened on June 8. Less than two weeks later, on June 20, Gregory and I were on the train to Southern California to live with my mother and my little brother and sister, whom I barely knew. This was a chance at a new life, without parole and probation, with no more sex offender classes. This was my chance to be close to my mom, sister, and brothers—something Greg would never allow when I was with him. A chance at a new life where I didn't know anyone and nobody would know my past. For the first time in my life, I could truly put my past in the past.

Chapter 32
Seven Years

I'd like to hold my head up and be proud
of who I am
But they won't let my secret go untold
I paid the debt I owed them, but they're
still not satisfied
Now I'm a branded man out in the cold.
—Merle Haggard, "Branded Man"

The more I learned to love who I was, the
more I could see and feel the love that
others had for me.—Wendy Barnes

GREGORY AND I MOVED into my mother's small two-bedroom apartment in Orange County. My first task was to find the local police station because I was required to register as a sex offender within forty-eight hours of moving from Portland. I was scared to again be judged by the police, who would fingerprint me and take my picture for the sex offender registry. I wanted to start a new life; how could I start a new life when this status followed me wherever I went? My mother, full of support and love, offered to drive me to the police station, but I decided to go alone. I wanted her to think that I was strong, and I knew I would cry before entering the police station. I didn't put on any makeup knowing the tears would wash it all away.

When I got to the police station, I sat in the car and cried, just as I had expected I would. I cried for the life that I wanted to live. I cried because I missed the other girls and I wished they were there with me. Surely, if they were with me, they would comfort me and then joke around with me and make me laugh. I was alone. Nobody was there who could possibly understand what I was going through.

After twenty minutes of sitting in the car, using up all my tissues to wipe my tears, I got out of the car and walked into the police station. It had a small open area with a desk on one end of the room and chairs lined up in rows, all facing the desk. Several people were waiting in the chairs; some of them looked like ex-cons, and others looked like regular people. Two police officers sat at the desk.

I walked up to the police officers and as softly as I could, I said, "I'm here to register as a sex offender."

They both looked up at me. I wanted to tell them everything so they would know. I wanted to tell them that I wasn't a real sex offender—but that wasn't appropriate and they probably wouldn't believe me anyway. Why should they believe me?

One of the police officers asked, "Do you have your paperwork?"

Oh, no, they didn't give me any paperwork. What am I going to do now? Will they not let me live in California if I don't have my paperwork?

"They didn't give me any paperwork. They just told me that I needed to register at my local police station within forty-eight hours."

He looked angry that I didn't have any paperwork and told me to have a seat. I found a seat away from anyone else. I looked around at the other people to see if they had heard the conversation, to see if they knew that I was a sex offender. I could feel my face was still red and tear-stained from the twenty minutes of crying. I sat quietly and waited to be called.

Another twenty minutes went by and a female police officer came out of a door and called my name. She told me that they need to fingerprint me and take my picture. This was not a surprise to me—that's what had happened every year. After the fingerprinting she had me stand in front of a wall where she snapped my picture. I did not smile. I never did. The pictures would only be used by the police to identify me if I was suspected of a crime. I knew that I would never be wanted by the police again, so there would never be a need for anyone to look at the ugly picture of me.

I got on welfare while I looked for work. Having a little money coming in was encouraging, but I was nervous about The Question I knew awaited me on job applications. I thought about how I would explain my criminal record—if I ever even got a chance for an interview. At least now I had four years of college and an Associate of Arts degree to show for myself. After posting my resume on-line and applying for a few jobs as a data entry clerk, I received a call from a temp agency to come in for an interview.

I walked into the office, obtained the application and quickly looked for the dreaded question. I hadn't practiced what I would say, but I knew I wasn't going to lie. Searching the application I didn't see any question regarding past crimes or criminal records. I made it through the interview with no mention of the feared and dreaded question. I was hired as a temp-to-hire at an aerospace company only three miles from where I lived. I enjoyed my job even though it was very low pay. I kept to myself most of the time, concentrating on doing a good job in the hopes they would offer me a permanent position.

One co-worker, Linda, took a particular interest in me and invited me to lunch. Not knowing what types of questions she would ask or how to communicate with a human being in a normal workplace, I stuck to the topic of my recent four years of college after being a "stay-at-home mother." Except for my family and the police, nobody in California knew about my past, and I planned on keeping it that way.

I enjoyed being a parent to Gregory and showing him how much I loved him. Before I was arrested, I didn't know what love was, and I didn't know how to be a parent, even though I did try. I had been a pathetic excuse for a parent—and now I had the opportunity to make up for lost time. Parenting Gregory was a struggle, but I didn't think he was any more difficult than any other teenager. He attended an alternative high school because he wasn't able to adapt to regular high school. He felt out of place in Orange County, and I completely understood his frustrations. Considering how things could have turned out for Gregory given his childhood, I thought he was doing pretty well.

Even while I was in prison, my older brother, Steve, had not trusted me to break off with Greg. Steve had been faithful to his resolve not to be part of my life while I was in that destructive relationship. Other than a few times at family Christmas gatherings and couple of times when I was briefly living with Greg's mother in California—for example, when Steve drove Latasha and me to visit my mother and meet her new baby—Steve and I had had very little contact for several years. When we had seen each other, he always encouraged me to leave Greg and always made sure that I knew he loved me. Through our mother, he had continued to keep tabs on me through the years.

During that time, Steve had gotten married; but the relationship did not last, and he ended up moving in with our mom after his divorce. I was also living with my mom at the time. Although the house was crowded, it was nice that Steve and I were now able to build our relationship. He knew all the things I had accomplished after I got out of prison. I looked up to my brother for the choice that he made to distance himself from my life with Greg. I understood his decision and loved him for it. Living together at our mom's gave us time to talk and play and become brother and sister—not like when we were little kids, but the brother–sister relationship I had always wanted. Still, Steve now lived by very high ethical standards; he had set a high bar for me, and I knew I still had much to accomplish to succeed in his eyes.

In March 2005, my life was stable enough that Juanita allowed Mikey to come down for a visit. Because Mikey was too young to travel alone, my mom agreed to pay for his Uncle Jerome to accompany him on the trip. Soon, Mikey and Jerome arrived from Seattle. Latasha, who by this time was living in Texas, drove to California for the visit. For the first time, I was with all three of my children and we were free to bond with each other.

Mikey was six years old and I did not feel like a mother to him. He called Juanita "Mom" and called me "Wendy." I understood the emotional bond he had with Juanita and I respected that. I was comfortable to be an auntie-type figure in his life. My mother's presence and support made it possible for us to enjoy our time together. Although Mikey and I did not yet feel comfortable with each other, my mom did have a good relationship with him. She was an excellent grandma to all three of my children, and she had made many trips up to Seattle especially to develop a relationship with Mikey. My mom also made sure we had lots of videos and pictures of our time together. She played an important role in keeping us all connected.

The mother–child bond I had with Gregory and Latasha was strong and stable. Seeing us together, Mikey knew that I was, at the least, a good person. After the week-long visit, when it was time for him to leave, Mikey told me that he thought I was a fun person and that he liked me. I couldn't wait for the next time we would see each other, and I immediately started planning our next visit together.

Linda continued to invite me out to lunch and over to her house for small events with her Buddhist group. I enjoyed being with her but felt like I was living a lie. One day as she was asking me questions about myself, I hesitated.

"Linda, there's something I need to tell you about me."

Seeing the concerned look on my face and, trying to make me feel better, she joked, "What? Have you been to prison for murder?"

"Well," I confided, "it wasn't for murder."

At first she looked stunned, but then her look softened into curiosity.

"What happened?"

After hearing my story, she was very understanding and compassionate about my situation. I discovered that my secret actually brought us closer together, and it felt so good to be free to be myself with her. I even told her about the sex offender status. She was appalled.

"You have to do something about that. You need to write letters to the governors and congressman. If you tell them the situation, I'm sure they will fix it."

With her help, I wrote letters to many congressional representatives and other government officials, but I did not receive even one response.

I had been working at the aerospace company job for almost a year when Linda encouraged me to find a job that paid more money. She would frequently tell me, "Wendy, you are too bright and too great of a worker to be working for such low pay." Still, the fear of someone finding out I was a felon and asking questions about my life consumed me. Finally, I took her advice and again posted my short resume on-line. I applied for several listed jobs and received five interviews, which I carefully scheduled for the same day so I wouldn't have to take too much time off work.

One lady called me the day before the interview and asked me if I was available for a phone interview. After talking for twenty minutes she said, "Go ahead and come in tomorrow for the interview, but don't worry, I like what I've heard and you basically have the job." The woman sounded excited, but the thought crossed my mind that my criminal record might prevent her from hiring me.

I knew that the person conducting the interview usually could not waive a company policy against hiring felons. I gathered up all my nerve.

"I need to ask you a question, though, and I'm not sure how you are going to take it because I have never done this before. I'm kind of testing this out on you to see how you react.... What is your company policy on hiring a person convicted of a felony?"

I held my breath while I waited for her response. I didn't know how she was going to react to this question, and I was scared that it would not be good.

I could tell by her voice that she was somewhat thrown off by my question.

"I don't know, I've never been asked that question before." I also heard in her voice that she wasn't upset or mad. "Well, let me look through my handbook here. Oh, here it is. There is a list of crimes that we would not be able to hire you for. What was your crime?"

Feeling ashamed and embarrassed, I answered, "Promoting prostitution."

"Wow, there are four pages here.... I'm not seeing anything so far....Oh, some of these are just stupid. I didn't even know this one was a crime!" I could hear that she was smiling. I continued to be quiet, and I felt on pins and needles as she continued down the list, from time to time reading the names of crimes.

"Okay, I'm on the last page and I haven't seen it yet, I think we're good. I really want to hire you. I hope it's not on here." After finishing the list, she said, "That crime is not on my list. I'm so happy.... Oh, wait. Was it a felony?"

"Yeah."

"At the very bottom of the list it says 'No Felony Convictions.' I am so sorry, Wendy. You would have been great for this position."

"May I ask you what you thought when I asked you that question?"

"I actually had a lot of respect for you coming out and asking. It shows me that you're honest and you don't want to waste our time."

We talked a little more, and she told me that it was her understanding that after seven years crimes no longer show up on your criminal record. She encouraged me to try again someday.

"Once your seven years are up, please apply again. I would love for you to work here."

After thinking more about the conversation, I decided to approach all my interviews in the same way. One by one I called the people with whom I had scheduled interviews the following day. When each person answered the phone, I simply said, "Hi, this is Wendy Barnes. I have scheduled an interview with you tomorrow. I don't want to waste your time or mine, so I need to ask you a question. What is your company policy on hiring a person convicted of a felony?"

Every person expressed appreciation for my not wanting to waste her time, but the appreciation did not change the fact that of the five interviews I had scheduled, four of them would not be able to hire me with a criminal record. The last place I called was open to the possibility.

"It would depend on the crime and the situation. Please come in for your interview tomorrow."

I went to the interview and told the story of my life to the Human Resources manager, Janet—this complete stranger who had the power to either offer me a job with higher pay or turn me down for the past I had lived. I was in luck; she offered me a position as a data entry clerk making three dollars an hour more than the aerospace company job. I accepted on the spot.

Again, it was a slow integration into a new world. This time I had Janet's support; she knew my situation and was willing and happy to help me any way she could. Because my past wasn't a secret from the boss, I was free to tell my co-workers if and when I was ready.

One day I heard on the news that the public could now search the sex offender website. I typed my name into the site, and staring me in the face was my grim, ugly picture. I was horrified, not only because I was in a sex offender database now viewable by the public, but also because of the way I looked.

My first thought was to run. I needed to move out of California because anyone with a computer could find out that I was a sex offender. The site did not explain the circumstances; in fact, it did not even state the crime—only my name, address, and my ugly picture. The next day at work I went to Janet and in despair told her I was going to have to quit my job. By this time I had worked at the company for six months. I was happy there; I loved my job and enjoyed my co-workers.

Janet kept asking me what was wrong. Through my tears, all I could tell her was that I had to move, that I couldn't live in California anymore. With patience and understanding, she gently drew out my real concern. I had told her about my crime, but I had never revealed to her that I was a registered sex offender. When I told her about the website, I expected her to be disgusted. Instead, she responded with kindness.

"Wendy, wherever you go this is going to follow you. Right now is your opportunity to stand your ground. You have a stable job with many co-workers who love you and care about you. Your job is secure; this is not going to affect your job. With our support, we can fight this. I think we should go through the steps of getting you off that list."

She looked on the internet to see my picture.

"Wendy, you look horrible. Next time, you should smile for the picture."

Her encouragement was contagious, and I vowed that in my next picture, I would have pretty makeup and a smile on my face.

My brother, who by this time had moved into his own place, heard about the posting on the website and called me to comfort me.

"Wendy, I am so sorry this is happening to you."

By this time, I had calmed down enough to realize that the situation was a consequence of the choices I had made.

"It's okay, Steve. You know... if I hadn't made the choices I made, this wouldn't be happening. It's a consequence that I need to learn how to face."

There was silence on the phone and I started to think that our connection had been broken.

"Wendy, I am so proud of you right now. You're taking responsibility for your actions and facing the consequences. That shows me how much you have grown and matured. I am so proud to have you as my sister." He then added, "Still, Wendy, you do not deserve to have your picture on the sex offender list, and I am sorry that you have to go through this."

I had so much respect for my brother and admired all the things he had done and how he had lived his life. I never thought in a million years that I could earn his pride in me. When I hung up the phone, I was for the first time confident that I was doing something right in my life. I knew I was on the right path and walking in the direction of a good, healthy, respectable life.

Fortified by Janet's encouragement, I again wrote letters to all the members of Congress for whom I could find addresses online. I also wrote to the judge and the attorney in my case. I contacted several more people than I had when Linda had helped me, including Arnold Schwarzenegger, who was then governor of California, and Oprah. This time, I did receive a few responses. One congressman wrote back and said he was sorry to hear of my situation but Congress had nothing to do with it and couldn't make any changes. Another official telephoned me to say he was going to use my story as an example of all the injustices happening with the sex offender status, but he also informed me that it would be years before the laws would change. He offered little hope that anyone could do anything that would free me from the sex offender status and prevent my picture being viewed on the website.

Even though I had little success with my letter-writing campaign, I felt buoyed by Janet's confidence in me and began to share my story with some of my co-workers. The work environment was very close-knit and almost everyone knew each other on a personal level. I didn't like feeling as if I were living a lie. My past was a part of who I was.

I still didn't feel that I fit into this world. I was uncomfortable, sometimes overwhelmed, every time I went anyplace new. Meeting new people was still unfamiliar and difficult for me—especially men, whom I was compelled to categorize into "pimp, trick, or gay." Although by this time I had met many good men who had helped me, in my core I believed that the only good man was a gay man. I didn't know how to be normal. Always an outsider, I sometimes felt like a foreigner in a strange land.

Gradually over time, I would reveal my secret and discover that I was still accepted and even loved, like I belonged. This was the case with my smoking buddies, the co-workers who gathered outside on breaks to smoke. Even though some of them were men, I would let my guard down and join in their conversation, talking about our lives.

One day, someone brought a Hacky Sack to work and started kicking it around on his break. I had never played this game before. It looked like fun but I was shy about participating. They continued to invite me to join their circle and wouldn't stop bugging me when I said no. Finally, I gave into the urge to allow myself to have some fun even though I would probably look like a fool. Over time, even the nonsmokers would come out to play Hacky Sack, and we would all go out on the weekends to play on our free time. Even though I wasn't all that good at the game, I was included in the circle. We all laughed, talked, and learned to trust each other. Unlike the neighborhood kids when I was a child, who made me feel odd and excluded, these guys showed me what friends are really like. The men in our Hacky Sack circle gave me further reason to believe that there are good men in the world, men who did not fit into the pimp, trick, or gay paradigm.

Within the next six months, I had shared my story with about half of the fifty people who worked in the office. Every time I revealed my secret, I was scared of the potential response, but my fears were unfounded in this group. Everyone I told was compassionate and appreciated that I had shared my life story with them. They told me that I offered hope that people really could change. They were much more understanding when I would run around the office buzzing like a bee with happiness, because they knew I was feeling free and appreciating every aspect of life.

Living with my mom was really wonderful. We were able to see each other in a different light. We weren't so much mother-daughter as we were two human beings walking the journey of life together. My childhood memories of her being a "bad mom" faded as I learned more about her and the situations she had faced. She had been through a lot in her life. *I* had put her through a lot, and she still loved me unconditionally. I could plainly see now that she loved me immensely. Why had I not been able to feel that love as a child?

Chapter 33
Jumping Hurdles

History, despite its wrenching pain,
cannot be unlived, but if faced with
courage, need not be lived again.
—Maya Angelou

THE SEVEN YEARS OF SHAME would soon be over, and my past no longer loomed as an insurmountable obstacle—but there were still a few tall hurdles blocking my way: I would to be on the sex offender list forever, I did not have my family together, it was still challenging for me to communicate with co-workers—especially the men—and in less than two years, Greg would be released from prison.

The most difficult obstacle to endure was the physical and emotional distance from my youngest child. Although Juanita would allow me to talk with Mikey occasionally, communication was sporadic. A court order gave me the right to see him in person twice a year, but visits had been completely blocked. It seemed that even in prison, Greg was calling the shots.

Even so, my self-confidence continued to grow, nurtured by the people who believed in me. When my birthday came around in February, with the annual journey to the police station for fingerprinting and my mug shot, I remembered Janet's advice. I put on my makeup, did my hair in a pretty up-do, and smiled broadly for the picture. If my picture had to be on the sex offender website, it would be happy and beautiful—just like the life I was creating for myself.

My supervisor, Jimmy, was a young man, twenty-two years old. During my first year of working at the company, I slowly told him about my life. He showed interest by asking sincere questions as I shared my story. When the "in crowd" at work went out after work to the bar, he invited me, and with his encouraging presence, I opened up to the others.

On August 3, 2006, I was at my desk, typing away doing my work when suddenly tears started falling freely down my face. I felt emotionally numb, and I didn't understand why I was crying. At that same moment, Jimmy came to invite me to go on a break and saw that I was crying. I looked up at him and put my finger over my mouth, signaling to him not to say anything and that I was okay.

After he left for his break, I was trying to pull myself together when a thought came to me: *I only have a year left to live.* The thought was at first inexplicable, but it was only a second later that I realized that Greg would be released in one year. I had been certain all this time that when Greg was released, he would find me and kill me. I had dreamed about leaving the country, but those thoughts were fleeting since I had no money. At the very least, I needed to have a restraining order against him before he got out of prison, but I had done nothing to prepare to protect myself and my family.

When Jimmy finished his break, he called me into his office. I shared my epiphany and he helped me come up with a plan to get a restraining order. He found the applicable websites and started me on the process. He was very encouraging and told me how much respect he had for me given all I had been through and how he admired my coming out the other side. He was gentle and kind—like Dominic, my first parole officer.

My son Gregory started struggling more in Orange County and he wanted to go live with his sister, Latasha, who by then had moved back to Seattle. I sent him with the hope that his being somewhere where he "fit in" better would help him solve some of his challenges. I missed Gregory and wished I could see all my kids more often.

In late October, I was greeted with a piece of mail from the California Department of Corrections.

What do these people want from me now? Will they ever leave me alone? I was nervous to find out what was in the letter. I thought maybe it would announce a new condition related to my sex offender status, perhaps another one of the ever-changing requirements about where I could and could not live. I ripped open the letter.

> *Dear Ms. Barnes:*
>
> *This is notification that your requirement to register as a sex offender pursuant to California Penal Code section 290 has been terminated by the California Department of Justice (DOJ).*
>
> *As a result, the Department of Justice has updated its records and your name has been removed from the California Sex Offender Registry. Additionally, notification concerning this termination has been sent to the appropriate law enforcement agency(ies), i.e., the agency at which you last*

registered. Please retain this letter as your documentation.

I started jumping up and down, screaming, "*Oh, my God! Oh, my God! Oh, my God!*" I ran to the computer, opened the California Sex Offender site, and typed in my name: WENDY BARNES... "No name found" floated before me like an apparition. I searched by ZIP code and by city. "No name found" again appeared.

I wasn't there. I was free! I was no longer a registered sex offender. I was on my way to being a normal citizen of the United States. I was no longer society's maggot. I was thrilled and called everyone I knew, proclaiming the great news.

In preparation for Greg's release and with Jimmy's help, I had applied for a restraining order against Greg. The court again allowed Greg to attend the hearing by phone. By the time Greg was done talking, the judge gave me a restraining order for the longest time allowed, ten years. Even so, I knew that when he was released, the restraining order would not be enough to make me feel safe. Greg had long ago convinced me that a restraining order would not stop him if he wanted to harm me.

So after Greg was released, I relied on the connections I had built with people in the corrections field to keep me informed of his whereabouts. They would let me know if he was "missing" from Oregon. Whenever I went near Disneyland, I would be extra careful because I knew that would be where he would bring the girls to work if he was in California.

Every few months I would receive an email alerting me that he had broken his probation and was back in jail. He would stay in jail for a few days to a few months and be released again. My fear of him subsided after time, but I still remained vigilant. I wondered what would happen if he ever found me. My mind played out every scenario I could imagine, including his killing me and my killing him. I wondered if I would ever be able to live feeling completely safe.

In time, I started to feel comfortable in my own skin. It was a roller coaster ride for sure, with many ups and downs. Slowly, I met more people and developed friendships. I felt that I was navigating my way through this thing called life. There were moments of uncertainty to be sure, but more and more, I felt that I did belong.

My children were also making their ways through the world, predictably struggling with the effects of their childhoods but also taking positive steps to recreate their own lives. I had feared for Latasha's safety because she had also cut all ties with Greg after he wrote her a hateful, threatening letter. I convinced her to move in with my mom and me in California, where we shared a two-bedroom apartment. Although it was cramped, we got along great. Many people would ask us how three generations of women were able to get along so well. I didn't know for sure, but I told them that our secret was that we first respected each other as roommates and then loved each other as family.

At first, Gregory stayed in the northwest after Latasha moved to California. Trying to find himself, he moved around a lot—sometimes living in Portland, sometimes Seattle, and sometimes with me in California. He struggled with his childhood memories and the difficulties inherent in his not having had a stable father figure in his life. Even though the two of us had some difficult times, our love for each other remained strong, and we always knew we could count on each other when we truly needed each other.

Mikey continued to live with Greg's mom, who had always taken good care of him. Once Latasha was with me in California, Mikey felt much more comfortable visiting me in my home. Every year, he would visit us for two weeks, and we would go to Disneyland and all the other theme parks. Although I was still "Wendy" rather than "Mom" to him, we developed a positive relationship.

My mom passed away in 2011, with all four of her children and Latasha by her side in our shared apartment. She had lived long enough to see me get my life together and to know that Latasha and I were happy. She also knew that I had strong, healthy relationships with everyone in my family: my dad, stepmom, stepdad, brothers, sister, and children. With my share of her small life insurance policy, I was able to buy myself a gift that I knew she, too, would have treasured: a white grand piano.

Greg did not stay clean for even a moment after he was released. In his arrogance, he continued to build his empire and destroy the lives of countless women and girls for another five years. Finally, justice did prevail.

FEBRUARY 12, 2013

Portland pimp gets life sentence after third conviction

--Aimee Green, *The Oregonian*

http://www.oregonlive.com/portland/index.ssf/2013/02/portland_pimp_gets_life_senten.html

A 45-year-old pimp who was convicted for the third time of prostituting teenagers was sentenced Tuesday to life in prison with no possibility of release under Oregon's get-tough law on repeat sex offenders.

Judge Edward Jones sentenced Gregory Hightower Sr. after studying Hightower's history of enlisting teenage girls as young as 14 or 15 as prostitutes in Oregon and Washington and after listening to what Hightower had to say.

Hightower told the judge that he wasn't sorry for his most recent crimes because he victimized no one.

The judge said Hightower's words helped confirm the sentence he already was thinking of giving him. Under Oregon law, the judge could have given Hightower as few as about six years in prison.

"The evidence showed that since he was a teenager, he's been involved in some shape or form of sex trafficking," said J. R. Ujifusa, the deputy district attorney who prosecuted the case. Hightower was first convicted at 19 of pimping a teenage girl in the Seattle area.

In his most recent case, a Multnomah County Circuit Court jury found Hightower guilty in December of prostituting three women — including his wife. He also was found guilty of engaging in sexual acts with a 16-year-old girl. All four victims testified against Hightower — saying that he showered them with affection and love.

He got one of them to start working as a prostitute for him by promising her a trip to Disneyland when she was 18, the woman testified. He drove her south toward Anaheim, but when they got there, he claimed that the car was broken down and that she would need to make money to fix it by having sex with men. She did her part, he took the money and they returned to Portland—never visiting the theme park as promised, she said.

Jurors saw videos that Hightower made of himself referring to his Lincoln Town Car as the "pimp mobile" and bragging about all of the "dough" his victims were making for him.

He found johns along 82nd Avenue and through word of mouth.

In Hightower's defense, he claimed that he made an honest living as a limo driver, and that he was a benevolent big-brother figure to girls and young women who came from troubled homes.

"She had black eyes," Hightower told jurors of one young victim, during hours of testimony. "(Her dad) was beating her up so bad. That's why she'd always run to me for safety."

Jurors found him guilty of encouraging child sexual abuse, second-degree sexual abuse, compelling prostitution and promoting prostitution.

Not only was I now free from the threat of Greg's terror, the world was set free from this man. If only he were the only one...

I swore never to be silent whenever and wherever human beings endure suffering and humiliation. We must always take sides. Neutrality helps the oppressor, never the victim. Silence encourages the tormentor, never the tormented. —Elie Wiesel

Chapter 34
Creating My Tomorrow

*I believe that everything happens for a
reason. People change so that you can
learn to let go, things go wrong so that
you appreciate them when they're right,
you believe lies so you eventually learn to
trust no one but yourself, and sometimes
good things fall apart so better things can
fall together.*
—Marilyn Monroe

*We create our tomorrow with our words
and actions of today.*
—Wendy Barnes

I LOOK BACK ON MY LIFE and realize how blessed I have
been to be rescued from the human trafficking
nightmare. Because I know what life with a sex-
trafficker is like, I treasure every moment in life. I
continually learn from my experiences, knowing my
emotional growth cannot be compared to other
women. Sometimes I struggle. There are times that all
I want to do is hide in my closet where I feel safe,
wanting to stay there forever and cry. I then look at

my surroundings and, remembering the past, I feel blessed and happy to be where I am today.

I no longer cut myself, although I did on a regular basis for about a year. I didn't know how to deal with the emotions that built up when I would have haunting visions from the past or I would miss Greg or the girls. When I cut, I was cutting my emotions, becoming a robot in order to function throughout the day, to go to school and do my homework. The following year, I cut myself a few times; but after I moved to California, I never cut again.

When Greg was released from prison in August 2007, I feared that he would come looking for me. For years, I moved more than anyone I know. Today, with Greg sentenced to life without parole, I finally feel safe enough to settle into a place and make it my home.

I spend a lot of time observing other people, mostly to see what I could be and what I don't want to be. From the painful lesson of re-creating myself from scratch, I have learned that I am able to adjust my behavior to be the best person I can be. I have observed too many people who don't appreciate life enough. They are too busy—and I am from time to time also guilty of that—to see the beauty of the world and the opportunities that arise every day to affect this world in a positive way.

When I feel myself starting to get too busy and bogged down with the worries in the world, I find a patch of grass to sit in. I run my hands over the grass and run the blades softly between my fingers. I close my eyes and I remember the mixed feelings of despair and freedom I experienced my first day in prison. As I open my eyes I see how much better my life is now, and I feel grateful and happy.

I like sitting in a patch of grass during my breaks at work and letting the sun warm my face. It seems there will always be someone who walks by and warns me, "You're going to get a grass stain." Maybe that's what's wrong with the world today? Too many people are worried about the grass stains and not able to appreciate the stillness of one moment in time.

When a butterfly flaps its wings in one part of the world it can cause a hurricane in another part of the world. —Unknown

The sex offender treatment I received was harsh, but today I see how beneficial it was to me. Today I see how I am responsible for everything I think and do. I am also responsible for how my actions or lack of action affects other people. I see now that standing by and doing nothing when I know injustice is happening is just as bad as doing wrong yourself. Over the years I have integrated much of what I was taught in the counseling sessions into my world view. Like the butterfly flapping its wings, every one of my actions and inactions has an effect in this world— either in a positive or negative way. I do have power, we all have power. Most mornings I wake up and ask myself how I am going to affect the world today, hoping that by the end of the day I will be able to give a positive answer. It can be very simple and still be meaningful: a hug, or genuinely asking people, "How are you doing?" And when they answer "Fine,'" I look deep into their eyes and ask again with a smile, "How are you doing?"

Loving oneself is crucial. If we do not love ourselves, how can we love others? —His Holiness the 14ᵗʰ Dalai Lama

When my counselors first handed me the pack of affirmation cards, I believed every word was a lie. Having succeeded in resolving the negative through the offender treatment, I was able to turn to the affirmations with my heart open to my positive qualities. Today, I believe that I am beautiful, even when my hair is messy. I believe that I am worthy of love and that I am special and unique.

I know I have a purpose in this world—I know this because I created the purpose myself. After being released from prison, I wrote a half-page mission statement for my life. When I lost the piece of paper, I forgot my purpose. I had made it too complicated. So instead I made a mission statement so simple that I would never be able to forget it. A mission statement that gives my life purpose and reminds me of the actions I need to take every day: "Inspire others to care and to lead by example." All I have to do is care about other people. I do that naturally, and the rewards are great.

I have had a hard time writing this book. Remembering the experiences was like reliving them, even to the point that during certain stories I started to forget my confidence and believe the "reality" that Greg had beaten into me. The affirmations help me to regain connection with my inner strength so I can be a positive resource for myself and others.

Happiness can be found even in the darkest of times, if one only remembers to turn on the light. —Dumbledore, in J.K. Rowling's Harry Potter and the Prisoner of Azkaban

Isn't it odd the things we remember the best? I most treasure the people who took the time to care about me, who believed in me, and who didn't give up on me—and I do my best to offer that to others. Much of the credit for my positive progress goes to people who shared their kind and generous hearts. I remember what I felt like when that police officer in Seattle cared about me and when Dominic believed in me. I remember Janet, the Human Resources manager who encouraged me to stop running from myself; thank God for her and her ability to calm me down and help me regain my footing. I wonder where my life would be now if she had not been there at the right time, encouraging me to stand strong. Please don't ever underestimate how much it means to a person who feels unloved and unworthy to have someone care, even in just the smallest of ways.

Today I am free to act on my choices whenever I choose. I know that the qualities I exhibit today and the beliefs that I hold create who I am. Sometimes I want to put my past in the past and never discuss it again—but I also know that my past is a part of who I am today, and I refuse to deny it. I choose to speak out because I want to help others understand why and how young girls (and boys) end up in situations like mine. I hope that through my story, other people will develop a level of compassion and understanding that will inspire them to do what they can to put an end to the injustice that exists in our world. I hope also that children who end up in dangerous situations will gain hope through my story—that my story may even prevent others from being trapped. I choose to accept my past for what it is, to embrace all that life has given me.

And life continues.

Appendix: Resources

"The National Human Trafficking Resource Center (NHTRC) offers a broad selection of resources for various actors within the anti-human trafficking movement including educators, medical, legal and governmental professionals, service providers, law enforcement personnel, community members, potential victims, and those at risk for human trafficking." —Polaris

Hotline: Call 1 (888) 373-7888

or text HELP or INFO to BeFree (233733)

National Human Trafficking Resource Center

Hours: 24 hours, 7 days a week

Languages: English, Spanish

Hotline website: traffickingresourcecenter.org

Polaris website (including links to extensive resources): http://www.polarisproject.org/